LIFE
IS A
BANQUET

LIFE IS A BANQUET

BY

Rosalind Russell

AND

Chris Chase

Random House  New York

Library of Congress Cataloging in Publication Data

Russell, Rosalind.   Life is a banquet.

Includes index.

1.   Russell, Rosalind.   2.   Actors—United States—
Biography.   I.   Chase, Chris, joint author.   II.   Title.
PN2287.R86A35   791.43'028'0924 [B]   77–6001
ISBN 0–394–42134–5

Manufactured in the United States of America

4 6 8 9 7 5

Designed by Anita Karl

*Grateful acknowledgment is made to the following for permission to reprint
previously published material:*

Encyclopaedia Britannica: Excerpt from "Linkages" in *Encyclopaedia Britannica,* 14th edition (1973), 14:79.

FAIRCHILD PUBLICATIONS, INC: Excerpt from interview of Anita Loos by Howard Kissel, *Women's Wear Daily,* August 1974.

ROBERT LESCHER: Excerpt from "An Interview with Chanel" by Joseph Barry.
Copyright © 1965 by Joseph Barry, *McCall's,* November 1965.

LITTLE, BROWN & CO.: Excerpt from *Evelyn Waugh: A Biography* by Christopher Sykes. Copyright © 1975 by Little, Brown & Co.

NEW DIRECTIONS PUBLISHING CORP.: Excerpt from *The Crackup* by F. Scott
Fitzgerald. Copyright 1945 by New Directions Publishing Corp.

THE SOCIETY OF AUTHORS: Excerpt from *Candida* by George Bernard Shaw.
Permission granted by The Society of Authors on behalf of the George Bernard Shaw
Estate.

TIME, INC.: Excerpt from the review of *The Women.* Copyright 1953 by
Time, Inc. All rights reserved.

UNIVERSITY OF CHICAGO PRESS: Excerpt from *The Odes of Pindar* translated
by Richmond Lattimore. Copyright 1947, Copyright © 1976 by The University of
Chicago.

VANGUARD PRESS: Reprinted from *Auntie Mame,* a new play based on the
novel by Patrick Dennis, by permission of the publisher Vanguard Press, Inc. Copyright © 1957 by Jerome Lawrence and Robert E. Lee.

*To my son Lance and
my new daughter Patricia
With love*

PREFACE
by Frederick Brisson

TOWARD THE END of this book, in a chapter about rheumatoid arthritis, Rosalind says that in September of 1975 it was discovered "I had a couple of tumors which had been growing for years." She devoted only a few paragraphs to the cancer which eventually killed her, and when she was asked why she hadn't gone into more detail, she said, "One disease to a book is enough."

After she died I found a petition she had tucked away in her prayer book. It said in part, "Keep my mind free from the recital of endless details; give me wings to get to the point. Seal my lips on aches and pains. They are increasing, and love of rehearsing them is becoming sweeter as the years go by."

She never wanted to bore an audience; she never wanted anybody else to bore an audience on her behalf. Being a proud and doting husband, I had added to her catalogue of professional credits (actors always need to supply these "bios" to newspapers and magazines) a list of one hundred and fifteen awards, citations and honorary titles she'd achieved, as well as a list of ninety-four civic and public-spirited activities in which she'd been involved.

She hated my lists. "Will you quit handing out that thing to people, Freddie? It's embarrassing."

She never won an Oscar until 1973—when the Academy of Motion Picture Arts and Sciences presented her with the Humanitarian Award—but you won't find a word about that honor in these pages either. She only recounts the four times she was nominated—as a performer—and *didn't* win. She used to say, "Always a bridesmaid, never a bride."

We decided on the title for her book not simply because she

created the character of "Auntie Mame," but because Mame's first-act curtain line summed up Rosalind's philosophy. "Live, live, live," Mame would admonish her listeners. "Life is a banquet, and most of you poor suckers are starving to death!"

When I saw her on the screen in *The Women*, that aliveness of Rosalind's bowled me over. That's fun, I thought, that's for me.

(Long before I met her I'd caught a glimpse of her at the theatre. It was in London—she'd come over to make the movie of A. J. Cronin's *The Citadel*—and this evening I had gone with a friend to a play, and suddenly a buzz went through the house, people telling one another that Rosalind Russell was in the fourth row, and my friend and I had stretched our necks to get a look at a famous American movie star.)

Rosalind tells the story of our courtship and marriage in the pages ahead, and I won't repeat what she's said, but I can add a few details.

In 1939 I was newly arrived in Hollywood on business from Europe, staying in California with my old chum Cary Grant at his Santa Monica beach home and wild to meet Rosalind, with whom Cary was then filming *His Girl Friday*. Cary assured me that it would be easy to bring us together. First he invited her for Christmas. She sent regrets. Then he invited her to our New Year's Eve party. He and I had each bought a case of champagne, we had twenty-four bottles sitting on ice in the bathtub, and New Year's Eve came and went, but Rosalind never showed. I found out later that she'd had a date with Jimmy Stewart; if Cary knew about it, he never wanted to tell me.

After a couple of weeks of failed hopes and dashed expectations, I again asked Cary when he was going to get me a date with his co-star. "I can't believe you're with her every morning from eight o'clock until seven at night. Can't you at least invite me onto the set?"

He said no. "The way we work, there's no time for that . . ."

Later in the book you'll come to Rosalind's version of our first meeting—the three of us, she, Cary and I, went out together, and at the end of that evening I made a speech: "Miss Russell, I do hope that one day you will give me the pleasure of inviting you to dinner." In those days you didn't get on a first-name basis the moment you met anybody. Miss Russell said, "Oh, yes, yes, thank you," in a vague sort of way.

For a month or so afterward she gave me a hard time. I would phone and the maid would say Miss Russell was out. I could hear Miss Russell in the background declaring she was out.

Then late one Friday afternoon I got a phone call from the set of *His Girl Friday*. It was Miss Russell's maid, Hazel. Miss Russell wanted to know if I would like to go to the races with her tomorrow.

"What?" I said. "The races? Yes. I mean, you mean, all day?"

Hazel answered quietly, as if to a slow child. "Yes, all day," she said.

Now I was getting really nervous. "My car, it's just a little thing I brought with me from England; she'll want to go in some big wagon . . ."

"Never mind," said Hazel, who had a special nickname for Rosalind. "The Queen will go in your car."

Next morning I arrived at Rosalind's house, parked, and went in. She made a sweeping entrance down the stairs, gave me a very English-accented "Helooo, Mr. Brisson," came outside, took a look at my tiny Jaguar, said, "Oh, that thing?" and added, "All right, let's go." I told her I didn't know the way to Santa Anita, she said she would drive, and from that day on, for thirty-seven years, I never got a chance to take the wheel again. (I tried once, she said, "You're a dreadful driver," I said, "That's the way we drive in London," and that was the end of it. During the last three weeks of her life I *did* lure her out for afternoon spins, but she was still complaining about my style.)

Santa Anita was marvelous, and on the way home I got up my nerve to ask her out that night. "How about dining and dancing at Ciro's? Black tie, of course."

"Might be amusing," she said. "Call me when you get back to your apartment."

I clutched at my head. Oh oh. I'm going to get that Hazel again, saying Miss Russell's not in.

But when I called, Miss Russell herself answered the phone and confirmed that she and I had a date. Now, the fact was that I'd lined up another girl for that night—I had a nice little black book—and I had a nine-o'clock reservation at Ciro's. But Ciro's, Mocambo and the Trocadero were the big spots, and they saved their ringside tables for stars, and magnates like Louis B. Mayer. God knows where my reserved table would have been; I was not a Hollywood insider. So the minute I hung up on her, I phoned Ciro's and told them I'd be coming with Rosalind Russell. "I assume," I said, "that you'll have our ringside table ready . . ."

The date was fun. We laughed and danced and made all the gossip columns. "Who's this guy with Hollywood's Number One Bachelor Girl?" was the gist of most of the copy. A week later, on Valentine's Day, I stopped at a florist's shop. In the window there was an enormous heart, meant for display, not for sale. "What are you going to do with that thing?" I said. "What do you mean, do with it?" said the florist. "I'm going to throw it out."

It was big as the wall of a barn, that heart. "I'll give you ten dollars for it," I said, "if you'll deliver it to Rosalind Russell in Beverly Hills."

They delivered it. They leaned it up against her front door; she had to walk through it to get inside. "What the hell is this?" she said when she saw it, but she was amused.

The next week she invited me over for lunch, and I began to feel the ice breaking a little. She wasn't free with her dates, though; I still had to battle to see her. She never visited my first apartment (after I moved from Cary's beach house), so once I felt she was beginning to care for me, I got a new place. The reason was that she said she would not come to call if another woman had been there before her.

The first time I proposed, she didn't accept. I persisted. "I'm going to write your mother and ask for your hand." And I did. "There's no way I'm going to get rid of you, is there?" Rosalind finally said, laughing. But when she gave up, she gave up on her own terms. "I don't like any of these proposals after you've had an evening out. I'm not interested in that nonsense. If you want to propose, then come around at seven o'clock in the morning, and put a white handkerchief on the ground and kneel down and ask for my hand."

At seven o'clock the next morning Roz at last accepted.

Right up until the ring was on her finger, she kept me unsure. On our wedding morning I looked out of my motel window in the little village of Solvang and saw my bride-to-be marching up the road in the direction of San Francisco. I yelled out at her, "Where are you going? What are you doing?" "Running away," she said.

I went after her and brought her back. She was always very deep into anything she did, and I think she just wanted to be alone for those last few hours to think about the changes she was making in her life.

Cary Grant, who was my best man, claims she almost married Arthur Hornblow, Jr., one of the wedding guests, but that was because Cary and I were having trouble getting into the church. Rosalind was to come down the main aisle, while Cary and I were to enter from a side door and meet her at the altar.

Cary and I were standing outside this side door, immaculately dressed in our Hawes and Curtis morning suits. Rosalind had insisted on my wearing spats, vest, foulard tie, tie pin—what she used to call the full Balenciaga. In our buttonholes we men sported little sprays of bouvardia (a small, exotic white flower we had flown in from Hawaii for Rosalind's wedding bouquet). From inside the oldest mission in California we heard the wedding march begin, and we knew that Rosalind and her brother James were starting down the aisle. Cary tried the side door. It didn't open, so he rattled it. Typical of an actor. (Nobody else in the world would have thought of testing the props.) By now his actor's timing tells him that Rosalind is halfway down the aisle and he can't get the door open, and he begins to work at the knob.

Our friends were sitting there listening to the racket, and Rosalind heard it too. She slowed down her already measured steps. Then Hornblow came to the rescue. He got up, went in the direction of the rattle (an old monk who was the caretaker of the mission had locked the door from the inside so fans couldn't break in), turned a key in the lock just in time to let Cary walk in, with me, nervous as a mouse, behind him, as Rosalind arrived at the altar.

I had such fun at the reception that Rosalind had trouble getting me to leave. The champagne and music kept me floating, and Roz was saying, "Darling, we can't stay here any longer, we've got to go," and I was saying, "Roz, it's a wonderful day, and we only get married once, so let's enjoy it." I remember Rosalind bringing both her maids, Hazel and Blanche, and there was quite a to-do about which one was going to help her change from her wedding gown into her traveling suit. Rosalind settled the matter by saying Hazel could do the top half and Blanche the lower half, and I said, "What about me, girls?" and they laughed and said, "We'll do the same for you," and they came over and Blanche changed my shirt and Hazel pulled on my pants.

We were finally dressed, Rosalind in a wonderful grey traveling suit and a large hat, and we kissed and kissed everyone and drove off in our beautiful new Packard-Darrin with the top down. It was about seven o'clock (the reception had started at three-thirty) and we were headed for a little town called Santa Maria, some forty miles up the coast from Solvang.

We got to the old inn in Santa Maria, and there was a multitude of red roses to greet us. We had a little dinner and we toasted each other, and after that we went for a walk around the village in the dark, holding hands.

I remember later that night my bride, elegantly wearing a peignoir over her beautiful nightgown, coming to bed, and I, full of love, not to mention champagne, suggesting that she "take that damn thing off," and her exclaiming, in her "Auntie Mame" way, "You so-and-so, I have spent thousands of dollars buying a trousseau, you're supposed to enjoy looking at this . . ."

At about ten o'clock the next morning, there was a knock on our door. "Good morning, Mr. and Mrs. Brisson," cried a voice from outside, whereupon Mrs. Brisson leaped out of bed and shut herself in a closet, not emerging again until she had put on her honeymoon finery. The knock on the door had been delivered by Bill Powell, who entered now with a magnum of champagne, four glasses and his wife, Mousie. Bill and Mousie had been at the wedding, decided they'd drunk too much to drive home, and come to the inn at Santa Maria, where they were amazed to find that the bride and groom were already installed. They'd spent the night in the room next to ours, and Bill claimed to have heard through the walls everything Rosalind and I had said to one another. He began talking about getting off the negligee, and the more he teased, the redder Rosalind got. She was a very proper New England girl, and we had to drink almost the entire magnum before she started to think Bill was funny.

In the thirty-five years we were married, Rosalind and I never gave each other ultimatums; neither of us ever said to the other, "If that's the way you feel about it, I'm going to the Beverly Hills Hotel," or got on an airplane and flew to New York. Roz believed you should never go to bed angry. If she was real mad at me, and locked her door so I couldn't get in, I'd phone her. "I'm trying to live by *your* rule; unlock the door so I can come in and kiss you." She'd unlock the door, still looking a little angry, and we would hug each other and say goodnight.

Financially speaking, she gave up a lot for our marriage. When people ask me if it didn't make me feel loved, I have to say truthfully that what it made me feel was self-conscious. At the time she left Metro she was offered the same kind of contract Clark Gable had. They wanted to pay her seven thousand five hundred dollars a week, fifty-two weeks a year, and she said no. "If I sign a contract like that," she told me, "the next seven years of my life will belong to Metro, and not to us."

In 1943 Rosalind had a breakdown. She didn't go into detail about that in her book any more than she went into detail about her bouts with cancer, and I write it here only to stress what an unwhining woman she was. Our tough problems started early on. I'm talking about health. She lost her sister, the Duchess, to protracted illness, and she lost her brother, John—both during the early years of our marriage. When you say in sickness and in health, you'd better really mean it.

Be that as it may, we had the most marvelous time together, because Rosalind was a life affirmer, a fighter, and like Scaramouche, she had been "born with the gift of laughter and the sense that the world was mad." We argued about this and that, but when it came to business, she made her own final decisions.

We helped each other. Once, when she was in New Haven and they were trying out her Broadway musical *Wonderful Town*, I ran backstage to offer an opinion. Now, there's nothing more dangerous than going to an actor or a director during a tense period and telling them you don't like something. Particularly if you happen to be related to the actor or director. Rosalind, who'd been in movies for twenty years before she'd suddenly decided to do this song-and-dance show, didn't come offstage exactly relaxed. Keyed up, perspiring, touchy, she listened as I began—"Roz, the dress for the finale doesn't work, you look terrible in it"—and halfway through the sentence she gave me a look that would have hurled a smarter man back to Southern California.

I rushed ahead. "It's the end of the show, you've been in character all night, now people are interested to see you as you are." I reminded her that Galanos had created a marvelous sparkling dress for her in a picture called *Never Wave at a WAC*. "And the shot of you wearing it lasted on the screen exactly thirty seconds. That's the kind of dress you need—and it would still be in character."

"All right," she said. "You're so smart, why don't *you* go talk to Mainbocher about it? I've got other problems, thank you so much."

I didn't go talk to Mainbocher, the costume designer, but I sent home for the Galanos dress (Rosalind and I owned it; *Never Wave at a WAC* had been made by our independent production company), and when it arrived, she put it on and wore it at one of the dress rehearsals.

Mainbocher was sitting in the middle of the empty theatre, his coat draped over his shoulders, European style, half watching the finale, and suddenly he shot up as though a stick of dynamite had gone off under his seat. He ran backstage, crying, "What is this, Rosalind? What have you got on?"

"Well," she said, "I'm just trying something I thought would be more suitable for the ending."

"But, darling," he said, "this is *my* show. What about my reputation?" He went away muttering and unhappy, but in the middle of the night he telephoned Rosalind. "Darling, I think you're right. It's a lovely dress. Do me a favor. Get permission to let me copy it. I have a couple of ideas I would like to add to it so it becomes a Mainbocher creation."

Rosalind called Galanos, who said fine; he was flattered because he was at the beginning of his career, and Mainbocher was one of the top designers of the world.

In 1960, after she had had the first mastectomy, Rosalind went to Galanos. He says it was the only time he ever saw her break down. She had come to his office, very crisp, very businesslike. "I'm going to tell you something nobody in the world knows except Freddie and my doctor. I've had a breast removed, and I want to keep it quiet. So long as I can be active, I don't want to be thought a freak, I don't want people looking at me in person or on the screen and wondering about my sex life." (You have to consider the era. Women had not yet begun to go public about their mastectomies.)

"I want you to start thinking in terms of how I can now be dressed," Rosalind said to Jimmy, and then she began to take her clothes off. She started to cry, and he saw that she could hardly lift her left arm, it was so swollen, and he broke down too. From that day forward, he specially designed every piece of her clothing, and neither he nor his fitter ever told a soul.

You couldn't keep Rosalind down, or quiet, or even sensible about protecting herself. When she was recuperating from that first cancer operation, I caught her out in the greenhouse lifting heavy flowerpots (she had a green thumb and kept our garden with the help of our gardener, who has been with us for thirty-two years), although she—and I—knew that she wasn't supposed to pick up anything that weighed more than a powder puff.

In 1965 she had the second mastectomy, in 1969 she was hit by severe rheumatoid arthritis, for which she started to take medicines which have dangerous side effects, and in April of 1975 she got pneumonia, the symptoms of which were masked by these medications. It was in the fall of 1975 that the cancer recurred.

During the last two years she seldom lost her courage. One day in 1975, newly home from a sojourn in Cedars of Lebanon, she disappeared. Her nurse, who couldn't find her, was terrified. Rosalind had gone to the garage, got into her car, and backed it clear out to the front door. When the nurse said, in horror, "You're not supposed to do that, Mrs. Brisson," Rosalind laughed and told the nurse she wouldn't be needing her any more.

In July of 1976 she had to have a hip replacement; her mobility had been affected and pain prevented her from resting, even in bed. At UCLA Hospital, the night before the operation, although she'd been able to keep almost nothing on her stomach, she ordered an Eastern lobster, ate it with relish, and gave me orders. "Freddie, when you come tomorrow, bring the little portable bar so we can have a drink. It's no good you having to sit around here like this."

So many plants and flowers arrived at the hospital, but Roz gave most of them away just as she gave herself away all through her life, though she'd kill me for saying it.

I brought her home for the last time three weeks before our

x v

thirty-fifth anniversary, and she was already worrying about what to get me, what I needed. She had a new sports jacket on her mind, because I'd worn the same old number every day to the hospital, and it annoyed her. "I'm going to rip that off you and get one of the nurses to come in here and burn it," she'd threaten.

The morning of our anniversary I fixed her breakfast tray with a little wedding bouquet of bouvardia, which I'd ordered the month before, and beside it I put a four-page letter in which I'd tried to say all the things you can never really say.

That night she came downstairs to dinner. She'd been staying up in her bedroom, equipped with the things I thought she needed —a walker, canes, crutches, a wheelchair—but on our anniversary she dressed in her best hostess gown, and as a gesture to Lance and his wife Patricia and me, came to the table without any of the paraphernalia.

I'd ordered a dinner I thought she might be able to enjoy, and we drank a glass of champagne, and there was a wedding cake with Danish and American flags on it. Across the top of the cake it said, "Rosalind and Callemand, *Jeg elsker dig,*" which means I love you in Danish. (My name is actually Carl Frederick Brisson, Jr., and, in Danish, Callemand is a pet name for Carl.)

I'd also had a tiny bracelet made of very thin gold, with the number 35 spelled out in diamond baguettes, and when Rosalind opened the box and saw it, her eyes shone. She looked like she was twelve years old. She put it on and said, "I'll never take it off"—and she never took it off again.

She died on Sunday, November 28, at 10:20 A.M.

The year before, on a day when she was in a very good mood (she was in a period of remission), I'd broached a subject she didn't want to hear about. "The weather's good," I said, "and I'd like you to come on a little trip with me. I've taken care of something we've talked about all during our married lives, I've found a wonderful plot for us."

"Wonderful?" she said. "What's wonderful about going six feet under?"

"But it's beautiful, darling," I said. "The view—"

"The view!" she snorted.

Desperate, I threw in Metro-Goldwyn-Mayer. "As a matter of fact, it's very near your old alma mater."

The mention of the studio failed to charm Rosalind. "You're not burying *me* in the back lot," said my wife.

Right before Rosalind's funeral cortege hit the gates (which are surrounded by lovely trees and flowers) of Holy Cross Cemetery, I noticed with some chagrin a large white building standing nearby. I'd seen the building before, but never taken notice of it, and now as I looked over, I could make out the sign which said Internal Revenue Service. In my head I could hear Rosalind laughing and saying the two things we could be sure of were death and taxes.

My life goes on. The days are easier than the nights. I have a hard time sleeping, and at two o'clock in the morning I don't like to put the lights on and jar myself even wider awake, but I'm such an orderly man (Rosalind says in the book that I used to write it down every time I kissed her), I can open a drawer, find my ear stoppers, lay my hands on a sleep mask and pour myself a glass of water, all in the dark.

I've been in the dark a lot lately.

But Rosalind would not want to be remembered in sadness— "Give unto them beauty for ashes, the oil of joy for mourning," the Bible says—and I hope you will find some of her beauty and joy and spirit in this book. She was still editing it up until a few days before she died.

It is all Roz—had she lived, she might have made additions, deletions, corrected a misspelled name, a faultily remembered date, but the voice is hers. For that reason I'm pleased that it's being published as it stands; she talks to us in the first person, and often in the present tense, as though she were still here.

For me, she will always be here.

February, 1977

CONTENTS

INTRODUCTION

FOR A LONG TIME I didn't want to write a book.

I had my reasons. They were:

1. I couldn't write a sensational, confessional book, because for thirty-five years I'd been married to one husband. (Thirty-five years? And she calls herself a movie star?)

2. I couldn't write a lofty book emphasizing my patrician background (one of those "Skeffington Smythe Middlebaugh was related to John Quincy Adams, who was my great-great-great-grandmother's fiancé for six months" jobs), because my background wasn't patrician. I think my people were horse thieves, way back.

3. I couldn't write a book Swifty Lazar would agree to read. Swifty, a super agent and maker of big deals, told me my life simply wasn't interesting enough to write about. Too normal, he said.

Now I've written this book.

I know it's risky, because what if everybody is like Swifty Lazar? Still, several publishers offered me cold cash for my memoirs. Furthermore, I was around during what the film historians like to call Hollywood's "golden days," and there seems to be considerable interest in hearing from a country that doesn't exist any more, a country you can no longer visit.

But what finally convinced me to take a chance, to write a book, was the memory of another chance I took a long time ago.

On fall weekends, when I was growing up in Waterbury, Connecticut, my father would take us children to country fairs. Not the big commercial fairs, the little ones where you drank sweet cider and bought pumpkins and apples and baskets. We used to ride our horses to, say, Plymouth, Connecticut, which is pretty far—by hoof —from Waterbury, and we'd be trotting along briskly when suddenly my father would say, "The horses are getting hot, see, their necks are sweaty," and he'd make us slow down to a steady clunk, clunk, clunk. (Riding home later, in the dark, cold October nights, believe me, we galloped all the way.)

Anyhow, my brother John had a horse called Tom. He stood about eighteen hands, a great big animal, and one day, at one of these fairs, I entered him and me in a jumping contest. The moment came, and I, weighing a fast forty pounds, got up on Tom and galloped off. We approached the first hurdle, and instead of holding those knees in, going up with the horse, I lit out ahead of him. I took a terrific somersault right between his ears and landed *zoom!* on my feet, with the reins still in my hands. And when I heard the people applauding, I bowed, as if I'd done that flying leap on purpose. And the officials came out and gave me a cup for trick riding.

Sometimes you can get lucky.

LIFE
IS A
BANQUET

"...Until the Strangers Come"

I GOT THROWN OUT of the house with my prize cup because it was full of peacock feathers, and my mother thought they were bad luck. My mother was Irish and she was superstitious, if you'll forgive the tautology. She took one look at the feathers, cried, "Don't you bring those in here!" and banished me, my plumes and my bleeding knuckles (I hadn't been wearing gloves; I never could handle the reins of a horse when I had gloves on) to the tack room, and my brother John to the shower. She said he smelled of horse. Every time my brother John came around, my mother said he smelled of horse and sent him to take another shower.

As crazy as my father was about horses, that's how much my mother complained about them—they had to be exercised, they had to be fed and groomed, *eau de cheval* wasn't her favorite perfume— but my father always won. Even after the streets of Waterbury were full of Stutz Bearcats, my father was transporting us around in a horse and carriage. The people next door, the Hotchkisses, had red sports cars and bright yellow sports cars, and my father was still making us get into the surrey and go out with him. It was murder. You'd try to hide, ride with your head down because you didn't want your friends to see you, but my Dad loved it. I'm talking about way into the 1920's. "Automobiles are not good for you," my father would say. "This is good for you."

The age he lived in was right for him; he never should have been in any other. He went to church in the Prince Albert coat, and the tails at Christmas and Easter. He was infinitely patient with children (his library was never safe from invasion; while he sat trying to read the evening paper, we would climb all over him, comb his hair, plaster it down into his eyes, make curls of it—none of this bothered him) and he was infinitely civil with people of any stripe.

His civility used to embarrass me, because he knew everybody in town and he'd stop on his way home to talk to the street cleaner —"How's the new baby? Well, you've got to see to it that that young man goes on to college"—and the whole time the street cleaner would be pushing his broom along the gutter, and I, little snob that I was, would be looking nervously up and down the block, thinking, What if the kids from school see my Dad talking to the street cleaner?

My father wasn't old then, but when I read the Ezra Pound lines "They will come no more,/ The old men with beautiful manners," I think of him.

And while I'm quoting, let me plummet from the sublime to the practical. Somebody told me that Sophie Tucker at age sixty-nine delivered herself of the following wisdom: "From birth to age eighteen, a girl needs good parents. From eighteen to thirty-five, she needs good looks. From thirty-five to fifty-five, she needs a good personality. From fifty-five on, she needs cash."

Well, from birth to age eighteen, I certainly had good parents.

They were nothing alike, my mother and father, and I don't mean only in their attitudes toward horses. He was tall, she was tiny; he was fair and blue-eyed, she was dark as I am; he was calm, she was fiery; he loved the sea, she hated it, but she went on cruises with him anyway, because from the time he was fifty-five he was a heart case, and she wanted him to live.

(More than my brothers and sisters, I have reason to remember our parents' cruises. One day, after I'd begun my acting career, I said to my mother, "Isn't it amazing that you gave me a good theatrical name? I mean, everyone else is James or John or George or Clara or Mary Jane or Josephine—were you reading Shakespeare when you were carrying me?" My mother shook her head. "You were named after a boat," she said. "How demeaning," I said haughtily, and changed the subject. I fear there was a touch of the stuffed shirt about me in my youth. I now own a framed picture—a man on a newspaper sent it to me—of the S. S. *Rosalind*. She traveled between New York and Nova Scotia, and it cost thirteen dollars—steerage— to make the trip on her.)

When Henry James, Sr., first glimpsed the girl he was to marry, he told Emerson, "The flesh said, it is for me, and the spirit said, it is for me." I think it was that way for my father, a man already up in his thirties, when he met my mother, then twenty-two years old. His name was James Edward Russell, hers was Clara McKnight. They both lived in Waterbury, where he had a law practice, and every day, out of his office window, he saw her walking to the girls' school where she taught.

My father was a late starter at love—and at law—because his parents had died young and he'd had to go to work. He played semi-pro baseball to put himself through Yale Law School, and he wasn't graduated until he was twenty-seven. He took care of his younger brothers, too. That's the way they worked out their lives in those days. But everything was simpler then. My father used to say if you went to church, got through law school and hung out your shingle, it was automatic that you'd get along.

My Grandfather McKnight had reservations. He liked my father, but he thought he was too old for my mother to marry, and he never let the lovers forget it. (If my father took my mother out in the buggy, and didn't bring her home till eleven o'clock, my grandfather would get furious. "You should know better, a man of your years . . .")

They got married anyway. They wanted a big family, and they planned it. They had seven children, born about two and a half years apart. There were three older than I, and three younger. I'm the middle one, the ham in the sandwich.

I think lives are terribly alike, according to your background, your religion, the way you're reared. We were comfortable financially, so we had the same things as other families in our economic stratum. They put the braces on our teeth whether we needed them or not, and my father was great for keeping us physically active. We rode, we swam, we went to dancing school, and in the summers he rented a great big house at Laurel Beach on Long Island Sound. The house looked like a ship, all grey shingles with balconies around it. The Sound was still halfway clean; we used to dig for clams and have potato races and canoe races and go to the casino to listen to the band on Saturday nights.

They were shining days at Laurel Beach. And they left me

((5))

with claustrophobia. Because I almost drowned one afternoon. My mother and I had gone out together, and I had left her sitting on the sand while I swam out past a gully and a sand bar, and then on to a raft. I was very young and not much of a swimmer. (My mother was no swimmer at all. She could do a breast stroke to my father if he was standing ten feet away from her and holding out his hands, and that was about it.)

After a while I decided to come in from the raft, and I got as far as the sand bar and touched my toe down and felt I could make it. Next thing I knew, I'd fallen into the gully, and I couldn't reach bottom any more. There was a woman swimming in closer to the beach—she was facing my mother and I was behind her—and my mother was gesticulating wildly to her while I was gulping water. The woman was a mute. By the time she finally understood my mother's frenzy and turned around and reached for me, I was going under for the third time.

And if that isn't enough to explain my dread of confining places, I can blame it on a big wicker bathroom hamper. Whenever I felt they were being mean to me at home, I'd go climb into the hamper and pull the lid over me. I planned to die in there, and then they'd be sorry when they found me. They'd open the hamper to put the dirty linen in and I'd be down there dead.

But it takes strength of character to stay in a hamper and expire; I'd get to wishing I had some fudge (we children were always making masses of rotten fudge; it was sheer sugar with some chocolate in it) and I'd decide to live a while longer.

I was born in a house on Chestnut Avenue, and when I was four years old I ran away from home. Or at least I walked away, and found myself clear down on the Green, in the center of Waterbury's business section. A neighbor who saw me there, swinging on a hitching post, stopped short and cried, "Rosalind, what are you doing here?"

"My name is not Rosalind," I said. "I'm from out of town."

Four-year-old traveling fibbers don't get too far (the neighbor went straight to my mother and told her where I was), but the episode hints at my future theatrical bent. I always had a wild imagination.

We moved from Chestnut Avenue while I was still small. The house I grew up in was right in town on a boulevard called Willow

Street, but we had a barn, and a backyard with some pear trees and a rose garden and a big bed of lily of the valley. (I was forever picking flowers and taking them to my teachers; it didn't do me any good.) A former governor of Connecticut had built the thirteen-room Victorian mansion (with a fireplace in every room) and it was the bastard architecture of all time. The ground floor was of grey stone, the second floor of clapboard, and there was fretwork on the top floor, with gargoyles looking down over the whole business. (After my father died, and most of us had left home, my mother sold the place to a man called Snyder, who ran a funeral parlor. "Snyder?" I said. "Snyder? What kind of people does he bury?" "Dead people," said my mother.)

Set back from the street behind a lawn, we had privacy, even though streetcars (which in time gave way to buses) clanged past our front windows. We also had a pigeon problem. The second and third floors were forever having to be repainted, and though my father wouldn't allow my brothers to have rifles, they all had BB guns, and my mother knew it. She never said a word when they got out the BB guns and went after the pigeons.

My father always walked home from his office (the better to talk to the street cleaner, I supposed); he'd come in and stand in front of the great big glass doors that made the house look like a church, and we'd all run to meet him, and he'd pick us up in the order of our appearance—or at least, in the order of our having appeared: he did it according to age—and hug and kiss us. While he was greeting my older brothers James and John, and my sister Clara, I would jump up and down and squeal, "Look at me! Look at me!" and cross my eyes.

"Railroad," my father would say (he called me Railroad because my initials were R.R.), "Railroad, your eyes are going to stay that way." The warning never stopped me.

(Long afterward his nurse told me that my son Lance had been crossing his eyes, and I thought, How funny, here he is, fighting for attention the same way I did several hundred years ago.)

The need to be plucked out of the crowd, to be recognized, applauded, if you like, is surely why I wound up in the theatre. My family says I was a great exhibitionist, always on, making noise, running things, and in school I went out for cheerleading, and trimming the halls in the middle of the night, and leaping around basketball courts—I broke every bone in my body on the left side, and then started in on the right—and I dived and I toe-danced and I ice-skated. We used to take our ice skates and go out to Hamilton Park, and if anybody admired my form—I had ordinary long blades, nothing fancy, but I could do a few twirls—I'd say, "I'm from the Hippodrome in New York."

I'd been taken to the Hippodrome, a great big amphitheatre where they held circuses and pageants, when I was tiny, because my father was nuts about the theatre. We used to come in from Waterbury —it was ninety miles—on the train, and my Dad would usually give each of us girls seventy-five cents extra for the parlor car, which had lovely red plush seats. They didn't miss a show, Mother and Dad. Or a concert. And he didn't miss a ball game. (Often my parents traveled to the city alone; he'd head for Yankee Stadium, while she shopped for all the kids they'd left in Connecticut. The only shopping she could get him involved with was buying shoes. He liked beautiful shoes, so he'd sit still to be shod, and then he'd go to the ball park and she'd go to Best and Company. I hated the dresses she bought for us at Best's. They were charming, and I hated them. I thought all that fagoting and tucking and gathering was babyish.)

In those days, as a matter of fact, you didn't have to journey to New York to find good theatre. Everything came to Waterbury on the circuit. Great artists played Temple Hall—I heard Heifetz there —and theatre companies toured all through New England doing one-night stands, and Waterbury even housed a resident stock company. I cut classes religiously (how else would you cut classes from a Catholic school?) to go to matinées of that company. It cost twenty-five cents to sit up in the gallery, and if I didn't learn what to do on a stage, I sure learned what *not* to do. That's why audiences have always been able to hear me in a theatre. I resented not hearing. (At one point in my public career I was given an award for speech, and my mother was impressed. "You know how Dad and I were always telling Rosalind to lower her voice because the tone was really loud and vulgar?" she said to one of my sisters. "Well, she's been given this award, so it shows we were wrong, and besides, Dad used to say, 'At least we can understand her.' " Every award that came to me, my mother believed I was the only one who'd ever got it. Or ever should have got it.)

((8))

I saw Valentino dance when I was a kid. He performed in Waterbury, someplace out of doors, he and a Russian-named wife. And I saw him as the Sheik in the movies, and he was wicked and marvelous, so Latin. I remember his taking the girl to his tent, carrying her in, doing marvelous depraved things to her. And there were others I adored—Richard Barthelmess, the Gishes, the Talmadges, Vilma Banky. I was crazy about movies. We weren't supposed to go, but my brother John took me to a little theatre called the Princess, where they had the serials with the girl tied to the railroad tracks. And *Birth of a Nation*, I remember seeing that. I'd sneak away as often as I could, but I wasn't an addict because I wasn't allowed to be. A lot of actors say, "I lived at the movies, I was an usher, I saw everything fifteen times," but they didn't have my father. The Russell kids were out every Saturday going to those fairs, riding those horses, or piling into our Uncle Jim's car and chugging off to the Yale Bowl for a football game.

Sundays were busy too. After church we'd come home, have the big dinner with the roast chicken and the gravy and the mashed potatoes and the peas, and then we'd go call on Grandpa (my mother's father). It was way to hell and gone on the other side of the city, my grandfather's house, and we had to climb a steep hill to get there, and then on the walk home (naturally we walked; we were with my father) we were given a treat, usually an ice cream soda.

Now that I think of it, Sunday afternoons were probably the only times my mother got any peace. She didn't go with us.

Even though we had help, my mother was constantly working to run the big household. She went downtown and picked out every grapefruit we would eat, she bought sugar and flour by the barrel, and she spent countless nights on the second floor sewing name tapes into our camp clothes. (Every summer two or three of us would go off to camp, and if our parents were going to travel that summer, we'd *all* be sent to camp.)

We children would be up on the third floor—we had a billiard room there; my father played billiards, not pool, and to this day I can shoot so well, people think I must have earned my living at it—playing games and racketing around over my mother's head, while she sat downstairs doing those name tapes. How she stood the noise, I'll never know. We had turned an alcove on the third floor into a bowling alley, and we also had a poker table.

My poor father, he never made a bet in his life, he didn't approve of betting, and he brought up a bunch of gamblers. After he died those of us who were still in school used to come home at different hours—sometimes just for weekends—and there was always a crap game going in my father's library. My mother permitted it, and stayed to supervise. The dice were going all the time, and I remember arriving late one Friday night and having a chum of one of my brothers, a young man who didn't know I was a member of the family, warn me against the Russells. "Do you know these people?" he whispered. "Be careful, they're all sharpshooters." And in the background my relatives were yelling, "Get your money up, get your money up, it's all cash here . . ."

Since we were Roman Catholics, my parents were reasonably strict, and during the summers when we didn't go to camp my father made the boys work hard. Once they'd reached their teens, each of them had to spend a month of his vacation doing farm labor. But we had a happy childhood, with roller skates and noise and music, and racing down the back stairs to the kitchen to make hot chocolate on cold winter nights.

We were reckless too. We used to walk on top of a train trestle (it was a long drop to a dirty river), and if the train had come along, there would have been nothing we could have done about it, but we'd cry, "Let's see if we can make it," and we always made it. We jumped our horses over brooks, each time at a wider place, daring one another —"Bet you can't get across *here*"—and half the time the poor animals would go into the drink. Oh, the chances we took. When you're young you just think you're going to live forever.

If my mother or father had known of our exploits, we'd have got spanked. By her, not by him; he wouldn't touch us. They'd be entertaining guests downstairs, playing whist and drinking punch, and we'd be upstairs jumping on the beds and fighting with pillows and stealing each other's marbles—we all played marbles; we'd chalk out territory on the honey-colored parquet, and you'd hear this *chk, chk, chk* when we got down to serious shooting—and yelling and chasing around the rooms. And my mother would come to the foot of the stairs and warn us: "If I have to call up to you children one more time . . ."

Our bedrooms were blazoned with college banners—flags saying Yale, Princeton, Dartmouth—flying from canes, and those were the instruments of punishment my mother favored, once her patience was exhausted. She'd whack the canes against our legs, but I have to say we deserved whatever we got.

They were clever, my mother and father. Wanting us to entertain at home, they made it easy for us. There was a sleeping porch out back with five or six beds in it—to this day people meet me in the street and say, "I slept with you"—and there was always room for our friends. A bunch of us went to sleep one night after hanging strings out of the window, with the other ends attached to our fingers. Some grownup had promised to pull on the strings and wake us at dawn so we could go down and watch the circus come into town.

My mother not only felt responsibility for us children, she fretted constantly about my father because of his heart. He was director of a bank in Waterbury, and each time he had to go to the phone to discuss various loans the bank was making, my mother would grit her teeth. "That bank will kill your father," she would mutter. I think she was relieved when it failed.

Mostly, though, she was full of gaiety. She came to football games with us, she was always invited to be a chaperone if a crowd of kids was going up to Dartmouth for the Carnival or spring holidays, and she'd try to remember our favorite foods for our birthdays. (My brother George preferred lima beans, though most of us inclined more toward lobster. When we had lobster we didn't have to drink milk, for some reason.)

All birthdays were celebrated alike. The dining room was hung with crepe paper, swirls of it stretched overhead from corner to corner, and the presents were put in the chair of the birthday person. The table was decorated with frilly paper cups full of salted almonds and we used the Sunday china (there were corner cabinets in our dining room holding everyday china, Sunday china, and very good stuff for the fancy guests) and we had ice cream molds in the shapes of little animals, like squirrels or rabbits.

((11))

It's funny what you remember. George and his lima beans, Annie Dorgan and the pink celluloid toilet sets. Annie was our cook. She weighed two hundred pounds, she stayed with us for twenty-two years, and at Christmas, she's all I can think of. We children would go to the five-and-ten with our limited funds, and we'd buy Annie those celluloid sets in underwear-pink. I'd give her the hair receiver, and one of my brothers would give her the comb, and another the brush, and somebody else would come up with the tray. They were the worst-looking things. (We adored Annie, and abused her shamelessly. She had a beau with whom she used to sit on the back steps. The poor fellow nipped a bit, and we'd hang out of the nursery window and drip water on him. When Annie made love to him—he didn't pay any attention to her, just sat there leaning forward as though he was about to be sick—she'd put her arms around him and pull him over to kiss him, and we'd splash away.)

Everything with the Russells was a celebration. We looked forward to Easter and the Easter baskets, and then we looked forward to the Fourth of July and Roman candles, and then we looked forward to Thanksgiving and turkey and sweet potatoes with marshmallows on top, and white turnips and yellow turnips and pies. I think that's good. I love the ritual, I love the feeling of family. Even after we grew up and went our separate ways, we all corresponded with one another, and with our aunts and uncles too. While my mother lived, I wrote her at least two or three times a week. Sometimes I still wake up in the night and think, I have to get a letter off to Mother . . .

Nowadays people just pick up a phone, everything's accelerated, it moves so fast. I don't like it as well.

My family was very Irish in the middle of New England Congregationalists—there was a great distrust of Catholics; we couldn't go into their churches, they weren't supposed to come into ours—but fortunately, my parents didn't approve of the hellfire and brimstone which was widely preached in my youth. Even so, I've always been afraid of death. I was in a retreat, on a day of recollection, when I was a very impressionable thirteen or fourteen years old, and a priest told a group of us girls that we had to think about burning in hell for eternity. By the time he'd finished describing eternity, our hearts were pounding, some of us were crying. I doubt if any of us ever fully got over the experience. I can see that priest now; I've never forgiven him.

In a family with a lot of kids, it goes without saying that there's competition. My sisters and I were supposed to share things—there would be two bikes instead of four—but we weren't very good at that, and I was envious of my older sister Clara because she was noticed —and noticeable—so when I wasn't crossing my eyes in a feverish bid for glory, I was pushing the younger girls around. My sister Mary Jane tells about herself and me staying with an aunt—when my mother and father traveled, we'd be rented out to various relatives—and being sent into the kitchen to wash and dry the dinner dishes. "All you did was snap the towel at my legs," Mary Jane says. "I'm still scarred from you with that dishtowel." She also vows that I whined to our aunt about her living conditions. "This street is too quiet, nothing goes on here," I'm reported to have said before I mushed out into the middle of the road to interrupt some boys playing ball and insist on their letting me into the game.

There was laughter in our house—thank God for the Irish sense of humor; it gets you through tight places—and no talk whatever about sex. I didn't know anything, and I was terrified. When a contemporary of Clara's came tearing into my room, closed the door and whispered that she'd kissed a boy and she thought she was pregnant, I studied her solemnly. "Yes," I said, "you could be pregnant. Maybe you are going to have a baby." Another girl had told me babies came out through the navel, that that's what the navel was about. Some education we got.

We heard rumors, of course. There were certain whispered conferences between my mother and father regarding my Uncle George. He was my father's brother, and he was very popular with the ladies in Connecticut. And probably with the ladies in Massachusetts and Rhode Island too. I think he had a few of them in trouble, as they used to say. So my father, acting *in loco parentis*, shipped George abroad. He was sent to Vienna to become a doctor. It made perfect sense; he knew quite a bit about the body. Every summer my father would travel to Europe to check on his younger brother, most often leaving my mother behind (since she was usually carrying a child), and on his way home he'd stop in Belgium to pick up a present for her:

a little diamond clip, a bar pin, a tiny heart set with matched stones.

Uncle George's exploits notwithstanding, I still had no idea where babies came from. Though boys were a good deal on my mind. I'd met a few boys from Taft (a prep school in nearby Watertown) at dancing class, and now and then I'd see them in Waterbury having luncheon with their visiting parents at the Hotel Elton, and sometimes I'd even take a streetcar up to Watertown and get off and walk around the movie theatre where the boys went. I looked at them, but I never spoke, and they never spoke either.

I had a sassy face and a lot of curls, and I was terribly conscious of being in the shadow of Clara, who was born glamorous. I stole her clothes, and I got into some kind of purply rouge my mother had—though I can't remember ever seeing that rouge on my mother's face—and I got caught. I always got caught, and had my face scrubbed with Pear soap. I was finally kissed by a boy up in our barn, and it was smelly there and he had fuzz on his face, and I didn't care for it at all.

The only thing I remember liking less was a handyman's chopping the head off a turkey one of us had won in a raffle. The turkey began running around the yard without its head, and turned me into a lifelong vegetarian. My family ate meat three times a day. Not me. My mother would say, "Finish your vegetables and drink your milk and eat your jello and you can go out to play," so I got away with it, and Mary Jane says now, "No wonder you were so healthy, you were eating the right things and none of us knew it."

I *was* healthy, and because I never had a proper norm against which to measure my energies, I thought they were limitless. I didn't need a lot of sleep, and I couldn't bear to lie down for fear of missing something.

Sometimes in my head I hear my father's voice declaring, "Balance is the art of living," and it makes me smile. Yes, Dad. That was one lesson he couldn't teach me.

My father was big on catch phrases, very Horatio Alger. "A quitter never wins, and a winner never quits," he would say. Or: "Beware the person who doesn't have an enemy. If you don't stand for something, you'll fall for anything."

He used to pay us not to drink alcohol—we charged for being virtuous—and he was passionate about keeping his family together and suspicious of the intentions of any boy who came around to see Clara more than three times. He didn't want his girls to marry. *His* girls. He was very Irish in that way. He didn't want anything to change our lives, and he summed up his fear almost wistfully. "It'll be all right until the strangers come," he said.

The Duchess

WHEN MY DAD used to say that to my mother about the strangers coming, I thought it was an expression of narrow-mindedness, a remark which revealed, despite the many excellences of my father, his limitations.

I'm not so sure any more. My sister Clara, who had a wonderful mind, instinctive flair, a gift for making people happy—men were wild about her, she'd float into a room and their faces would light up—went through two divorces, and while there's probably no connection, died too young of a stroke.

Still, Clara's legacy was—is—joy, not gloom.

In the family, we always called her the Duchess because even when she was a little girl, she was extremely grand. She was forever saying, "You're on your feet, dear, would you hand me that book over there?" or, "It's the phone, darling, and you're on your feet . . ."

My father adored her, which was undoubtedly the reason I went around crossing my eyes all the time. She didn't have to cross her eyes to be noticed, she had only to gaze out of those large sapphire-blue orbs, under those long black lashes, to melt the hearts of men.

There's a picture of the four earliest-born Russell children at a time when I was the baby, a two-year-old in a long christening-style dress. Brother James (was he eight? nine?) sits soberly in a wicker armchair, feet done up in white socks and shoes tied like ballet slippers around his ankles; brother John stands behind my chair, fair, sturdy, keeping his own four-year-old counsel; but it's the Duchess, stage center, who commands your eyes. An enormous ribbon bow sits, like the propeller on a biplane, on top of her short blond hair; her face, heart-shaped, serene, elegant in its bones, even at the age of six, is a face out of time. You could have set the Duchess down anywhere, in any span of this world, and she would have made her audience laugh, and feel better. (When the typewritten manuscript of *Auntie Mame* was first sent to me by its author, Patrick Dennis—the book hadn't yet been published—I sat up till late, reading it, and since I was due on a movie set early the next morning, Freddie fumed. "Put your light out, you'll have such dark circles the cameraman will kill you." But I was bemused. "Somebody has written my sister," I said. "Somebody has written the Duchess." I could have played Mame with one hand tied behind me: I'd been living with her all my life.)

As I mentioned before, my father had mixed emotions about Clara's popularity; he loved the fact of it but he didn't want the same fellows hanging around every Saturday. "Wasn't that young man here last week?" he would demand if he spotted a familiar presence among the boys who swarmed down from New Haven to buzz around the Duchess.

She called them all "Darling," and like an accomplished juggler tossing plates, kept them passing one another in midair and gravitating back toward her fingertips.

One of her Yale admirers was Rudy Vallée; I can see him now, wearing that raccoon coat.

The Duchess relished her salad days; she may have been green in judgment, but pink was the color of the filter through which she remembered them. Even after we were grown and she had become a fashion editor on *Town & Country* magazine, we'd have idiotic arguments about The Way It Had Been. "Dad was always saying, 'Oh, I envy the man who's taking you out tonight,' " the Duchess would start, and I would scoff: "Dad didn't talk like that, you imagined it."

I argued with her and I learned from her. She introduced me to career women, to the merchandising ladies, who were a special breed. Some were married, some supported drunken husbands. They were always going to quit after the fall collection. They were rough ladies in a rough business. Some of them were brutes to work for, never letting the salesgirls sit down; some of them were tragic, fighting hard in what they thought was a man's world. But they all had taste. And you can't buy taste, and you can't send away for it out of a catalogue. The Duchess had instinctive taste.

I remember one trip down Madison Avenue with her—it must have been in the forties, and she *owned* Madison Avenue, knew everybody—during which she was being older-sister bossy. She was waving to a girl who passed and crying, "Margie dear, call me, don't forget," and shaking hands with another woman and saying, "I'll see you Thursday," and in between these greetings she was trying to correct my taste. "Now, darling, you can't wear these Hollywood hats; in New York we're more conservative." (I think we all got our passion for hats from Mother. Once, when it wasn't legal to own such a thing in this country, Mother, ordinarily the soul of rectitude, had come home from Paris with an egret hidden on her person, sewn up in one side of a red silk coat.)

The Duchess was going on about my Hollywood hat and my shabby handbag—"Is that an old one of mine?"—when a man came by. She hailed him with great glee. "How have you been?" demanded the Duchess. "You don't need to tell me. I can see just by looking at you, you're in the best condition of your life. And how's your mother? Give her my love, she's one of my favorite people, always has been, always will be. Still going away weekends to the countryside? Well, it's wonderful to see you. Goodbye, dear."

The man had nodded to me, asked, "How are you, Roz?" We'd shaken hands, and now Clara and I were walking on down the street. "Darling," she said, "I know just as well as I know I'm walking here who that man is, but I can't think. Who *is* he?"

I stopped dead and looked her right in the face. She's not gonna pull both my legs, I thought; one at a time is enough. Then I realized she was in earnest.

"Now, Duchess," I began, but she was nattering on again: "I know him, I know I do—can't you give me a clue?"

"That was your first husband," I said.

"Oh my God!" she screamed. "Don't tell anybody. I'm going to stand right here until you promise. Raise your right hand and say, 'I will not tell anybody this story.'"

"I'm gonna tell everybody this story," I said.

"Now, that's mean," she said. "They'll think I'm senile or something."

"You're something," I said, "I can tell you that."

I've heard this same tale with other casts of characters—

Truman Capote wrote about Gloria Vanderbilt not recognizing *her* first husband—but I *know* it happened to the Duchess; I was there.

She was allowed to grow up fast, and she seemed to me so chic, so fabulous. I worshipped her and envied her; she had an enormous influence on me. My mother, who kept me under somewhat tighter rein, used to try to comfort me. "Now, now, your turn will come," she would say.

The first dance I ever went to—at Canterbury, a boys' Catholic prep school in New Milford—Clara wore a white satin sheath with a red satin insert, prefiguring Jean Harlow, while I was gussied up in a frilly peach number. Peach was my most unfavorite color and the scallops of the skirt hit me right in the wrong place on my long skinny legs; and because the dress was sashed with silver, my mother had a little silver bandeau made for my hair and bought me silver slippers with baby Louis heels, those heels that look as though they're being crushed by the weight of your body.

I was too tall, too gangly, I had too many curls and a million freckles, and I sat on the sidelines trying to look world-weary rather than abandoned. I'll never forget it. Ellen Mackey was a chaperone, though she was only nineteen. She had a brother at Canterbury. She wore black velvet, cut quite low, and grew up to marry Irving Berlin.

A glutton for punishment, I now embarked on a feverish social life, all engineered by Clara. She would shop around among her beaux and set up dates for me, but I was the one who had to lie myself out of the house. First I'd approach my mother in her sewing room. "Dad says I can go to the prom at New Haven with Clara and two boys," I would say. My mother would gaze at me thoughtfully. "If your father has lost his mind, he will have to take the entire responsibility for such an enterprise." Then I'd tear downstairs and into the library. "Dad, Mother says I can go to the prom at New Haven with Clara and two boys."

He'd look surprised. "At your age? Your mother agrees to a thing like this at your age? Well, your mother's a very sensible woman, and if she feels your older sister will look after you, you may go."

The year I was sixteen Clara got us invited for a weekend at Princeton, and the only gown I owned was still that damn peach-colored affair. I'd been so miserable wearing it that my parents said I could have a new dress. Not only was I given the money with which to buy it, I was also permitted to go to New York to shop. Clara came to the city with me; she was supposed to take me to Best and Company and help me select something suitable. Then we'd carry our suitcases and our purchases to Pennsylvania Station and take the train down to Princeton.

Somehow I talked the Duchess into letting me shop by myself. I promised to meet her at the information desk in the station at an agreed-upon time, and off I went, my ears ringing with instructions. Clara was a fountain of instructions. "Don't talk so much, wipe off that lipstick, they don't do this at New Haven, they do this at Princeton . . ."

She had a green chiffon dress, so I went and bought a white one. It was a humdinger. I cheated a little on the price, and used the money I'd held back to buy a black satin coat and a black satin hat that sat way over on one side of my head, and I wore them to the station. Can you imagine going off to Princeton in a black satin coat? In broad daylight? But oh, I was pleased with myself.

Of course I was late getting back to the information desk, and we missed our train, and Clara was fit to be tied. She took one look at my new vamp suit and started bawling me out. "Whatever have you got on? Does Mother know you've bought a coat like that?"

We boarded the next choo-choo headed for Princeton, and all the way down, Clara rained instructions. "There are no fraternities at Princeton, there are eating clubs at Princeton. Take off that rouge. We're going to Tiger Inn tonight, and then tomorrow there are the boat races"—it was a spring weekend, as I recall—"and Saturday night . . ."

But I wasn't listening about Saturday night. It seemed too far away. I had it in my mind that I had to get in there fast and make a big impression on Friday night, or the whole weekend would be a bust. I'm going to wear the new white chiffon Friday night, I thought, and then if I can meet up with something that takes to me, he won't mind the peach job on Saturday.

So we traveled, my sister's voice an obbligato to the fantasies being woven under a black satin hat clinging perilously to a clump of wiry curls.

We arrived at the house where we were to stay in Princeton with just enough time to dump our bags and come down for tea. The tea was so we could meet and mingle with the boys. On the way to our room I spied a pool table, and by the time Clara had powdered her nose and come looking for me, I was already in action, cue in hands, one leg up on the table, threatening to sink two balls in separate pockets as part of my I'm-a-better-man-than-you-are act which so endeared me to the male sex.

Thick is the only word for it. Despite my studying Clara faithfully, I was a slow learner. (When I came to do *Wonderful Town*, my girlhood experiences stood me in good stead. I asked Betty Comden and Adolph Green to write me a number about how I couldn't get a man, and they went off to put one together and came back with a blues song. "No," I said. "No, no, that's a song for after you've had a man, and he's done left you, and you sit at the bar and say set 'em up, Joe, with the cigarette hanging out of your mouth. This character hasn't had a man." They went away again, and came back again and said they'd been struggling but they couldn't get what I wanted. "Listen," I said, "let me tell you the story of my life. If I went out in a car with a boy, and that car sputtered and stopped, the boy would say, 'I think it's the carburetor,' and I'd say, 'Oh, get away from there, it's dirt on the points, I'll take care of it.' And I'd take care of it, and I'd never see that boy again. If I went to a football game with a boy, and he said, 'The next play is going to be a forward pass,' I'd say, 'You're crazy, it's gonna be an end run, can't you see the way old number seven is fading back?' And they'd run an end, and I'd never see *that* boy again. If a boy tried to kiss me, I'd say, 'Are you kidding?' and make a repulsive face. Of course I was sorry after I did it, and I'd spend the next few days waiting by the phone, but the boy wouldn't call again." We got a hit song—"One Hundred Easy Ways to Lose a Man"—out of Betty's and Adolph's talent and my suave techniques with the opposite sex.)

That Friday night at Princeton, Clara hauled me away from the pool table, and we how-dood the young men. She knew them all anyway—it was Tom and Joe and Bruce and ooh, darling. (That ooh of hers can't be reproduced on the printed page. It was a kind of mixture of whoop and coo, followed by flutey laughter.) Then she and I went back to our room to lay out our dresses and take our baths.

I spread the white chiffon on the bed. The Duchess' eyes narrowed. "What's that? Does Mother know you have that?"

"Well, Dad gave me the money—what did you think I was shopping for?"

She studied the dress, and then she studied me. "You're not wearing your peach tonight?"

"No, I'm wearing this tonight."

"Hmm," she said. "I'll take my bath first."

Naturally.

Out of the tub at last, she stands there, my pink-and-white sister, all rosy, with the straight yellow hair I grudge her, and while I'm getting ready for my soak, she's talking. She lights a cigarette, and she never stops to take a breath, making me a gift of her endless instructions. "First we go to such-and-such a club, but don't eat too much, because later we'll have scrambled eggs at such-and-such a place . . ." And all the time I'm saying to myself, That's what she thinks. I'm going to dump her as fast as I can; I'm going off on my own in a blaze of white chiffon.

Blaze, indeed. Call it an unfortunate burst of intuition. Clara leaned over the bed to put her shoes on, cigarette still in hand, and the next thing I saw was my chiffon dress in flames.

My heart broke. All I could think of was, That means the peach for both nights.

My sister was stomping out the fire. When she had finished, there was a fine hole clear through the front of the bodice, over the bosom, and out the back. Of course, I had the kind of bosom you could expose and not know whether it was front or back, but still—

I couldn't help it, I started to cry. "Look what you've done!" I sniveled, and the Duchess genuinely felt bad. "Now, now, don't give up, wait a minute, let me think," she commanded, and grabbed up our cloche hats. Each of us owned a rhinestone pin, one was shaped like an elephant and one like a rabbit; they'd been fastened on our cloches to perk them up. The Duchess tore the pins from the hats, gathered my chiffon, and pulling together the edges of the hole in front, stabbed the elephant pin through the mess. Then she pulled the edges of the hole in back into a tiny bunch and skewered them with the rabbit. "There," she said, proudly displaying her handiwork. "It's just decorated, and you'll be all right."

I wore it. A glittering clump on my chest, a glittering

clump between my shoulder blades, and a little evening bag held up to my collar bone, with the vain idea that it—and my two arms—might disguise the improvements the Duchess had wrought in my costume.

I never saw her again that night. She was going to be punished. Let her worry about where I was. Let her think there had been rape in the bushes, and wonder how she was going to break the news to my father. I wasn't going anywhere with *her*.

I toddled off with the boy she'd arranged for me, and we went from one club to another, dancing a few dances in each place. In those days everything was the stag line, and you looked desperately around, hoping unattached males would find you attractive and cut in on you. And every now and then I'd hear the "ooh, darling" and the flutey laughter, and I'd know my sister was arriving. "Let's beat it out of here," I'd say to my date, and we'd leave by a side door.

When I got back to the room I shared with the Duchess, there was a good deal of suspicion and "Where have you been?" but I could tell her exactly what kind of music they'd been playing at Tiger Inn and what kind of food they'd served at another house, so she knew I'd really been to those places, and she was mollified.

Next day the boat races, and another dust-up. "You're not wearing that satin coat," she said. I realize now she saved me from horrible embarrassment, but while she was dragging out my traveling outfit—the sweater and skirt I'd been wearing when I'd got on the train in Waterbury—and pushing my reluctant body into it, I was sulking.

Once before I tried to write about the Duchess. I made some notes, but she's hard to capture. Because she was at once totally sophisticated and absolutely naïve. (This is Auntie Mame's character too.)

Example: I didn't drink till I was about twenty-four, but two or three times when Clara and I were still living at home, I'd splash whiskey all over me like perfume and come in and put on a drunk act for her. An unspeakably bad, broad drunk act.

"Hullo," I'd say, staggering. "Wha' you doin' there, readin' that apple?"

((23))

Every time she'd fall for it. She'd drop her book, grab me. "Oh, come in here, close that door, oh, this is terrible, what if Mother saw you like this?"

She was so sweetly dumb. And so smart. She was an authority on the Irish poets (how many loved *her* moments of glad grace), she was always reading Macauley, she was funny and she was easy. My darling Duchess, I still miss her.

"We're Tenting Tonight on the Old Campground, Give Us a Song to Cheer…"

WALTER KITTREDGE,
"Tenting on the Old Camp-Ground"

IN THE SAME WAY that I remember myself being overshadowed by the Duchess, my younger sister Mary Jane remembers being submerged by me, as I have only just, to my amazement, found out. The way I found out is, I sent Mary Jane the first pages of these reminiscences, hoping she might set me straight if I had garbled any of the facts of our childhood. I told her I thought I had presented an honest account, even to telling the truth about how I'd flicked at her scrawny legs with that old dishtowel. Well, I got a letter back in which Mary Jane—exaggerating ferociously—says she was bossed by me to the point where I "dragged" her to summer camp. "You make it sound as though we kids were constantly abandoned while our parents gallivanted," she writes, "but the fact is, you *liked* camping."

It's true. I liked camping. When I was fifteen I frizzed my hair, put on makeup, and went to New York to meet the owners of a new Catholic camp called Jeanne d'Arc, in the Adirondacks. I wanted a job as riding counselor, and I told a lot of lies, like that I was nineteen and owned something called the Greystock Stables. They'd never heard of the Greystock Stables. "Why, they're some of the largest in the East," I said, and they hired me.

When I came home and told that story, Dad, who always matched our earnings—if we made a quarter sweeping the walk, he'd give us another quarter—threw back his head and roared. "I hope I don't have too much to match," he said, and I said, "A hundred and fifty dollars," and his mouth fell open. He knew I'd never taught anybody how to ride a horse—I'd never even bothered to read a book about it.

I'd also told the Jeanne d'Arc people I had a younger sister who was dying to go to camp. It was the last thing in the world Mary Jane wanted to do; she liked boys and loathed competitive sports, and she spent the ensuing summer wishing she was back at Laurel Beach with Milton Hollister and her other boyfriends.

Milton Hollister had a crush on me. Once he and Mary Jane were out shooting baskets beside our barn—she was trying to get the ball in, and missing, and cooing "Oh, you must help me" to old Milton—and I came along and picked up the ball and went plop, plop, plop, plop, four tries, four baskets. Milton Hollister looked at me with big calf's eyes and then he said to Mary Jane, "Why can't *you* do that? *She's* a girl."

"She's not a girl," Mary Jane said. "She's a monster."

By the end of the Jeanne d'Arc summer, my story about the Greystock Stables had been worked up from twenty to ninety-six horses (in my fertile brain, they were breeding fast), and Mary Jane made the mistake of going to Philadelphia for a weekend with her friend Rosalie, who came from a really horsy family that had stables with grooms and Arabian stallions.

"Daddy, this is the sister of our riding counselor," Rosalie said, introducing Mary Jane, and Daddy's eyes glittered. "Yeeeeees," he drawled, "the one who owns the Greystock Stables. I understand she has the only women's polo team in the world."

At Jeanne d'Arc the girls had to pay ten dollars extra for riding lessons, but I got bored and decided to give a play on horseback. I wasn't supposed to have anything to do with dramatics, but I had those kids rehearsing all summer. Everybody was on horses, carrying ribbons and surrounding me while I played Jeanne d'Arc. I wrote the play too.

Once I took fifteen girls, including Mary Jane, on an overnight horseback trip. The camp authorities weren't sure it was such a hot idea, but I told them I had arranged for food and knew where there was a little cabin to sleep in.

We set off, me with all these eleven-year-olds on the dumbest camp horses, and we went further and further and it got darker and darker. We were practically in Canada. When Mary Jane and the girls asked me where the "little cabin" was—we'd been riding eight hours and we were tired and hungry—they got no answer. Mary Jane rode up alongside me and said, "Are you sure you have enough food?" and I waffled. "Well," I said, "it's not gonna be a *big* supper . . ."

It started to rain, and I bedded the girls down in a meadow —luckily they'd been made to carry ponchos as part of their camping equipment—and a couple of drunks appeared out of nowhere. "Loo-kit all these girls in here," one of them said, and I snarled, "You go away, or I'll call the police." There was nobody to call, except maybe the Royal Canadian Mounties, but the drunks took to their heels.

Next day, on the trip home, it was still raining. Twenty miles we'd come, and we had to go twenty miles back again.

Mary Jane didn't like anything about camp; for her, it lacked Milton Hollister. And she kept brooding because our older brothers never had to go to camp, and Clara only went for a few weeks, once. She left in the middle of the season, by popular demand. (A boy named Bill Jones had come up to see her, and she went over the fence, stayed out too late, and that was the end of that.)

I used to sneak out every night when I was a counselor. Who needed sleep? I'd blow taps, put the younger kids to bed, then beat it, and get back in the morning in time to blow reveille. I had an old car called the Thunderbolt (you had to start it with a hairpin) and I'd drive over to Lake Bombazine and dance.

My bugle calls were a riot, anyway. When I applied for the job, in addition to horsemanship, musical ability was required. "Do you play the bugle?" they asked me, and I said, "Of course." Then I came home and borrowed a horn from a musician working in the local music hall and practiced an hour or so with him. I didn't know

((27))

one tune from another, but I bluffed it through. I think I was doing that "Come and get your beans, boys, come and get your beans" call for reveille.

Mary Jane says I was as bossy at home as I was at camp, that I insisted people call the parlor the music room ("But it's the parlor," Mother said) and that I also changed her (Mary Jane's) name. She had been christened Mary Russell, but I thought that sounded dumb, so I stuck the Jane in the middle.

When George and Mary Jane went away to boarding schools, I wrote them portentous advice. "I want you to remember, you must always go forward, there is no standing still in life, you must make something of yourselves." I had a big thing about mediocrity.

Sometimes it must have seemed to Dad that there wasn't *enough* "standing still in life." Everything kept getting more complicated. I remember the day he stopped slicing roasts at the table. He looked around, said, "There are too many children," and handed Mother the knife. "From now on, Clara, you carve."

And I remember as we children got older and started playing phonograph records, instead of improving ourselves with intelligent discussion, it drove Dad wild. "What is all this lollygagging about?" he would cry. "Go out, do something."

And I remember the time I set the house on fire. A man who saw the smoke came and knocked at the door and said to Dad, "Mr. Russell, your house is on fire," and Dad turned him away. "You've been drinking," Dad said. "Now you just go right along."

Next thing you know, somebody else came and said the house was on fire, and it was true. I had been smoking a cigarette on the porch and had set the shingles ablaze.

For smoking, for sneaking out at night, for not exercising the horses when I'd said I would, I was forever being marched "upstairs, please" to be switched with those Yale banners. Annie Dorgan would follow Mother and me and wrap her huge arms around me to protect me from my punishment. "Dawn't you touch 'er, Mrs. Russell, dawn't you touch 'er," Annie would say, and Mother would sigh in exasperation and beg Annie to mind her own business.

We kids led charmed lives. I never hurt any of us in a car, though I sometimes wonder how on earth we escaped. Before I got the Thunderbolt, before I even had a driver's license—because of

((28))

Dad's prejudice, none of us was trained to drive while he lived—we had highway adventures. The Duchess had so many beaux, and they all left their jalopies parked in our driveway with the keys in them, and I'd say to the younger kids, "Come on, we'll go for a ride," even though I didn't know the brake from the gas pedal when I started.

Once we ran out of gas in Oakville—we hadn't been aware that the Duchess' gentleman caller had left so little fuel in his tank —and I drove right into a gas station and said, "Fill it up." The fellow did, and then said, "That'll be three dollars and forty-two cents." "We don't have—" George started to say, but I was quicker still. "Shut up," I said, and turned to the attendant. "Young man, what kind of cigarettes do you smoke?"

"Lucky Strikes," said the young man.

"Oh," I said, "good," and handed him a package, holding it upside down with my palm over the torn part so he couldn't tell that it had been opened and was only a third full. I had the car in gear, and I drove away, with George and Mary Jane sitting astonished in the back seat.

The Thunderbolt was named after the roller coaster at Savin Park, where we used to go as children. I paid thirty dollars for it, ten dollars apiece to three boys who were being graduated from Yale and wanted to get rid of the piece of junk. The Thunderbolt had no keys, and it went chug, chug, chug all the way home. On the days when it made it home.

One of my first drives in the Thunderbolt, I took Mary Jane down a hill, and there was a stop sign at the bottom, and I went right through it and across the street and into a stone wall. Very gently. It didn't demolish the car, but it certainly didn't help it either. "Roz," Mary Jane said, pointing back to the lethal corner, "that's a stop sign there."

"Damn well should be," I am reported to have said.

The older kids were never involved in the Thunderbolt high jinks; by then Jim was busy singing "Hindustan" in his college play, and the Duchess, well, she just thought we were clowns.

I've never minded being a clown. Clowns make people laugh, and that was always something I loved to do.

"A Nice Catholic Girl Doesn't Do That..."

THOUGH WE LOST my sister Clara, and we lost my brother John, these blows were dealt to us as adults; our childhood was uninterrupted by tragedy.

True, we were asked to be aware of kids who didn't share our privileges and pleasures. My Dad said it wasn't enough to dole out five dollars to a charity once in a while; each of us had to pick—and to serve—a cause bigger than himself. (Seeing a lame child walking the streets of Waterbury, I chose my cause—or it chose me. Then until now, I've worked for crippled children through whatever means—The March of Dimes, Sister Kenny—presented themselves.)

But mostly the little Russells had fun. I tried never to let school interfere with my serious education (like studying the leading lady's blue eye shadow from way up in the third tier), no matter how many nuns might telephone complaining that Rosalind had not been to St. Margaret's Grammar School today. Or, later, to Notre Dame Academy. (A Catholic girls' high school is always called an academy.) But by the time I got to Marymount College, at Tarrytown-on-Hudson, where I boarded, it was necessary to evolve more elaborate schemes for achieving freedom. You couldn't just not show up, because you *lived* there. And because I was rebellious, I was always being confined to the school grounds for some misdemeanor or other; I'd never have got a weekend at home if I'd had to earn one, so I took to killing off my Aunt Mary Jane. And this is how dopey I was—I had her die about three times, the first year I went to Marymount. She always met her Maker on a Friday morning. I don't know why I could never think of another excuse. I'd have one of my sisters send a telegram: "Mary Jane died today, come home for funeral." A little death could break a girl loose, even a girl who'd been grounded, but why an uncle's name, or a different aunt's name, never occurred to me, I still haven't figured out.

I was expelled from Marymount four or five times my freshman year. Once it almost took. I'd got clear into the taxicab, when the Dean, Reverend Mother Girard, came down the front steps, opened the taxi door, and without saying a single word, hooked her thumb over her right shoulder and gestured me back upstairs.

The trouble was, I had to bust any rule I thought was silly. Make a rule, and I'd push against it. Heavily. Many of the rules *were* silly. When you think of putting college women eighteen years of age to bed at nine or nine-thirty, it seems insane. We weren't supposed to have food in our rooms, either, and I ran a whole delicatessen out of my bathroom. As a result, I had a few mice, but mice have never bothered me. I'd wave at them and throw them a little cheese.

I stocked all the cheeses under the sun, and I was always caught, because Russell's Deli was open seven days a week and the traffic gave me away. I didn't mind too much when the shop was finally shut up for good; it was too tough to collect my money, what with everybody yelling "Charge it" as they fled, mouths full, down the halls.

Marymount was really a country club (though I'd better watch what I say; they've just given me the first of their outstanding alumnae awards in place of the degree I didn't stay around long enough to collect). All the lace-curtain Irish went there. There, or Manhattanville. The Kennedys put Manhattanville on the map, but some pretty fancy fillies matriculated at Marymount. There was another silly rule I just remembered. If you were going to a dance, you had to submit your dress for the nuns' approval. Well, of course you showed them a dress with the neck up around your chin, but you never took that dress to the dance, you took the lowest-cut one you could find, or you left the zipper undone. It didn't mean a thing, showing your dress.

These days they don't have such strict rules in most schools. If you want to stay up till all hours and make a wreck of yourself, they let you, and I think that's better. So does Lance, who was born in 1943. When he went off to prep school at Hotchkiss, he found the boys weren't allowed to smoke, so he'd sneak into the woods and light up. (He doesn't smoke at all, now it isn't forbidden.) And when it came to the opposite sex, he was as slow as I had been.

He once said to me—he was about seventeen—"You know, Mom, I'm not very fast with girls."

He was attractive, too, not one of those really grungy ones with pimples. But from the time he was fourteen until he was eighteen, he seldom dated a girl. I think that's wrong. He went to one dance at Bennington, traveled on the bus with other Hotchkiss boys, didn't like the girl he'd been matched up with, and for the next three years, stayed away. I'd say, "Darling, why don't you go?" He'd pretend to be uninterested. "Oh, they're a bunch of dogs over there." And I knew from experience, the poor girls were just as confused as he was.

If this sounds like a vote for coeducation, it is.

At Marymount, I was a demon athlete. Our basketball team had beaten Manhattanville and another Catholic girls' school, so we considered ourselves great Olympic material. Our prowess came to the attention of Marymount's benefactor, a Mr. Butler who owned the Butler Stores (they were like the A&P stores) and a famous race track up in the Bronx. Butler Hall (the senior hall at Marymount) had been the Butlers' Tarrytown home, and during my sojourn there, the head of the school was Mr. Butler's sister, the Reverend Mother Butler.

Mr. Butler had lost his son in World War I, and on the anniversary of the son's death I took my bugle to the chapel and played taps for him. (The chapel at Marymount was beautiful—pure white, with a blue carpet, a runner that led to the altar, very simple, very nice.)

Anyhow, Mr. Butler was kindly disposed toward us girls, especially toward us bugle-blowing basketball players, and he said if we could win an upcoming game against a certain physical-education school, he'd treat our team to a trip to Europe. (The Marymount nuns also ran a school in Paris; their order had originated there.)

The team was elated. We went to the beauty parlor before the game. Then we dressed in white blouses with Peter Pan collars, put our Marymount blue jumpers over them, added clean white socks and clean white sneakers.

When we took the court against the players from the physical-education school, we were amazed. We'd never seen anything like those girls. They were wearing short shorts and sweat shirts, pared down for action.

Even so, we held our own. At the half, the score was 24 to 24. We rushed to a telephone and called Mr. Butler. "We're going to win, get ready for Paris, you can count on us."

Then we went back for the second half, and I noticed that I had a different guard. I was playing forward, because I was tall, but this guard was about six foot six. Clearly, we'd been up against the school's fourth team, and now they'd got tired of toying with us and had sent in their second team. They didn't have to bother about their first. We never touched the ball again, not even at tip-off. They just kept going bum, in, bum, in, bum, in. The final score was something like 112 to 24. I never forgot that game. We were such ninnies, thinking we could beat those big apes.

➤ Life was pretty much all games for me until I was nineteen. Then my father died. He stood up to open a window in his office, dropped to the floor, and was gone. Everything about death is so complicated—in the middle of the grief and the drama, something will strike you funny. We held a wake for my father—wakes have more or less gone out of style, thank the good Lord—and since he'd been a friend to everyone for miles around, all these people with shawls over their heads came to the house. And when my sisters and brothers and I, in our black suits and dresses, opened the front door —we were trying to save my mother from being commiserated with by the whole town, trying to keep her upstairs because she had an eye infection and crying was bad for her—the shawled mourners would walk right past us, and keep marching through the whole downstairs until they got clear to the kitchen. There was Dad, laid out in the music room, surrounded by piano, Victrola, little gold chairs, and everybody who'd come to see him was going right past him in the wrong direction, and we Russells would start to say, "Excuse me, wait a moment, this way, please," and find ourselves doubled over with unseemly, uncontrollable hysterics.

My father's will made the law journals. It said that his children could have as much education as they wanted—and could be supported while they were getting it—but once they were out of school, no more money until they'd worked for three years. When this was first read to us, we thought it meant only the boys, that Dad was trying to tempt them to stay at their books in preparation for making a living later. But the will said "all my lawful issue." Girls too.

The baby of the family, Josephine (we call her Phine), had no intention of going to work—and she didn't, for years—so she's the most, if not the best, educated of us all. Phine signed up for any kind of lesson that came down the pike—Dad's will wasn't restrictive—and there were months when she studied crewelwork, and other months when she turned to embroidery, and painting on porcelain, and stamp collecting. I think she pasted two stamps in a book, then exhausted that interest. Once, after not having seen her for a while, I asked Phine what she was up to, and she beamed. "I'm taking smiling lessons," she said.

I figured it was probably true. "That's good, that's fine," I said. "How are you getting on? Do you think you'll get your degree?"

Unlike her, I was eager to be employable and employed, but what I wanted was the theatre, and I didn't know quite how to broach that to my mother. I'd done some acting in my first year at Marymount—I played St. Francis Xavier, wore a beard, flagellated myself—and loved it. I wanted to quit college and go to the American Academy of Dramatic Arts in New York City. But reared as I had been, I didn't dare to think of becoming an actress. I knew what the nuns would say. "A nice Catholic girl doesn't do that . . ." Because actresses were known to be, if not drug addicts, at least heavy drinkers.

I finally had an inspiration. I told my mother I wanted to teach speech. We all knew about my good loud voice. Miraculously, she thought that was a good idea. "You'll have nice long vacations," she said.

Fine. For once I was going to break out of a school with permission of the proper authority. So long, Marymount; hello, God knows what.

That night, up in my bedroom, I peered out of the window through the darkness. For so many years this room had been the heart of my world. When I was very little I'd stood there by the same window, listening to the sounds of Willow Street, the trolleys and the automobiles and the sometime laughter of girls passing by with their young men. And always I had known there was something more out there, and I was anxious to know what that something might be. And always I had known I would get out, that I would go.

"It Must Be Obvious
That You're Not Wanted
in the Theatre..."

I CAME CRASHING down on the American theatre the same year as the stock market. It was 1929 when I was graduated from the American Academy of Dramatic Arts and began sitting in the Shuberts' office, hoping to be noticed by the Shuberts. Sad to say, though Lee and J.J. used to pass me on their way in and on their way out, that was as far as our relationship progressed. Sometimes I would go from the Shuberts' office to the office of an agent named Chamberlain Brown, and sit in *his* reception room, just for the change of scene.

I was in the Brown office trying to look professional—without ever having had a professional job—the day the old lady appeared. She was all bent over, wearing a long black coat, and she doddered up to the desk behind which the office boy was planted. It was like a scene out of a B movie; the office boy had his feet up, he was reading *Variety,* and he never lifted his eyes from the paper, just said, "Nothing, nothing for you today," and the old lady shuffled out again.

Filled with self-righteousness, I sprang to my feet. "Did you have to speak that way to that old woman?"

This time the office boy looked up. I can still see his face behind big horn-rimmed glasses. "You're new, aren't you?" he said.

I declared that that had nothing to do with it. "You could have been kinder—"

He interrupted what promised to be a lecture. "Let me tell you something," he said. "That old woman made up her mind a long time ago to be an actress. And she's had plenty of chances and she stinks. She ought to wake up to the fact. She should be selling ribbons down at Macy's. So you just forget about her."

I went back to my chair and sat down, and a cold sweat came on me and an awful fear. I could see myself fifty years from now trailing yards of dusty woolen with the hem down, staggering into this very office, a pint of gin in one hand, a pleading look on my seamed face.

A terrible question assaulted me: What if you just *think* you're an actor, and you aren't one? Nothing at the Academy had prepared me for that moment. I lived to learn that most performers face this terror at some time or other; in a play called *Epitaph for George Dillon*, the actor-protagonist says there's something worse than having the "disease" of talent, and that is "having the same symptoms as talent, the pain, the ugly swellings, the lot—but never knowing whether or not the diagnosis is correct."

That day, in Chamberlain Brown's office, I made a pact with myself. I was going to have a five-year plan. I'd serve my apprenticeship, play bit parts, maids, whatever I could latch on to, and try to work my way up, but if I hadn't made good in five years, I'd go back to the idea of teaching.

My stint at the Academy had equipped me to show other students how to stand, how to sit, how to fence, how to walk into a room without looking down at their feet, how to step over a doorsill without tripping. Art, being unteachable, was something else again, and probably wouldn't be expected of your garden-variety instructor. (Though in my day there was one great teacher at the Academy—his name was Jellinger; we referred to him as Jelly—who managed to communicate both method *and* magic to his students.)

I know some actors sneer at dramatic schools, say they're nonsense, but I feel a school gives you the kind of confidence it would take you years to acquire anywhere else. When I was at the Academy, the boys—particularly the boys—were agonizingly shy. We'd all take our coats off, hang them on hooks in the cloakroom, but if a girl tried to engage a boy in conversation—"Good morning, I see Columbia beat Brown yesterday"—he would choke on an answer. Inhibited as those boys were, a dramatic school could only be good for them, could help them to find their voices so that even if they went on to become shoe salesmen, they'd be better shoe salesmen.

But I wasn't fixing to sell shoes, I was going to be a Broadway star. After two years at the Academy, I got the lead in *The Last of Mrs. Cheyney,* our graduation play. The cast was encouraged to invite theatrical friends to the performance, but the only theatrical person I knew was Lucy Monroe. She was famous for singing "The Star-Spangled Banner" every place in the world. I asked her and her mother.

Next day, on the stage of the Lyceum Theatre, Edward G. Robinson, a former graduate of the Academy, addressed us new-minted actors, and then my mother and I went back to a dressing room to pick up our coats.

A man was standing there waiting. "Miss Russell?" he said. I said yes.

"I have a stock company in Greenwich," he said, "and I'd like very much for you to join us this summer."

Silence. Fellow students who'd been milling about stopped dead. My mother stared. I was so startled I didn't know what to say. "How much do you pay?" I heard myself asking.

"A hundred and fifty dollars a week," said the man.

I gasped—I'd never known a beginner could get that kind of money—and the man shrugged. "Well, I know you have a lot of clothes . . ."

(He knew I had a lot of clothes—most of them handed down by the Duchess, who was already working in New York writing copy for Best and Company—because he'd been to the school to inquire about me and because he'd seen *The Last of Mrs. Cheyney,* but I didn't find this out until afterward.)

Thrown though I was, I thought I'd better bargain. I'd been warned that bargaining was one of the rules of the game. "I don't believe a hundred and fifty dollars is enough," I said.

With that, the man started backing out of the dressing room. He kept looking at me and just going and going and going and going till he backed right through the door, and I watched him with my mouth open. I was sick. I knew I'd never again be offered one hundred and fifty dollars in my whole life.

My mother and I went to have tea up at the old Ritz-Carlton

on Madison Avenue, and there we met some friends, and my mother told them the news. "Rosalind was offered a professional job in a professional theatre. A hundred and fifty dollars a week. Just now. I was there, I heard it, the professional theatre, not the amateur theatre."

Sick or not, I felt a pang of happiness. My mother was proud of me, and I could quit worrying about being a teacher. I knew now she wasn't going to be mad if I tried to become an actress.

But she wasn't going to be patient, either. As a graduation present she took me to Bermuda for a week, and when we got back she went off to Waterbury and left me in New York to find acting employment. Four days later my telephone rang. It was my mother. "Now, Rosalind," she said, "it must be obvious to you by this time that you're not wanted in the theatre, so come home."

I begged her to suspend this fierce judgment for a little bit longer. By then my office sitting had begun, and as I watched the Shuberts mushing into their private chambers and slamming the door behind them, I used to fantasize that they spent long, useless afternoons sniffing the delicious smells that wafted up from Sardi's while going out of their way to ignore the brilliant talent—me—in their anteroom.

Here I was, willing to serve my apprenticeship, and nobody cared. Then I met Ed Casey.

For some reason—an appointment? an audition?—I had found myself in an old rehearsal hall on 44th or 45th Street, a building cut up into dozens of studios furnished with practice barres and mirrors and camp chairs. Plaster cracked and fell from the ceilings like the gentle rain from heaven; paint peeled down the sides of the rackety radiators; half the ivory facings had been knocked off the white keys of the venerable upright pianos; the vocalizing—mee-ee, may-ee, ma-ee—of unseen sopranos came through the walls to quarrel with the sharp counts—1-2-3-4, 2-2-3-4—of chorus dancers, and sometimes you could pick up a casting tip in the halls.

This day I heard a fellow talking to a friend. "No," he was saying, "he doesn't cast till the end of May." I butted in. "Excuse me, may I ask whom you're speaking about?"

He looked suspicious. "A guy named Ed Casey," he said

reluctantly. "He has a company in Saranac Lake." Pressed for details, he offered one further fact. Mr. Casey lived someplace on Long Island.

I tore down to the lobby. Under the stairs on the ground floor there was a phone, not in a booth, just on the wall, and nearby, several worn, torn phone books. I attacked the Queens directory.

I found the right Ed Casey in Forest Hills, and told him my name. "I understand you have a company in Saranac Lake," I said.

He'd been around the track before. "I don't cast for another month," he said wearily.

I asked when he was coming to town.

"Well," he said, "I'm coming to town tomorrow. To go to the dentist, if anybody cares. But I won't be casting—"

"I think you ought to see me," I said. "Because I have to go on a trip." The trip was to Waterbury, but he didn't need to know that.

After a bit of an argument he agreed to meet me in the Astor Hotel. In the lobby. He'd be finished at the dentist's at about four o'clock.

Next afternoon I was skulking behind the potted plants in the Astor lobby, ruminating on Ed Casey—would he be young? old? fat? thin?—when a voice sounded in my ear. "Are you Miss Russell?"

Mentally I assigned him points for brilliance. It didn't hit me that the number of young women bobbing around in the Astor's bushes at any given moment was probably limited.

"I have to go away," I said hoarsely, "so could you sign me now if you think I'm right for anything in your company?"

"Well, what do you play?" said he, clearly fascinated.

"I play anything," I said. "I mean, I think I'm right for the second woman."

"I don't need a second woman," he said, "I need a leading woman—"

"That's really what I am," I said, "but I didn't want to start by telling you that for fear you'd think I was conceited." (Females in a stock company consisted of leading woman, second woman, character woman and ingénue, but I was going to be whatever Ed Casey wanted.)

He asked me what I'd done, and I said I'd worked in Hartford at the Parsons Theatre. I thought maybe I could get my brother John to phone somebody there who'd be willing to cover for me. "Also," I said, "I worked in a stock company you never heard of. In Pennsylvania."

"I like you," said Ed Casey. I was so new at the game I didn't even realize it was a miracle. Two weeks out of school, and a producer liked me. Wouldn't everybody? "But I want my wife to see you," Mr. Casey was saying. "She's going to meet me here."

Mrs. Casey came along; he and she did a good deal of whispering—I knew they were intrigued, because from where I was watching I could see Mrs. Casey's head nodding up and down—and then he came back to me and said I had the job. "What's your salary?"

I was a quick learner. "A hundred and fifty dollars a week," I said brazenly.

"Whew!" he said. "My partner's going to have a fit. He has in mind a girl who'd never cost what you cost—he thinks we could get her for thirty dollars a week, but I'm going to take the gamble."

The minute I'd left the Academy, I'd rushed to join Actors Equity (these days somebody has to want you and hire you before the union will let you in; in those days if you could stand up, you could sign up), so I told Mr. Casey I had to have my contract. Now. I don't know how I convinced him of the necessity for speed, but I wasn't going to turn back into a pumpkin if I could avoid it. At five-thirty on that still-wintry April afternoon—it was already dark in the streets —I dragged the amiable Mr. Casey to the Equity office, where we signed a contract. I carried my copy around in my fist for days.

Dissolve to June. Rosalind Russell, leading lady, steps off the choo-choo at Saranac Lake. The rest of the acting company is there to meet her. Her appearance is greeted by an unearthly scream.

What is it? she wonders. What *is* it?

"It" was Casey's partner, a man named Dick Bartel. "That's the one," he howled. "That's the one I saw at the school in *The Last of Mrs. Cheyney*. That's the one I told you we could get for thirty dollars a week. She's never worked anyplace in her life!"

Lesson Number Two: Never lie, because you always get caught. Not to mention Lesson Number Three: Never walk through a performance, even at school, because you don't know who's out there looking at you. (Lesson Number One is: Never haggle over salary unless you can afford to watch the guy back out the door.) Actually, I'm not so sure about Lesson Number Two, because lying sometimes pays off. Obviously.

The theatre in Saranac Lake was in a tent, the stage and the box office fashioned of birch bark. (I once told a boy that I began in a tent, and he hooted, "You must have been a scream in tights." "It wasn't a circus, you jerk," I said, "it was a stock company.")

The town of Saranac Lake, set down in New York State's northern Adirondacks and known for the sweetness of its cold mountain air, was a haven for tuberculosis suffers. In 1876 a doctor named Edward Livingstone Trudeau had come there to die, but was so revived by the climate that he lived to found a sanatorium, and after the first World War, Edward Albee (the playwright's father) put together an association that built a hospital to take care of sick vaudevillians.

Ed Casey himself had had tuberculosis, which was why he'd formed his company in Saranac Lake. Now the question seemed to be, had he survived a dread disease, only to be murdered by an outraged partner? Luckily, Mr. Bartel decided it was funny for one dumb kid to have outsmarted two seasoned entrepreneurs, and during the whole summer season that I played for him and Casey—twenty-six plays in thirteen weeks—he brought me thirty dollars every Friday night. (We got paid in cash because they took the salaries right out of the box-office receipts.) I'd get the other one hundred and twenty dollars later, but first Mr. Bartel would have his joke.

Stock producers never liked to pay much for the rights to plays (new scripts cost more, especially if they're fresh from a Broadway run), so we'd open up the season with a fairly recent number, but once the bait had been snapped up, we switched to old warhorses. It's been said thousands of times, but I'll say it again, the stock company was marvelous training for an actor. I got to handle leads of every description. In the ingénue parts I was totally ghastly. I was too tall not to find it embarrassing having to be coy, to sit on someone's lap, saying, "Dickie, shall we play tennis?" When it came to the tougher stuff— a wronged but still unbroken prisoner complaining, "You took my name and gave me a number!"—I was far better.

At Saranac Lake we did an incredible amount of work, rehearsed every morning, played golf every afternoon, put on a show

I was the baby in this picture. James is in the armchair,
John stands behind me, and that's Clara, the Duchess,
stage center with the big bow in her hair.

Baby Rosalind at age one.

With George and Mary Jane
at Laurel Beach
(I'm on the right)

I was about
thirteen years old here.

My father, James Edward Russell.
This was taken at the time of
his marriage in 1900. He was
thirty-eight, and his eyes
were bluer than the Duchess'.

Portrait of my mother.

My mother, Clara McKnight, at
about age sixteen, costumed for a
Highland fling at Notre Dame
Academy. She was very proud
of her Scottish ancestry.

Clara

Mary Jane

Three sisters. An early portrait of Clara the Duchess in one of her high-fashion hats (she used to say, "Darling, you can't wear Hollywood hats, in New York we're more conservative"), and Mary Jane in her wedding dress.

Rosalind

Irving Chidnoff

My brothers during World War II.
George on the left, Jim on the right,
John down in front.

I'm front row left in an
all-girl version of *La Bohème*
at Marymount College.

Me on the left
in *Garrick Gaieties*,
Theatre Guild, 1932.

Vandamm

With William Powell in *Rendezvous*.
I felt self-conscious. I thought he
wanted Myrna Loy for the part.

With Robert Taylor in
West Point of the Air.

With Ramon Navarro and
brother George during filming
of *The Night Is Young.*

1935: *The Night Is Young*. I was acting this scene with
Edward Everett Horton and Ramon Navarro. Sitting in front
of the camera is the director Dudley Murphy, and standing
behind him is the cameraman James Wong Howe.

Reckless, with Jean Harlow and Bill Powell.
I loved Jean, and oh, she was a stunning creature.

The Citadel, with Robert Donat.
The English Labor Unions had wanted
an English girl to play my part.

China Seas, with Clark Gable. I played
a lot of "Lady Mary" parts and I was
always taking Clark Gable or Bob
Montgomery away from Jean Harlow
or Joan Crawford. Temporarily.
It was ludicrous.

With Robert Montgomery, with whom I made *Night Must Fall* in 1937.

Virgil Apger, MGM

Under Two Flags, with Ronald Colman. I kept swallowing Listerine so he'd kiss me.

A night out with Spencer Tracy, his wife Louise, my sister Mary Jane and Tim Durant. I think this was 1938.

The Women, with Norma Shearer. This picture
brought me acceptance as a comedienne, and I loved it.

With Loretta Young
at the Hollywood Press
Photographers' Ball, 1940.
We came as the Toni Twins.

With Louella Parsons, 1940.

Photo by Irving Lippman. Courtesy Columbia Pictures.

Time out for birthday cake during the filming of *My Sister Eileen*, 1941. Shirley Temple was visiting the set. At right, Alexander Hall, our director, and Janet Blair, who played Eileen.

With Ralph Bellamy and Cary Grant in *His Girl Friday*, 1940.

Photo by Irving Lippman. Courtesy Columbia Pictures. (From His Girl Friday. Copyright 1940 by Columbia Pictures.)

With Blanche, my maid, at right,
on the set of *My Sister Eileen*, 1941.

Jack Koffman

Take a Letter, Darling, with
Fred MacMurray, 1942.

© *Universal Pictures.*

This Thing Called Love,
with Melvyn Douglas, 1941.

Photo by Irving Lippman. Courtesy Columbia Pictures.
(*From* This Thing Called Love. *Copyright 1941 by Columbia Pictures.*)

Photo by Willinger. Courtesy MGM Inc.

Photo, Courtesy Columbia Pictures.

Samples of the glamour shots we used to pose for in the golden era of movies. We'd spend whole afternoons at a photographer's studio, changing gowns and earrings for publicity pictures.

Jack Koffman

Hazel Washington, who had worked for Greta Garbo before she came to me, nicknamed me "The Queen."

every night. And our first leading man nipped quite heavily (he was later replaced), which meant I had to learn his lines as well as mine.

He could be absolutely smashed, draped across a desk, in another world, and I'd be making speeches like "I know what you're thinking, you're thinking you don't love me, you're about to say you don't want to see me again, but you mustn't say it because I tell you that you will feel differently tomorrow, and I shall be here at nine o'clock, dressed for the opera . . ."

I got so slick, he didn't have to grunt if he didn't want to. It was rough, but it was fun.

The character woman in the company was older than the rest of us. Her blond hair was badly dyed, the dark roots showed, and she changed her one good dress from show to show by putting a scarf on it, or a sash, or a string of beads. She'd come to Saranac Lake because she was taking care of a niece who had tuberculosis, so she worked mighty cheap. One morning when she stopped by my hotel—she'd call for me and we'd walk to rehearsals together—she noticed a lot of stuff in my mailbox, packages as well as letters, so she guessed, rightly, that it was my birthday.

"Please come to my place after the show tonight and we'll celebrate," she said.

I protested no, no, she mustn't bother, but she wouldn't be deterred.

That night she led me through the streets until we came to a mustardy-yellow frame building. It was a boarding house—Saranac Lake was filled with them—and we climbed four flights of stairs and went into her room.

She pulled a cord, which lit a bare bulb hanging over a round wooden table in the middle of the floor, and she boiled water on a hot plate in the corner. She had one cup and one spoon, and she brought me tea in the cup and drank hers from a glass. Then she brought out a tiny white cylinder and put it down in front of me. The light was so dim I couldn't identify the object. It's a can of cold cream, I thought in confusion.

It wasn't. It was a cupcake. All that woman's salary—and it was meager—went to support her niece, but she couldn't let my birthday pass without my having a party, so she'd spent fifteen or twenty cents for the cake. And she didn't own two cups.

((43))

Years later I saw her walking across Broadway, and we stopped and talked. She's long since gone to the old actresses' heaven, but I still think of that party. She gave me the dearest birthday of my life.

Nineteen twenty-nine a bad year? What were they talking about? My fortunes held. Incredibly, I went straight from summer stock in Saranac Lake to winter stock in Boston. Chamberlain Brown had sent me (no, he did *not* do it just to get me out of his office) to see a man named E. E. Clive who ran a company at the Copley Theatre, right near the Copley Plaza Hotel. Mr. Clive (called Clivey by those who knew him) produced shows featuring English casts; Leslie Howard and quite a number of other well-known actors had played for him, and in 1929 John Emery was his leading man. When he interviewed me, I was so teddibly British I could hahdly understahnd myself. I think he got wise to me before the fourth line was out of my mouth, but I was hired anyway.

(At some future date I had Mary Jane up to spend a weekend, but I was so worried that her Waterbury accent might give me away that I never let her say a word. "You can talk to me," I said, "when we're alone, but when you're introduced to any of *them,* just smile and say, 'Hmm.' Don't open your mouth." John Emery came with me to the train station to meet Mary Jane, and he must have thought she was simple-minded. She kept going "Hmm, hmm," and grinning, for two days straight.)

It was a nice job. Positively restful, after Saranac Lake. Clivey would run a play as long as the box office held up, so sometimes you did the same show for five, six, seven weeks. Every year he put on *The Ghost Train,* a terrible but famous old melodrama that audiences loved. (If a character in the play saw the Ghost Train, he died; that was the plot.) Again, because of the money involved, most of Clivey's shows had a little age on them.

Downstairs in the theatre basement, where the dressing rooms were, the kettle was always boiling with water for tea, and my fellow British actors sipped and sniped. We had tea, tea, tea, tea—which I loved—and they roasted America, a pastime which I didn't love. Those English actors could think of more ways to pan the colonies and the colonists than I could stand to listen to. Because I was the flag-waving, Statue of Liberty, rah! rah! America type, they drove me crazy, and one day I blew my cover.

((44))

"Listen," I burst out, "I want to tell you I'm a member of one of the colonies, and I'm sick of listening to you people. If you don't like this country, go back to England . . ."

None of them left, but I was rewarded for my patriotic fervor. Clivey was about to put on a play (by a man named Ian Hay) which featured an American girl in England—the story had something to do with show business—and I got a nice new part.

By now, though I'd been working a year and wanted more money, I didn't know how to approach Clivey. Having suffered the experience of graduation day, I wasn't anxious to see yet another manager backing out of a room gasping like a fish and trying to get his breath to call the cops. But I knew I deserved a raise. So I turned in my two weeks' notice, in writing. It'll kill 'em, I thought. They'll fall apart; the theatre will have to close.

And I waited. The first week went by. Nothing happened. Nothing. I started gibbering to myself. Soon we were into the second week, at the end of which I would have to leave. Miss Smart-Ass, hoist by her own presumption.

Clivey was not only our director, he sometimes acted with us, and he happened to be in the Ian Hay play. I started timing my entrances for the curtain call so that I'd walk up the stairs right in front of him. Or I'd stand next to him in the wings, ostentatiously asking him how he was tonight. On the stairs he didn't chat; in the wings he said only, "Fine, Rosalind, very fine."

It came down to the matinée of the last performance. My two weeks were up. I knew I'd have to go to the hotel—I was living at the Copley—and pack. After the curtain fell, Clivey finally spoke to me. "Come into my dressing room for a minute, will you?"

In his dressing room he was a kindly uncle. For two weeks he'd been teasing, now he really wanted to know. "Why have you done this?" he said. "Has somebody been rude to you?"

"No, no," I said. "I just feel I should have some more money."

"How much more money do you think you should have?" he said. My original plan had been to ask for a bundle, but I settled on fifty dollars. "Fifty dollars a week."

"I'll give you twenty-five," he said. "Now go back to work."

Work is the operative word. I get letters from people who say they have talent, their teachers think so, their mothers think so, they were dandy in the class play. I answer fine, but do you also have self-discipline and good health? That's what you need if you want to last in show business. (Naturally, a lot of color is provided by the people who *don't* have self-discipline, who burn themselves out with drink or drugs and who sometimes die of the pain or the pills without ever learning how to say no to a party.)

Talent is wonderful, but I've played with actors who have more talent than I, and you can't hear them in the fourth row, they just don't have the energy, nothing in the belly, nothing in the guts that brings it all out and sells it across the orchestra pit and into the twenty-third row.

In Boston with Clivey's troupe—I couldn't do it at Saranac, I didn't have the time—I used to sit on the stage apron and watch every rehearsal I wasn't involved in. I'd be thinking, Why can't he get a laugh on that? It's a funny line—and taking the thing apart in my head to see why it wasn't working. Half the pleasure of doing comedy in the theatre is that even before you hear a laugh, you sense where the laugh should be. Something happens in the audience, you feel it, you go to work on it. Until one day, all of a sudden, you're rewarded with a titter. You keep working on the line and finally you get a real belly laugh. After that you generally push too hard and lose it, and you have to pull away and inch your way back.

(Sometimes you get a laugh you didn't expect and haven't earned. Once in stock I was playing Linda in Philip Barry's *Holiday*, and I had a line which went "I know what you've been doing downstairs, talking behind my back." I said, "I know what you've been doing downstairs, talking to my behind." The audience screamed, and I had no idea why.)

In the summer of 1930 I went back to Saranac Lake and reopened the theatre for Casey and Bartel, but after that I felt it was time for me to move on. I returned to New York City. If an agent was willing to send me anywhere, I'd go. If I heard about anybody's putting on anything, I'd go. And when somebody told me Phil Loeb, who'd been one of my teachers at the American Academy, was directing a show for the Theatre Guild, I hiked over there to find out what was going on.

Their subscription list was very important to the Guild—they were trying to hang on to it, to build it, and that season they didn't have enough plays. They'd already produced *Green Grow the Lilacs,* they'd got Nazimova to re-create one of her famous roles, and now they'd decided to put on a new *Garrick Gaieties* that would be a potpourri of Richard Rodgers' numbers from several old *Garrick Gaieties.* The *Gaieties* shows had always been done down in Greenwich Village; this one was going to be presented on Broadway.

Had I known it was a musical that Loeb was involved with, I'd never have shown my face; as it was, I rushed right in smiling. There was a big rehearsal hall at the top of the Theatre Guild building, and when I pushed the door open, Phil, who was conducting auditions, looked at me and waved. "Everybody take ten minutes and rest," he said. "There's a very fine musical actress who's just come by to sing for us—"

"Will you please stop it?" I said.

"Now don't be shy," he said, and confided to the others, "Miss Russell has been with the Chicago Civic Opera, and she doesn't want everybody to know it, but she's going to render us a number or two."

I was ready to maim him. There were the three pillars of the Theatre Guild—Philip Langner, Theresa Helburn, Armina Marshall —sitting in rocking chairs, and Phil going on and on, enlarging the joke, and I finally got so embarrassed I stood up. "I'll prove to you I don't sing," I said, and I launched into "Stormy Weather" with this gargle that passed for a voice. Everybody laughed, I sat down, and Marshall, Langner and Helburn disappeared. A few minutes later they sent up word that I was to come to their office.

I went to their office, and they said they'd like me to join *Garrick Gaieties.*

"What as?" I said.

Well, they said, I could do the sketches. I agreed that I probably could do the sketches. It was the start of my musical—if we can use the word loosely—career, and it was my Broadway debut. I even sang a couple of numbers and opened the show. We played only ten days in New York, then went on the road. Which was paved with gold. I was earning three hundred dollars a week, a fortune in 1930. Imogene Coca and Sterling Holloway were fellow players, so was Phil Loeb. We had our own train, and our own musicians traveled with us to Minneapolis, Chicago, St. Louis, and we had the kind of fun you can only have when you're young and strong and you think your luck is going to last forever.

It doesn't. It can't. The next few years were frightening, because the depression had settled in and people had to be concerned with brute survival; for most, theatre was a luxury. There was very little work for actors, and while my situation was less desperate than some—my mother wouldn't have let me starve; on the other hand, if I couldn't make good on my own, I could kiss acting goodbye—it wasn't all that easy.

Unemployed actors used to hang out in a drugstore on 44th Street, where you could nurse a nickel cup of coffee and a doughnut all afternoon. We clung to one another, commiserating, encouraging, but I couldn't sit—not in a casting office and not in a drugstore—as long as some of the others. I had to keep moving, trying, pushing.

I was very much registered with Chamberlain Brown (who'd got me to Clivey), and his agency kept sending me out, thinking I would go cheaper than other people. I would, too. I'd fight for the money later, but first I'd get the work. I kept every appointment, I moved my dainty derrière around the Apple, I took stock jobs—with William Brady's company in Red Bank, New Jersey, with the Tech Players in Buffalo, New York, with a Massachusetts outfit that played Worcester and Boston—and dreamed of cracking Broadway again.

It happened. I got a good part in a show with Mady Christians. We finished the dress rehearsal and the management closed us down. We never opened. Then I was cast in a play called *Company's Coming*, with Lynne Overman and Frieda Inescort. I attempted a Southern accent. The play lasted eight performances. I don't think my accent was to blame, neither do I think it helped much. When I was at college I'd known a girl named Angel Allen who came from Atlanta and talked way up high. "Ah'm up No-th gonna skooo-il," she'd squeal. In *Company's Coming*, I tried to sound like Angel Allen, but it came out more like Step'n Fetchit. Reviewing the offering, John Mason Brown, himself a Southern gentleman, said, "There is a young lady who plays a Southern belle. Her name is Miss Russell. Miss Russell's accent deserves a prize. A gag, perhaps."

(Some years later, when we were both out entertaining troops during World War II, I was introduced to John Mason Brown on a train siding in Texas. "You almost put me out of business," I said. He laughed, but he didn't know what I was talking about. I accused him of adding insult to injury. "I thought I was bad enough so you'd at least remember me.")

In 1934 I took a job—took it gratefully—on the subway circuit. The subway circuit had been started by two men named Wee and Leventhal who sent plays around not only to places (like Brooklyn) that could be reached by subway, but also to out-of-state places that were only short train hops from Manhattan. I think the enterprise began in the 86th Street Theatre and expanded from there.

Some of my drugstore friends told me I was crazy. "You worked for the Theatre Guild! How can you go to work for Wee and Leventhal?" they said. "That's very bad."

I thought it was very good. Mr. Leventhal offered me thirty-seven dollars and fifty cents a week (union minimum) but I held out for five dollars more. It was a question of pride; four years earlier the Theatre Guild had paid me three hundred dollars a week and I wasn't going to settle for minimum now. Mr. Leventhal took my pride into consideration. I got my forty-two dollars and fifty cents.

Ever since I'd left the Academy, whether I was in town or out of town, I'd been hanging on to a ground-floor flat in a brownstone on East 54th Street. My apartment was in the rear of the building and it had a garden. When I was flush I poured resources into that garden, trying to coax something green out of the rock pile. I also had a living room, a bedroom, a kitchenette and a bath, all furnished by Bloomingdale's department store, five blocks away. I liked to live well, which was easier said than done working on the subway circuit. Though I picked up some extra cash gambling with Mr. Leventhal.

I will now explain that statement.

Subway circuit shows closed on Saturday nights. It meant that no matter where I'd been playing during the week, I got to go home to my apartment for what was left of the weekend. Every Saturday night Mr. Leventhal would show up in Philadelphia, or Newark, or wherever we were, carrying our pay, along with a brown paper bag in which he had a sandwich.

Then he and I would ride back to New York on the train together. We always took a drawing room—it cost us seventy-five cents extra apiece—and had a card table set up, and we ordered a big bottle of ginger ale, I remember it was brown ginger ale, and lots of ice, and he shared his sandwich with me. He taught me to play pinochle, and then let me beat him at it. He always let me beat him. I'm sure he did, because I didn't play that well. We'd get off the train at Penn Station, and I'd catch a taxi up to East 54th Street and forget about *Murder on the Second Floor* (in which I was working with Cesar Romero) or *The Second Man* (in which I was working with Bert Lytell) until the following Monday afternoon.

It was on one of those Monday afternoons—I was due back in Newark that night—that I got the call from the Chamberlain Brown office. I'd been seen in *The Second Man* by a talent scout for the movies. "Universal Pictures," the secretary said raptly. "They want you to come to Hollywood . . ."

Two Weeks Behind
the Camera, or the
Universal Joint

"Universal joint, used for joining two intersecting shafts. Unfortunately, a varying angular speed ratio results when the joint connects shafts at an angle, though this defect can be minimized by . . . an intermediate section of shafting."

ENCYCLOPAEDIA BRITANNICA

HAFTING. That was about the size of it. God knows, I was all angles, and when Universal and I tried to connect, it hurt me more than it did them.

To begin with, I didn't want to go to Hollywood. At least I thought I didn't want to go to Hollywood. I wanted to become a Broadway star. An instantly recognizable, very important Broadway star. And I'd been told that important Broadway stars looked down on film. Katharine Cornell looked down on film, Helen Hayes looked down on film, so I was prepared to look down on film too.

But a job was a job, and I couldn't get out of the habit of keeping any appointment the agency set up. Which was why I reported to a room in the same building that housed Radio City Music

Hall and talked to a man from Universal Pictures. It developed that I wasn't the only genius who'd been spotted in Newark and environs; Universal had also sent for fifteen or twenty other actors. And what they were prepared to offer me was a really rotten contract—seven years of nothing.

Now, all New York actors knew about the extravagant, after-us-the-deluge life styles led by the Hollywood chosen, and some of what we knew was even true. (I recently met a sixty-two-year-old man who'd worked for Gloria Swanson forty years ago. "I started at nineteen," he said. "Miss Swanson trained me, and I was the fourth butler. There were three butlers over me. She also had two chauffeurs and three Rolls-Royces, one white, one maroon, one black, and the chauffeurs dressed in uniforms to match the cars.")

Gazing at the man from Universal, a representative from that other planet, I told myself to act large. You have to act large with these people, or you're dead, I silently advised Rosalind. Then I spoke. "I want seven hundred fifty dollars a week."

The Universal man wasn't offering half that, so I went home.

By the time I reached the apartment, the phone was ringing. "Let's talk some more," said Mr. Universal.

I knew I had him.

"You don't know anything about me," I said, "and I don't know whether I can act in films. I don't even know whether I want to. But I'll tell you what I'll do. I'll go to Hollywood and you can test me. You can test me every day for two weeks. You'll pay my fare both ways, my hotel expenses, and a hundred dollars a test. If you think I'm worth it after you see the tests, you'll sign me at seven hundred fifty dollars a week. If you don't like me after you see the tests, I'll come home."

He agreed.

I went chugging West on the train, and was met at the Union Station by a man who took me directly to the studio. Bags and all.

At Universal, I was wheeled into the office of a guy named Kelly, head of casting, and abandoned there. I'll never forget Mr. Kelly and I'll never forgive him. I stood against the door in his office and he never looked up. He was too busy playing big executive. It was like seeing the man on whom Chamberlain Brown's office boy had modeled himself in order to be able to turn away old ladies in long black coats. First Kelly phoned everyone he knew, along with a few people he didn't know but thought he'd like to meet.

I didn't move, and I didn't say a word. I would have stood there till kingdom come, he was going to have to speak first.

He clicked away at his telephone. Yes, he'd join so-and-so at the Brown Derby at noon, and yes, he'd look at those character men at three o'clock. When he ran out of telephone numbers, he called his secretary and asked her to bring him a two-cent stamp.

It was pathetic. He was putting on this great show, and I couldn't even get him a nomination for an Academy Award. Eventually he deigned to glance in my direction. "Who are you?" he said.

By now I didn't care about charming anybody. Especially him. "Let's start with who are you?" I said.

"My name's Kelly," he said.

"My name's Russell," I said. "And I have just gotten off a train. I'm hot, I'm dirty, I'm tired, and I want to be taken to my hotel—"

"Oh," he said. "You're that actress from New York."

"That's right," I said. "I'm that actress from New York."

I didn't like that man at all.

Sighing, Kelly got up. "Well, come with me," he said, "I hear we gotta make some tests."

He showed me around the Makeup department, and he showed me around Hairdressing, and he took me into an office where a couple of songwriters were sitting. One of the songwriters cried, "Quick! Give me a title for a song!" It was straight out of *Once in a Lifetime*. Then Kelly went to lunch and I took a taxi to my hotel. I had no idea when my screen test would take place.

Brooding, I sat in the hotel for maybe three days until the call came. I'd be making the test with John Stahl, a very important director, and the studio was sending over a script so I could learn my lines.

The morning of the test I got to Universal at the crack of dawn. It was six A.M. when I went into Makeup. The makeup man was reading *The Hollywood Reporter*, a trade paper I'd never seen before, and he said he couldn't take me. "I got a big day ahead of me, honey."

I walked on down to Hairdressing, and there was this dame teasing her own hair in front of the mirror, and she couldn't take me either. "I gotta do Gloria Stuart," she said. (That's not Jimmy Stewart's wife; there was an actress named Gloria Stuart.)

I went over to Stage 19, where the test was to take place. It was cavernous, empty, dark. I sat there in the dark for most of that day. Toward evening a couple of men wandered in and hit some lights. Then on came Mr. Stahl, the great white father, with a shock of snowy hair. He looked around, tapped the camera, an old Mitchell, and called out, "Where is this actress who's supposed to work with me?"

When I emerged from the shadows, he gaped. "Where's your makeup? Where's your hairdo? Are you the girl who's supposed to test for me? Don't you know that I can't use you like this?"

On certain days I have more guts than brains. "Now let me tell you something, Mr. Stahl," I said. "Nobody would make me up, and nobody would do my hair, but I know these lines and I'm going to say these lines, because I get a hundred dollars for saying them!"

Mr. Stahl yelled a little bit more, and then he solved his problem. He put me under the camera, where I sat and fed cues to an actor who was hoping to play opposite Claudette Colbert in *Imitation of Life*. Talk about insults—I wasn't even getting a test of my own, I was doing Claudette Colbert's lines because she was already busy shooting the movie and Stahl was desperate to find her a leading man.

After that first bout of work I ran like a deer to the cashier's office and demanded my hundred dollars. Insulted or not, I wasn't leaving without the money.

Now a friend from the East, an actress named Charlotte Wynters, whom I'd met in stock, came to my rescue. She moved me out of the hotel into a house with her and her husband, actor Barton MacLane, and I began to feel less lonely, if not less humiliated.

Over the next several days I did tests for the Colbert picture with nine different men, and I was never seen on the film. Sometimes I'd sit under the camera, sometimes right next to the camera.

Before my two weeks' testing period was up, I'd collected nine hundred dollars and Charlotte had plotted out my future. There was a movie that was going to be made at MGM. Charlotte had tested for a part in it, but felt she was all wrong. "The girl who's staying with me, though, is absolutely right," she told the flabbergasted casting director at Metro. (It was no more usual then than now for one ambitious actress to push another.) She got the casting director, a man named Ben Piazza, to agree that I should test, and I sneaked over—technically, I wasn't free; I still had a couple of days to go on this half-baked contract with Universal—and Metro did a test of me in a great big head; the whole thing was a close-up. It turned out fabulous. I never acted so well in my life, before or since, and I was offered a contract, which went a long way toward soothing my damaged pride.

Then I got word that Universal was going to pick up my option and sign me for seven years. (To this day I don't know why.) The news made me miserable. "I won't do it," I said to Charlotte. "I won't go there! I'm going to tell them to take their contract and—"

"Stop!" Charlotte said. "If you walk out, they can keep you from making a movie anyplace for the next seven years."

"So what?" I said. "I'll go back to the stage."

But I wasn't being quite straight with her—or with myself. The big stage actress Rosalind Russell, the one who hadn't wanted to come to Hollywood, was more than half moonstruck with the idea of working at Metro—Metro, where Greta Garbo, Joan Crawford, Jean Harlow, Myrna Loy, Norma Shearer and Jeanette MacDonald shone and sang.

New developments followed hard upon this discussion. Carl Laemmle, Jr., the boss at Universal (his father was still alive, but had retired from any active part in the business), had been in Europe during my two weeks under the camera. Now he wanted to meet me. Tomorrow morning.

Charlotte and I sat up all night hatching and discarding ideas. There had to be a way to get out of the Universal contract without being punished by seven lean years. We phoned our friend Nedda Harrigan and everybody else we knew, trying to find out about Carl Laemmle, Jr. Nobody could help us much. Finally one informant said, "I know he likes beautiful women; he has a lot of girls."

It gave us the inspiration we'd needed.

When I went off to meet Junior Laemmle, I was a work of

art. I was wearing a cast-off dress, compliments of the Duchess, a red-and-white print with a boat neckline, bought on sale at Bergdorf Goodman. I was too skinny for it; my collarbones stuck out. I had added to this a white linen hat dug out of the bottom of my trunk, a good hat but quite creased, and white shoes, not perfectly clean. Charlotte and I realized we had to be careful, choose stuff of decent quality, because Laemmle was no dope, and if I'd gone too far, tried a fright wig and rhinestone bracelets, he'd have known something was up. We trod a fine line. I had shoulder-length hair, and we put Vaseline on it and let it hang down in strips around my neck. Bad, but not too bad. We smeared a trace of mascara under my eyes, my lipstick was runny, and we painted a little of it on my front teeth. Even my white gloves were weary. And I wore a tight bra that flattened down what little shape I had.

In Laemmle's outer office I was nervous as a cricket. An agent who knew me from New York was waiting there too. He said, "Hi, Roz," and kept studying me. I could feel his eyes on me wherever I turned.

When I was called into Mr. Laemmle's presence, I slumped on a couch. Mr. Laemmle tried not to stare. He failed. But he was a gentleman and he spoke politely. "Miss Russell, I hear you haven't really made a test for us, and I'm sorry about that. We're going to start your build-up—"

"Well," I said, "I'm just very unhappy here." I kept it nasal, barely opening my mouth; the words came out between clenched jaws, sort of "Oym just vairy unhairpy here."

"Pardon me?" said Mr. Laemmle.

"Oym vairy unhairpy here," I said again. "Oy want to go to New York, oy miss moy family."

He kept questioning me, because he couldn't believe that some idiot in New York had signed this creature in front of him with the dirty hair and the runover heels. In those days you didn't wear slacks on appointments; you wore pretty dresses, plenty of silk hose and high-heeled shoes. It wasn't like today, when kids go around in blue jeans, a rumpled shirt and disheveled hair, and you couldn't surprise anybody in a casting office if you tried.

A few more lonesomes and unhappys and references to my mother, and Laemmle breathed what had to be a sigh of relief.

"Well," he said, "if you feel that way, I guess we can let you go."

My adenoids came into play again. "Oy waant moy papers that say oy can go."

It occurs to me that I was forever haranguing some poor soul to give me papers, whether it was Ed Casey to sew me up, or Carl Laemmle to set me free, but I was scared to death to leave Universal without an official release in my hand.

"Don't worry," said Laemmle. "Just go sit in the outer office and I'll have somebody bring you your papers."

As soon as the release was sent up—it took about ten minutes —I was off and away. I got to Charlotte's place, showered, washed my hair, changed clothes, and raced straight over to Metro, where I signed my first real movie contract.

It was lovely. It was the beginning of a different life.

The Night I Slept
with John Wayne

ALL RIGHT, I never slept with John Wayne, but people expect a Hollywood chapter to be filled with sex and big names. Now that's out of the way, I'll tell you the epilogue to the Junior Laemmle story.

There used to be a club up on Sunset Boulevard, a so-called exclusive club where all the stars went. I wanted to go there too, and not being a star wasn't going to stop me. With my first paycheck from Metro, I bought myself a white satin dress and a white fox stole. What else? I was in movies. Then, carefully coiffed, new stole flung around my neck with an air, I hoped, of insouciance, I sauntered through the front door of that exclusive club. And bumped right into Junior Laemmle, who did three double takes. "Are you that same girl . . . ?" He was a good sport; he laughed and shook my hand.

In 1934 Metro was at the height of its power. The studio had perhaps twenty huge women stars and at least as many men, among them, Clark Gable, William Powell, Spencer Tracy, James Stewart, Wallace Beery. Metro made A pictures and B pictures, and they tried to turn out fifty-two features a year. They never made it, but they did average forty-six or forty-seven.

When the talkies had come in, in 1927, business had accelerated wildly, and the acceleration had been international. Within a few years the great director René Clair was already at work in France, the Odéon Cinema Circuit had been formed in England, and Rosalind Russell was bloody busy too, playing a meanie in *Craig's Wife*.

At that time most contract players were salaried forty weeks a year, not fifty-two—they worked six days a week and not five—and Metro didn't give you the money for sitting around, either. You were no sooner finished with one picture than you were reading your next script.

I had gone right into A's, playing second leads, "other women" parts. That pleased me. I guess I was afraid of playing a lead and doing it rotten and being thrown out; I wanted to protect myself while I was learning the business.

My first assignment was in *Evelyn Prentice*. It starred Myrna Loy and William Powell. There was a drawing-room set, and the script said "Enter Miriam," so I entered, walked right into the set and through it and was starting to walk out of it when Powell yelled, "Wait a minute, you have to hit those marks, those chalk marks."

"Oh," I said. "Is that what I have to do?"

Powell was a divine man and a great friend. Several epics later, when Myrna was off the lot getting more money, I was put into a movie called *Rendezvous* with Bill. I felt self-conscious. Powell and Loy had been a hit in *The Thin Man*, they were an unbeatable team, so my first day on *Rendezvous*, I tried to apologize. "I know you don't want me, you'd rather have Myrna—"

Powell denied it. "I love Myrna, but I think this is good for you, and I'm glad we're doing it together."

He was not only dear, he was cool. If an actor thought he could get any place by having tantrums, watching Bill Powell would have altered his opinion. I remember a story conference during which he objected to a scene that he felt wasn't right for him. He was at once imperious and lucid. "It's beyond my histrionic ability to do this," he said. I thought that was delicious.

I was never a top star at Metro. When I went there I was no eighteen-year-old, but already in my twenties, and I didn't fit neatly into the pattern of stars and the star system. I'm not saying this out of false modesty; it's a fact. There's an old story told by the playwright Samson Raphaelson about his hitting it rich and buying a yacht and going, in a peaked cap, to see his old Jewish mother. She asked him what the cap was for. "It's my captain's hat, Mama," he said. "I'm a captain." She nodded. "By me, you're a captain," she said. "And by you, you're a captain. But by captains, you're no captain."

According to my mother, I'm sure I was a top star at Metro,

but compared to Garbo or Tracy, I was no top star. I was in the second echelon. That was the way they ran the lot. I once said I never got a part at Metro unless Myrna Loy turned it down, and while that was meant to be funny, there was a grain of truth in it. They had me as a threat behind Myrna, the same way they had Luise Rainer behind Garbo. Every time Myrna asked for a change in her contract, or a raise, the brass could say, "Never mind, Roz Russell will do the picture," and this system worked very successfully.

Myrna used to live up a hill from me, and once at a dinner party I was teasing her about my having got all her rejects. "Those scripts," I said. "You'd wait until dark, shove 'em out of your house, and they'd roll down the hill and hit my front door, and that's the way they were cast."

Everybody at the table laughed, and then Myrna's voice, reflecting on one of the dogs *she'd* got stuck with, cut through the hilarity. "Well, you must have been out," she said, "the night I rolled you *Parnell.*"

During my earliest days at Metro, I was put into movies with Joan Crawford and Jean Harlow, and I was always taking their men away from them. Temporarily. It was ludicrous. There would be Jean, all alabaster skin and cleft chin, savory as a ripe peach, and I'd be saying disdainfuly (and usually with an English accent; I played a lot of Lady Mary roles) to Gable or to Bob Montgomery, "How can you spend time with *her?* She's rahther vulgar, isn't she?"

Sometimes I'd be the second lead in three pictures at one time. I'd run on the set in a bathing suit and somebody would yell, "No, no, the evening dress for this one, the bathing suit's on Stage Eight," and as soon as I was done on Stage 8, the director would say, "You're due on Sixteen," and turn to the cameraman. "Can we get one more shot with Russell here? She's gotta get over to Sixteen—"

When I wasn't disdaining Harlow or Crawford, I was at 20th Century-Fox disdaining Claudette Colbert or I was at Warner Brothers. Or Columbia or Paramount or Universal. Metro, as you can tell, loaned me out a great deal, and I got some damn good parts that way.

Robert Taylor started at Metro the same day I did; Jimmy Stewart and Maggie Sullavan had already been there for a while. It wasn't exactly like the silent days, when violinists had played on the sets to give the stars inspiration, but there was still plenty of glamour. If Joan Crawford was in the throes of a rage for Bing Crosby records, we'd have Crosby records playing all day long—sometimes until you thought you'd go nuts—and when Billie Burke, who was married to Flo Ziegfeld, came on the lot, great trumpets sounded. First you'd see an awful lot of dogs on leashes, and then the maid, and then the makeup man, and then some guys carrying a big tray with a potty on it. A potty all covered in satin, and monogrammed; that impressed the hell out of me. (On-set facilities stashed behind screens meant that stars didn't have to run to their dressing rooms.) Billie would follow in the wake of this entourage. Crawford had an entourage too. But listen, I wasn't without my followers. Those guys in the crew that I played poker with, they were always glad to see me stumble in.

Hollywood people used to pull lots of gags on one another. George Raft once bet with me on a football game, and I won. He had a potato sack filled with pennies delivered to my door. It was so heavy I couldn't lift it.

I'd got to know Raft when I was loaned to Fox for a number called *It Had to Happen*. I was supposed to be the richest girl in the world, Raft was a laborer slaving in the streets with a red flag, but we wound up getting married. Then I was kept on at Fox to do *Under Two Flags* with Ronald Colman. (It was another of my Lady Mary jobs; I never even got to meet Claudette, who played Cigarette.)

Colman sent white lilacs to my dressing room and invited me to tea in his bungalow. It was exciting; he had a butler, and the tea was served by candlelight and Colman was very handsome and I was very nervous.

For our big scene together, two stages had been opened up to make one huge desert set, and I rode out into it on a horse. I had a fantastic outfit—a velvet cape in a glorious shade of blue, and orchid veiling, studded in little tiny rhinestones, across my face. That getup was so flattering it could have turned Louise Fazenda into Hedy Lamarr, and if I say so myself, I didn't look like anybody's old radiator cap.

Ronnie and I were to meet by an oasis, a pool of water beside some old ruins. It was a beautiful set. On I came riding sidesaddle, and when I pulled up, the director, Frank Lloyd, told Ronnie to take me off the horse.

Ronnie helped me to dismount.

"No, no, no, no," the director said. "Slide her down your body."

Colman was a shy man, and he didn't know me from a hot rock, but I climbed back on the horse and went out and came in again, *diddyump, diddyump, diddyump, ump, ump,* charging toward the oasis, hoping to hit the marks with the damn horse.

I dropped the reins, we had some more of that slide-her-down-your-body business, and finally I was off the animal, and Colman and I walked over to the pool in which our reflection was supposed to be caught, kissing.

He wouldn't kiss me on the mouth. I kept trying to push my face around, but he just wouldn't kiss me. Between takes I'd go in and swallow half a bottle of Listerine and spray myself with perfume. The scene went on and on. It started to get late; some of the crew were restless and beginning to giggle. Finally the director said, "Maybe we'll just have to put this off until tomorrow morning."

Oh my God, I thought, I won't sleep. By now I'm reeking of Arpege and mouthwash, and I'm desperate. I finally just grabbed Ronnie, clung to him, would not let him go, and kissed him until he was purple in the face and the director was yelling, "Cut! Cut! Cut!"

What I didn't know was a) that a kiss full on the mouth doesn't photograph as pleasingly as an off-center buss, and b) that they'd been doing a glass shot, a form of dissolve. The camera wasn't even on us most of the time, it was on the camels, the desert, the sun going down, the sun coming up again to indicate that we've spent the night together. Colman, of course, was aware of the camera (he knew cameras like Wernher von Braun knows rockets), but all the time we were supposed to be standing apart making small talk—"How are you? How have you been?"—while they're shooting the camels and the sunrise, he's had this maniacal female clutching him to her fevered lips.

He was very nice about it.

Every leading man was different. Once in a while you'd come up against one who was good-looking, fun, but without depth, no layers to him. You'd go along thinking, When we come to the big scene, when the child dies, or the plague is upon us, then he'll really act. But nothing would happen, it just wouldn't be there. That's the kind of thing you find out much quicker on the stage. Life can take it away from you—passion, an ability to stretch, to reach—but no director can give it to you.

Back at MGM, where there was talent to squander, the A pictures sometimes featured ten stars in a single film. The Barrymores were around, and Charlie Butterworth and Bob Benchley, wonderful people to work with.

And I was in it, but not really part of it. I sort of kept going on my own. My experiences at Metro weren't shabby, the way my Universal fortnight had been, but even at Metro, if you didn't fall into a category the big wheels were comfortable with, you confused them. (Today it's different. There's no paternalism and employers don't think of long-term investments. They can look at an actress and say, "I don't give a damn if she's on drugs, she's good for this part, I'll use her for two weeks, then throw her out on her can.")

I know I confused Louis B. Mayer, the boss at Metro, because he said so. It happened one night after I'd been through a sitting at a photographer's studio on the Sunset Strip. A Metro publicity man had taken me there, along with a load of evening dresses, turbans, veils, earrings, and when we were done with the pictures it was about seven o'clock, so the publicity man said, "Come on, we'll go next door to the Trocadero and I'll buy you some dinner."

I was wearing a woolen suit and a sweater, and I said I wasn't dressed for nightclubbing—"I should at least be in black, with pearls" —but the publicity man said no, it would be all right.

It happened that Mr. Mayer was also dining at the Trocadero, and he sent a henchman over to our table. "Mr. Mayer would like to dance with you," the henchman said.

"If he wants to dance with me," I said, "he can come and ask me himself."

To my surprise, he came. And after a couple of turns around the dance floor, he spoke. "Why do you wear heavy tweeds? It's not much fun dancing with you."

I said these were working clothes, that I'd just come from a picture session. We took a few more turns. "You're a wonderful girl," he said, "but you represent yourself as a cold New England woman."

The analysis didn't faze me. If my style was off-putting, so much the better; it made my working life easier. Nobody chased me around a desk, I wasn't the type.

Actually, Mayer was a highly moralistic man—about everybody else, anyway. There was a stringent morals clause in every Metro contract, so when hanky-panky went on, it went on in the dark. Literally. Stars hadn't yet begun to demand that their lovers share their dressing rooms, or to brag to magazines about their illegitimate children.

(In the thirties reporters wouldn't put the blunt kinds of questions they ask now, but they always wanted to know about "romances," and I never made very good copy. I wouldn't tell a journalist about any romances; I'd been brought up to believe that this was a private matter and one didn't discuss such things, it wasn't cricket and it wasn't ladylike. The press finally settled for calling me a "bachelor girl," and when I married Freddie in 1941, it was "Number One Bachelor Girl Married Today." Pretty tame stuff.)

Though I had no casting-couch problems, I did go through a bad few days with one of my leading men. Since he's still alive, though perhaps too halt for chasing, I won't mention his name. He came to my house and made a small pass. I deflected it. From that time forward he behaved badly on the set. We weren't working well together, so I decided to take action, and one night I went clunking over to the men's dressing rooms—at Metro the men were separated from the women—stomped up a flight of cement steps, and pounded at his door.

"Who is it?" he called.

"It's Roz," I bawled back. You could hear me in the San Fernando Valley. "Come on, come on, open up this door."

Since he hadn't been barring it or anything, I must have sounded demented. He opened the door. "Yes?" he said frostily.

I went on yelling, "We have to get this thing straightened out!"

Terrified that my bellowing would bring studio guards, or his wife from their home in Beverly Hills, or Louis B. himself, he yanked at my arm. "Come in here." The louder my voice rose, the lower his fell. I let myself be drawn into his dressing room. "Listen," I said, "this is a lot of nonsense. We've got to make a picture and you're sulking like a child."

Once again my notorious noisiness prevailed. He promised to treat me with civility, if not enthusiasm. He'd have promised anything just to shut me up. And it wasn't even that I didn't find him attractive, but he was married, for God's sake, and I'd been to their home to dine, and what other reaction could a "cold" New England woman have than to think his conduct was disgraceful?

The first lead I played at Metro—it was forced on me, I went down hollering—was in a B movie called *Casino Murder Case*, with Paul Lukas. It was so bad, and I was so bad in it, that it gave my maid Hazel ammunition for seasons to come. "If you don't behave," she'd say, "I'm going to tell people about that *Casino Murder Case*."

Bad or not, after *Casino Murder Case*, I played only leads.

My course through Metro was so atypical that I'd been there for five years before Benny Thau, a top studio executive, asked me if I'd ever had a makeup test. When I said no, he just shook his head. "You should have," he said.

I didn't have my name changed or my teeth capped, or my hairline redesigned, either. In dealing with the studio, I suppose I should have been more difficult—somebody once said to me, "The trouble with you is, you never thought enough of yourself," and I didn't understand it at the time—but I was afraid of being too caught up in the total Hollywood scene. I wanted to be able to shrug my shoulders, walk away after my day's work, go dancing with a beau.

Sometimes, of course, the great female superstars could make you feel like Second-Hand Rose. Even when I worked with them, I was in their shadow, very much apart from them. To me, Joan Crawford remained an enormous star; we weren't intimates. I wasn't intimate with any of those women. They flicked across my life, touched my life, but we never sat down and dished, asked each other, "Where did you buy this?" or "Is that stuff any good for your face?"

I'll take that back. I was close to Jean Harlow. I loved her, and oh, she was a stunning creature. I remember sitting under a hair dryer in a beauty parlor one day, and sitting next to me was a child, also under a dryer. She was wearing shorts, and her little baby legs, perfectly formed, rested against the back of her chair while the nails of her little baby hands were being manicured.

My word, I thought, a ten- or eleven-year-old having that bright red polish put on, and suddenly the hood of the dryer went back and the child stood up and it was Jean. She was probably twenty-three at the time, but without any makeup and no eyebrows, she looked exactly like a little kid.

I guess you wouldn't think of her and me as apt to be friends, but her publicity man, Larry Barbier, sort of took care of me at the studio too, and Jean was very warm, very friendly with everybody.

Still, she had a fierce temper. One night her mother phoned and asked me to please come over, it was important. So I went, and when I got there, Jean wasn't even home, she was off on a date. Her mother kept babbling about how she wanted Jean and me to be good friends, while I wondered what in the world I was doing in that place. Eventually Jean came back, and she and I talked, standing near a bear rug stretched in front of the living-room fireplace. Half the bear's fangs were missing, and the ones he had left were sticking straight down toward his throat. "What happened to his teeth?" I said. "I kicked 'em in," said Jean.

She was a sad girl, driven by her mother, madly in love with a man who wouldn't marry her, and she spent the last nine months of her life drinking too much. I went into a lot of bars to try and get her out.

In 1935 we made two movies (China Seas and Reckless) together.

In 1937 she died. She was twenty-six years old.

When I first came to Hollywood, I gawked, like any other fan, at celebrities. I remember going to the Southwest Tennis Tournament on a September afternoon and seeing Gloria Swanson and Herbert Marshall there, and thinking what a perfect couple they looked, how elegant, how entirely like movie stars.

And I remember being at a party to which a well-known British actor had brought his actress wife. The wife had just closed in a Broadway show and flown West to what she believed was going to be an ecstatic reunion with her mate. They were standing side by side when the husband made a gesture in the direction of a famous, much-married star leaning against the curve of a grand piano across the room. "Do you see that woman?" he said. "I love her, and I want a divorce . . ."

Glittering people came and went around me, and I was fascinated, but I didn't share the world-well-lost-for-stardom drive that goaded most of them, maybe because I was sensible enough to know I wasn't a sex symbol and never could be. I was always a character actress.

Love scenes continued to be murder for me. I was no more convincing lying on a couch in Hollywood than I had been in Saranac Lake. I'd be giggling, and begging the leading man to take his elbow out of my stomach "and quit bending my head back like that." (The only man who could make a love scene comfortable was Clark Gable. He was born graceful, he knew what to do with his feet, and when he took hold of you, there was no fooling around.)

You can be sixteen years old and look ghastly in a shot if your face is all pulled to one side, so the mechanics of passion have to be carefully worked out beforehand. The director is standing over you, saying to the leading man, "Don't twist her neck! Is there any way you could put your arm near her shoulder? No, no, drop it down her back!" And by the time you finally get to the kissing, you're positively spastic, and it's very uninteresting stuff. Particularly when you're playing with an actor who ate garlic for lunch. Besides, how can you enjoy making love when you're being watched by two hundred men in their overalls?

Character parts, comedy parts are much more fun. Still, when I was starting out I did what my bosses told me to do, even if that meant an occasional love scene. I dealt with what I had to deal with, and I relished the work. (Obviously, since I made my way to some studio or other for forty years, more or less.) Every day at five A.M. I'd throw on a shirt and pants and an old topcoat, stumble out of doors, take a look at the garden, get into my car, and still half asleep, drive to the studio. We started shooting at nine A.M., but first came hair, makeup and wardrobe fittings. I didn't mind that. I love the early mornings.

Somebody once quoted me as having said, "God gave us from five to seven so we could get up and beat the traffic." I think that's funny, but the real reason I've always loved the morning hours is, it's the only time you can ever have alone, time that belongs to you, and not to the world or your house or your husband or your boss.

Little by little, as I learned more about my new craft, I also learned more about myself. Part of what I learned was that the second echelon suited me; I wasn't prepared to pay the price it would have required to get on the big Varsity. And I'm not just talking about having my teeth capped. I wasn't prepared to give up free time in order to cultivate important producers, to scheme, to become involved in the intrigue at Metro.

I enjoyed a challenge and I'd fight for a part (*The Women* would never have come to me if I hadn't fought for it, but that's a later story), yet I didn't care two cents' worth about being loved—personally—by the tycoons in the picture business.

To this day Freddie and I have never entertained a soul in our house that we didn't like. We've had a few love-her-hate-him couples—what can you do if your friends marry the wrong people?—but we've given no dinners for Mr. Cohn, Mr. Zanuck or Mr. Mayer. I don't even mean that we didn't like Mr. Cohn, Mr. Zanuck or Mr. Mayer, I just mean that we kept our business lives separate from our personal lives, and we kept our privacy that way, and I think our sanity too. Because Hollywood is made up of people with wonderfully exciting talents, but they're not always emotionally stable.

You *can* be a superstar and have a personal life, but you'll probably have to shift it around several times to meet the demands of your profession. If your husband doesn't want to be married to a studio, you get rid of the husband, not the studio. You have to be willing to sacrifice too much, and the end comes anyway. Your usefulness stops for one reason or another, the box office falls off or your health gives out, and you aren't able to work any more.

So I was always grateful that my career was really of a different kind. I had my cake and ate it too, and I'm very aware of that.

Between 1934 and 1938 I made fifteen movies, and when I got a day off I used to like to ride horseback in an area called the Riviera, which was the Will Rogers Polo Grounds, beyond Bel Air and before you get to Pacific Palisades. That section's all built up now, the bridle paths are closed, but in the thirties there were big stables and a polo field and you could ride up into the hills through woods that smelled of pine.

People were always asking me if I didn't miss New England.

Of course I missed New England. My sister Mary Jane still lives in Southport, Connecticut, with its marvelous harbor, and I was there last spring when the lilacs were in bloom and the dogwood was out on Sasco Hill, and on Congress Street (which leads to a church that's been depicted by every Sunday painter on the eastern seaboard) the old dogwood trees met across the middle of the road and made a bower. But even as I rhapsodized, Mary Jane brought me back to earth. "You forget," she said, "that we go through months of slush and ice to get these two weeks of beauty."

I think every place has its own kind of beauty. After the skies of New England, it takes some doing to accustom your eye to California and the splendor of the raw mountains and deserts, but you can set me down anyplace and I'll make the most of it. A doctor will tell you not to worry about things you can't change, it's like trying to affect the tides. I know people who are always crabbing about the weather; it's never right for them. Well, I don't understand that. If I plan a picnic, I go on it, whether or not I have to eat in the car. Or under it. You waste too much time fussing.

Moving (On).
A Brief Domestic
Digression

THE VERY FIRST HOUSE I rented when I came West was in Hollywood, up on a big hill. I took the place furnished, and was so lonely for my family that my brother George came out and stayed with me and went to USC law school for a year. After the year was up, George went back, and I decided to move to Beverly Hills. Just as I'd needed a white satin dress and a fox stole to make me believe I was really in the movies, now I needed to move to Beverly Hills, where the chauffeurs matched the cars, the swimming pools were filled with vichyssoise, and even the bicycle thieves made their getaways in silver Bugattis.

I know I said I wasn't prepared to pay the price to get on the big Varsity, but I never said I didn't like to live as well as those guys did.

I'd no sooner informed my Hollywood landlady that I was leaving than she slapped me with a lawsuit. She wanted three hundred and six dollars for damages to her house. She owned several houses, rented them out, and she had a nice little racket. Whenever a tenant left, she automatically sued him for whatever she could get. They were nuisance suits, and most tenants settled out of court. If I'd been willing to do that, the landlady would have had the money to paint two or three rooms, and she'd have been that much ahead when it came to getting my house ready for the next tenant.

But I could hear my father's voice telling us children that

anybody could sue you over anything—"They can sue you if they don't like the color of your dress!"—and that responsible citizens ought not to knuckle under to intimidation. "If you pay, you're guilty," he'd say. And, "If we don't use the courts, we're lost."

So I got me a lawyer and prepared to use the courts.

When the case came up, my lawyer and I spent quite a bit of time listening to my landlady testify. She said some valuable china had been broken; she said my dog had committed a nuisance (that's what they call it in legal jargon) and had thereby stained the living-room draperies; she said a bedspread had been torn; and she said that my cook, who was a big woman, had broken a bed.

As soon as the landlady came to this item in her bill of particulars, the cook, who had been sitting quietly in the back of the courtroom, sprang to her feet. "Ah didn't break no bed," she cried. "Ah'm heavy, Jedge, but Ah didn't break no bed. That bed was broke when I come in that house, and Miss Russell knows that and *you*"—by now she was shouting at the landlady—"and *you* know that."

I turned around and shook my head reprovingly. "Sit down, sit down," I hissed, but righteous indignation had put the cook beyond the call of reason. "Ah'm a single lady," she wailed, "a single lady, and Ah didn't break no bed."

It all went like that. The landlady's lawyer picked up the bedspread to show where it had been torn, and he opened it wide and tripped over it and fell into it and couldn't get out, and lay on the floor pitifully gazing up at the judge.

Depending on whether you were principal or audience, it was a nightmare or a riot. After the morning session everybody in the courthouse had started coming in on his or her lunch hour, hoping to see the judge hiding his face so he wouldn't be caught laughing out loud, or to hear the cook who got up at regular intervals and made a speech about how she didn't break no bed.

When my turn came to testify, I was worried. I'd never been to court in my life, but I'd seen those movies where the opposing lawyer keeps barking at the witness, "Just answer the question, yes or no."

"I don't know how to do that yes or no stuff," I told my lawyer, "so when I get up there, why don't you say to me, 'Just tell your story to the court.' You keep saying that to me any time I stop talking."

The judge's name was Caul and he was famous in town—the whole Caul family had been in the California judiciary for generations —and as I took the stand I was nervously aware of his black-robed presence. I was sworn in and said I worked at Metro.

"Now tell your story to the court," my lawyer said.

"First tell the court what I'm paying you," I said.

Obediently my lawyer turned to Judge Caul. "She's paying me five hundred dollars."

"It's a matter of principle," I said. "I'm supposed to owe this woman three hundred and six dollars. Now why would I pay my lawyer five hundred dollars if I could get out of this whole thing for three hundred and six dollars, unless it was a matter of—"

My lawyer interrupted. "Tell your story to the court." I had him so mixed up he didn't realize I *was* telling my story to the court.

I started over again. "I work at MGM studios. I get fifteen hundred dollars a week, and I've had to give up two days' salary to come down here. Now I have to ask you a question, Judge. Why am I doing that if I owe three hundred and six dollars? And if I owe three hundred and six dollars, why did this woman offer to settle for a hundred and fifty dollars last week? And why, when I came up the steps of this courthouse, did she offer to settle for fifty dollars?"

Warming to my own rhetoric, I grew more fierce. "Not only do I not owe this woman any money, she owes *me* money, and I'm here to prove it." Then I turned to my lawyer. "Proceed," I said grandly. "Ask me the questions."

My lawyer gaped, as though he hadn't known I was going to let him back into the ball game.

"Do you have a dog?" he said.

"Yes, I do," I said.

Before going on, I have to explain that it had already been established by my landlady that the curtains my dog was supposed to have stained hung three inches off the floor.

"What kind of a dog do you have?" asked my lawyer.

"A wire-haired terrier," I said.

"No, no," he said impatiently, "what *kind* of dog?"

"Oh," I said. I'd forgotten the point we were out to make, which was that a lady dog doesn't lift her leg to commit a nuisance, she squats.

((72))

Again the lawyer asked me, "What kind of dog?"

"A female dog," I said. "And if she could do what she's been accused of, I'd have a trick dog, and I wouldn't have to work in pictures, I could tour the world with her and make a fortune."

By this time the judge had swiveled his chair around and appeared to be studying an oil painting that hung behind the bench, but his shoulders were heaving.

My lawyer, tasting blood, perked right up. "About the bed in the cook's room, Miss Russell—"

From somewhere in the rear came the cook's voice, no longer filled with fire, but only mournful. "That bed was broke before I got in it—"

"Ask me about the china," I said to the lawyer.

He asked me about the china.

"Well," I said, "when I took this house, the landlady told me there was open stock on the china, and during the time I lived there two butter plates were broken and two cups. Now the landlady says they'll cost forty-five dollars to replace because they have to come from England."

I handed my lawyer a box. "Open it," I said.

He opened it, and he and the judge and the landlady's lawyer looked, and there were two cups and two plates and a bill of sale. I'd sent to England for the crockery and it had cost me—except for the mailing—forty-five cents.

The landlady's case was thrown out of court, and Judge Caul made her pay my lawyer and all costs.

I left the courthouse thinking about my Dad. Except for him, I'd never have got involved, I'd have paid the money and gone to work.

"If you pay, you're guilty," my Dad had said. I thought about that all the way to my new place in Beverly Hills.

Adventures with Hazel (a Dark Duchess), Winston (an English Knight) and Louella (a Hollywood Queen)

I MET HAZEL WASHINGTON when she was still on Greta Garbo's payroll. The first time Hazel ever rode in a car with Garbo, the driver pulled out of Metro's main gate and onto a public street, and Hazel found herself hurled to the carpet. G.G. didn't want to be seen by any civilians, and in her frenzy for privacy she knocked Hazel clean off her seat. "Pow!" Hazel said. "I was down there wrestling on the floor, and I didn't know what hit me."

Garbo was one of your better-paid actors—Hazel knew, because she used to take the checks to the bank—but she saved her loot; she didn't see any reason to support a maid when she, Garbo, was between pictures. (In the old days, before the union brought in wardrobe mistresses, a star's maid handled her wardrobe, ran back and forth between set and dressing room, fetching hats and gloves and furs, not to mention cooking the star's breakfast and lunch and bringing her glasses of water and ashtrays.)

Because I was willing to pay Hazel fifty-two weeks a year, she came to work for me. She was part Irish, part Indian, part black, and all funny. Once when my sister the Duchess was expected on a visit, the doorbell rang, and then somebody came through the front door. I peered over the staircase and in the half-light couldn't quite make out the figure below. "Who is it?" I said.

"It's me," Hazel said, "the dark Duchess."

She affected an Amos 'n' Andy dialect—"Why you do dat, Miss R.?"—and when I'd say, "Now, you cut that out," she'd break up. She was married to a policeman so smart the brass finally had to make him a captain (he was top man in his class seven times, scored the highest marks in every examination), but it took a while. He was the very first black captain on the Los Angeles police force. Hazel wouldn't approve of that description. "I'm a Negro," she'd say. "Don't you go calling me black."

Although she lived at home, Hazel came and helped me any-time I was in trouble, and she traveled with me more out of pity than because she wanted to go. (Once we left for Europe with her scream-ing, "I'm gonna drown on this here boat.")

Travel is a perk that comes with an acting career, and I got my first taste of this in 1938 when Metro sent me to England to make a picture called *The Citadel*. It had a tremendously polished cast—Robert Donat, Ralph Richardson, Rex Harrison, Emlyn Williams—and I don't think I was a very welcome addition to it, since the English labor unions had wanted an English girl to play my part. The rules are still strict about American actors working in England, but in the thirties they were even worse. King Vidor, the director, and I were the only two non-Britons involved in *The Citadel;* even so, my being there caused a furor.

It was during this stay in London that I was invited to the American Embassy. Joseph Kennedy was our Ambassador, and every-body assumed that I'd known the Kennedys in the United States. (I hadn't.) Everybody also assumed that the Kennedys had pulled a gaffe. "You're going to the Embassy? That's never been done before, they don't have actresses."

Rosalind, the social pariah, didn't care. I put on my long white gloves and off I sailed. The Kennedys were charming to me, and during the cocktail period (we weren't really given cocktails, only a glass of sherry apiece) Rose Kennedy brought a cherubic-looking gentleman over to meet me and said he would be my dinner partner. She introduced him as a Mr. Churchill, there was no Sir Winston about it. In fact, Churchill wasn't much in favor then. When people looked at him they tended to have this "remember the Dardanelles" expression on their faces.

The season was spring, the company distinguished—the guest of honor was the French Foreign Minister—and I chatted with various agreeable strangers until time to go in to dinner. Then Mr. Churchill came and offered his arm.

There was a long narrow table in the center of the dining salon, and seated right in the middle of this table were Ambassador and Mrs. Kennedy. At one end, far, far below the salt, were two chairs for Mr. Churchill and his dinner companion. After we'd taken our places, Churchill turned to me. "Well," he said, "I understand you're an actress from the United States, and I'm sure you're very fine, but still and all you can't amount to much if you have to sit down here with me."

After that, we never stopped laughing. Anthony Eden was at dinner too, a little further up the table; he and Churchill were obviously fond of each other and Churchill ribbed him constantly. "Even Eden got a better seat than we did," he boomed. He also groused about not smoking. "If they'd only finish this food. It's barbaric that you can't have your cigar during the meal."

A few months later Mr. Chamberlain came back from Munich, bringing a white paper and peace in our time, and soon Churchill and Eden were returned to power. Neither of them would ever again have to sit in the coffin corner at a party. But for me, that Embassy dinner is a lovely memory; I feel proud to have spent those hours with Churchill (he couldn't escape me; he couldn't just get up and leave after the soup) and I know the experience was salutary. Young actresses tend to think of fame as a permanent condition; to see a once-lionized man maintaining his grace when he was out (not down, he was clearly never down) was a valuable lesson.

Back home in California, the partying—though Beverly Hills didn't feature foreign embassies—was pretty fancy too. In the movie business, much of the social life was run by the heads of companies. Jack Warner gave parties at his Beverly Hills estate, Darryl Zanuck had parties at the beach, Louis B. Mayer gave big dinners, David O. Selznick, who was on the MGM lot in the thirties, entertained lavishly, as did Sam Goldwyn and his wife Frances, and various socialites

—like the Countess di Frasso, Dolly O'Brien, Lady Mendl, William Randolph Hearst—who always invited the movie people.

There was no such thing as a dinner for six or eight guests; everything was on a vast scale. In the summer, tents were put up over the lawns and the gardens, there were cut flowers everywhere and orchestras for dancing, and the guests enjoyed dressing up and making big entrances. The Basil Rathbones' parties were considered something special; it was really classy to be able to murmur carelessly "Oh, we're going to the Rathbones' . . ."

One night at the Rathbones', Fred MacMurray and I put on a show—he played the saxophone and I accompanied him with the human voice; it must have been awful, because I've blocked out of my mind the names of the songs we did.

I didn't really party all that much (as I keep saying, I was working my tail off), though from time to time I dated Jimmy Stewart, John McClain (the wittiest of men; he later became a Broadway theatre critic) and a bunch of others. Enough has been written—and documented, for that matter—about Hollywood orgies, so I can't swear they never happened. What I can swear is, I never got invited to one.

Maybe I put blinders on and couldn't see the razzmatazz that was erupting all around me. As recently as last year I heard of spectacular goings-on at the home of a man out here, so when he asked me to dinner, I accepted eagerly. At last, I figured, even if I'm of a generation that thinks when you're stoned it means people are throwing rocks at you, I'm going to find out who does what to whom. Well, the night I was there, nobody did anything. A couple of very nice authors were among the guests. Marvin Hamlisch, the very talented composer, also attended. There was very nice music throughout the evening. Then I went home. I'm still waiting to go to a wild party.

I think probably just as many wild parties go on in Southampton, Palm Beach or up and down Park Avenue as ever went on here. A life in Beverly Hills has good things, bad things, upsets, color, the same as a life in Red Bank, New Jersey.

In the years when the social doings of the Hollywood gentry were being chronicled by Louella Parsons and Hedda Hopper, these columnists could get any actor, big or small, to call on them. Right after I first came West, I was invited to Louella's home to do her radio show—Clark Gable was there too; Carole Lombard's secretary, Fieldsy, was one of Louella's best friends—and after I'd said my few lines, Louella strolled out to my car with me. Her house was still filled with famous guests, I was an unknown actress, new in the business, but she took the time to see me on my way. "Where do you live?" she asked, and when I told her up in Hollywoodland (in the house I went to court about), she was concerned. "You shouldn't be driving through those hills alone."

I said it wasn't dangerous, that my brother George would be there to meet me, but I went away thinking she had excellent manners. Our second encounter came after I'd moved into Beverly Hills (made it down off the hill, as they say) and I was playing bridge at a neighbor's place. Louella was my partner, and I trumped her ace.

This ought to give you some idea of the reckless abandon with which I frolicked through the middle thirties. (The century's middle thirties, not my own.)

Some years later I met Sir Charles Mendl, the British ex-Ambassador to France and a long-time fixture of Anglo-American society, and discovered I'd been doing the whole thing wrong. Freddie and I were married by then, and one evening we were to dine with Merle Oberon, who had a charming house in Bel Air. When we arrived at Merle's front door, Sir Charles was already standing there. He rang the bell, turned to us, and said, "This is where I draw into my lungs three or four big breaths of oxygen."

Pulling deeply at the night air, he demonstrated. "I always do that before I make an entrance," he said. "Into any room, any house. As I walk in I have this air down in my lungs—it only lasts long enough to greet people—and I say to myself, 'I'm as good as anybody here and better than most.' "

Freddie and I were tickled. To this day we seldom venture into a strange place without one of us turning to the other and saying, "Now take three deep breaths, darling."

I'm as good as anybody and better than most. It's a perfect credo, and in 1939 I found myself acting on it. I must have taken several particularly deep drags of oxygen the day I went after a flashy part in *The Women*.

The Women

MGM HAD TESTED EVERYBODY but Lassie and Mrs. Roosevelt for *The Women*. Even the maids' roles were being fought over. Norma Shearer, Joan Crawford, Paulette Goddard, Joan Fontaine, Ruth Hussey, Mary Boland were already set, when it suddenly hit me that I could wear a big black hat as well as anybody, and I got mad.

I came out of the Elizabeth Arden salon on Wilshire Boulevard, and instead of going home, drove out to Metro and marched straight into Hunt Stromberg's office (Stromberg was the producer for whom I'd done *Night Must Fall*, so I knew him) and told him I wanted to play the part of Sylvia in *The Women*. Sylvia was a gossipy gadfly, and she was funny. "Why haven't you tested me?" I said.

Stromberg sighed. "Well, Roz," he said, "you're too beautiful."

It caught me with my mouth open. Nobody'd ever told me that before (or since). "My God," I said, "bring your secretary in here, I'd like you to say that again in front of a witness."

"We want somebody," he said, "who gets a laugh just by sticking her head around the door."

I crossed my eyes, offered to put a wart on my nose, and asked him to give me ten minutes in Makeup.

He talked to me for quite a while, but he just didn't think of me as a comic. "You're a wonderful dramatic actress," he said.

I said some of my friends had been known to get a laugh out of me. "If I play a love scene for you, and it leaves you cold, then you have every right to say so, you paid your good thirty-five cents, and you weren't moved, but until I play that love scene, don't say anything. And I feel the same way about a comedy scene."

Stromberg was a fair man. He called me at home later and said

I was to come in and make a test for George Cukor, who was going to direct *The Women*. And who, it developed, was less than thrilled by the prospect of working with me. "I don't want you in this part," Cukor said. "I want Ilka Chase, she's a friend of mine, she played it in New York and she's right for it, but I have to make a test with you."

I told him I appreciated his being so honest, "but I'm going to do the best I can."

He said okay. We went onto a sound stage, and I asked how much footage there was in the camera, and somebody said two hundred and fifty feet, and I asked if they'd put in a whole load, which is a thousand feet. "I'd like to play this scene in more than one way," I said. And I did. I played it as drawing-room comedy, and then I played it more realistically, and then I played it flat out, in a very exaggerated style.

Next day Cukor informed me that I could start being fitted for Sylvia's clothes.

I was blissful until we actually began work on the picture and Cukor stopped me right after my first few lines. "No, no," he said, "do it like you did it in the test."

"Isn't this what I did in the test?" I said.

He said, "No, the very, very exaggerated version is the one I want."

I was horrified. "Oh," I said, "Mr. Cukor, I can't do that, the critics will murder me."

"You know," he said, "you have a big following at Loew's State in New York. But in Waukegan, Illinois, they've never heard of you. Now you do it the way I tell you. Because in this picture Sylvia's breaking up a family, and there's a child involved, and if you're a heavy, audiences will hate you. Don't play it like a heavy, just be ridiculous."

He was a hundred-percent right. I was frightened to death, but from then on, I did what he said, and everything that came to me from *The Women*—namely, my reputation as a comedienne—I owe to George.

He was marvelous to work for, he could think of a hundred bits of business for every moment. In one scene, where I was in a powder room with some other women, he said to me, "After they leave I want you to look at your teeth."

"What?" I said.

"Yes," he said. "When you girls make up in front of people, you make up one way, and when you're alone, you make up another."

So I waited for the others to leave, then bared my teeth at myself in the mirror, and eventually got credit for an inspired moment, courtesy of George Cukor. Another time he had me pick up a towel, say "cheap Chinese embroidery," and toss it away so quickly the whole thing was almost subliminal, but it helped to establish Sylvia's character.

On a Cukor picture, there's no rest. He keeps you so busy, you're spinning. You're rehearsing, you're running lines, you never get to go to your dressing room, or to the bathroom, somebody comes out and combs your hair right in the middle of the set, and it's great, it's stimulating.

One day I was sitting on the set chewing gum (I don't chew gum anyplace else, but I chew gum on the set) and practicing knitting because I hadn't knitted since I was twelve years old and I was going to have to knit for the fashion-show scene. I was also wearing glasses because I was going to have to wear glasses for the fashion-show scene. My head was bent over the knitting, the glasses had slipped down my nose, Norma Shearer and I were running over our lines, when Cukor said, "All right, all right, quiet, clear the set, we're going to make a take." Hazel started toward me with a piece of Kleenex to wrap around my chewing gum, and Cukor stopped her. "I want Miss Russell to chew gum in this scene. I've been watching her, and that's just what I want."

Norma Shearer (who was married to Irving Thalberg, the head of production and therefore the most important man at Metro except for Louis B. Mayer) couldn't believe her ears. "Just a minute, dear," she said to Cukor. "Is she going to knit and talk and chew gum and let those glasses hang down on the end of her nose in a scene with *me?*"

"Yes, she is, Norma," said Cukor. "Now let's go."

"Who can compete with that?" Norma said somewhat sharply, and I completely understood her irritation. "I don't blame you, kid, it's rough," I said, but I went ahead joyfully with my work.

Because Sylvia never shut up, the writer had already done a lot of that work for me. In my scenes with Norma she never got to say much more than "Please, Sylvia" or "No, Sylvia" or "Go away, Sylvia," while I was chattering on and on about "Have you heard this?" and "Did you know that?" and "Are you aware that your husband was out last night with Crystal?"

After the knitting scene Norma and I had a scene in a dressing room, and all the time she's being fitted in a dress, I'm talking a mile a minute. There's a woman down on the floor fiddling with a hem, mostly out of camera range, once they've established what she's doing, and then, as Norma turns around, there I am buzzing, buzzing, buzzing. "Just think of it like a bee," Cukor had told me. "Get into her ear, and if she turns away, get into her other ear."

In the midst of my buzzing, Norma left the set for half an hour. When she came back she was wearing a dress left over from *Marie Antoinette*. It had never been worn; it was black velvet and it had an enormous hoop skirt. "I just hated that other dress, George," she said, "so I put this one on."

He studied her, he studied the dress, then he said, "Take a few minutes," and told his crew he was going to change the scene.

Now, bear in mind that the set was a little tiny dressing room with a platform, and that once Norma was in the gown with the hoops, I wasn't going to be able to get anywhere near her ears.

"Rosalind," Cukor said, "I want you to stand on that platform." I stood on that platform. "Now pull those four full-length mirrors around her," he told the prop men. They pulled the four full-length mirrors around me. "Now, Norma," he said, "you go stand next to her as close as you can get." Norma came up beside me, and Cukor surveyed his handiwork. "Light that, fellows," he said.

It took some time to get the shot lit, with the reflections from the mirrors flaring into the camera, but when it was done, Cukor turned to Norma. "Now, instead of one Sylvia, you've got four," he said. It was tremendously effective, four people buzzing at her. Poor Norma, she was a terribly nice woman and a very pretty woman and a good actress, but what could she do?

The only thing I take credit for is keeping my mouth shut because I knew the break I was getting. Even though Cukor hadn't wanted me, he'd made my test with all the zeal under the sun, and he worked with me the same way throughout the picture. (Cukor and I became—and remained—close friends.)

Norma had it in her contract that only a man could be starred with her. On any picture. No woman's name could be up there with hers. For *The Women* she'd capitulated and said Joan Crawford might also be starred above the title, but when it came to me, that was another story. She must have felt she'd been pushed far enough. I, on the other hand, wasn't willing to settle for billing that said "with Rosalind Russell" underneath the title. I'd already starred in pictures and I didn't care to be demoted.

I thought about the situation. When it comes to a fight with management, a performer has only one weapon: he can refuse to perform. The employers have everything else: they have the lawyers, they have the contracts, the courts will usually back them up. But if a performer gets sick, what can his boss do?

About five weeks into production on *The Women*, I got sick. You couldn't pull that trick in the first few days, they'd just replace you. I never attempted it again in my whole career, and I only did it that once because I had a feeling I could make it work. There had been signs and portents. I'd gone to a luncheon where I'd met Louis B. Mayer, and he'd said, "I hear you're stealing this picture," and I'd said, "I'm tryin', I'm always tryin'." And *Life* magazine had been sniffing around again. And I just had this feeling in my bones.

(The first time *Life* had ever come to photograph me, I damn near killed myself jumping on and off a horse's back, showing off, and they never used the pictures. The second time they showed—*Life* was very important to the studios—I cooperated again. Again they didn't print a single shot. The third time I wasn't so impressed. I'd been working on *The Women*, rumor had spread that I was good in it, and when the *Life* photographers appeared at my door, I marched out of the house in a shirt and slacks—clean, but nothing special—stood in the driveway, said, "Snap it and go, because you're not going to use it anyway."

Naturally, it appeared on the *Life* cover. The date is burned in my brain, it was the issue of September 3rd, 1939. The Nazis had invaded Poland on September 1st, and on September 3rd, Britain and France had declared war on Germany, and back in New York, my sister Mary Jane, who was working as a researcher for Time, Inc., covered her ears so she wouldn't have to hear my name being cursed up and down the corridors. Editors had managed to snatch the celebrity-of-the-week from the cover of *Time* and substitute a picture of a Polish solider—they weren't ready with a shot of Churchill or anything—but it was too late to alter the cover of *Life,* which had already gone to press. "You've never been called so many terrible things!" Mary Jane said. "They were screaming, 'Get that cover changed, get that actress off!' I heard them all over the building.")

Norma Shearer wouldn't give in on the billing, so I wouldn't come to work. I wasn't holding up production, they had plenty to shoot, but I let it be known that I was going to be under the weather for quite a long time.

I lay out in my garden, looking up at the sky, and every day Benny Thau, who was in charge of talent and their problems, would phone and ask how I was coming along, and I'd say, "Not very well. I don't feel very well."

The last time he called—it was the third or fourth day of my strike—he said, "Oh, something happened this afternoon. Norma Shearer says you're so good in this film that she's going to allow you to be starred too."

"That's very nice of Norma," I said.

Pause. Then Benny spoke again. "Do you think," he said, "you'd feel well enough to come to work tomorrow?"

"Hmm," I said. "I'll call my doctor, Benny, and I'll make a stab at it."

(At the completion party for *The Women* at the Trocadero, I was dancing with Cukor when Ernst Lubitsch fox-trotted by and said to me, "If you want more close-ups in the picture, never mind dancing with your director, you'd better dance with Norma Shearer!" So then Norma and I did a turn on the floor.)

I loved *The Women.* I still do. *Time* magazine said that of the hundred and thirty-five actresses (were there that many of us?) in the picture, "Rosalind Russell is the one usually best remembered by the millions who saw it . . . She became firmly established as the idol of a generation of less-than-beautiful moviegoing girls who had to use smart clothes and bright chatter to lure men away from more luscious-looking females."

I don't know about that, but *The Women,* brought me acceptance as a comedienne, and *The Women* also brought me my husband.

Because when England declared war on Germany, Freddie, a

Danish-born Anglophile (reared in England, sent to English schools), tried to join the military, and the British turned him down; they weren't taking resident aliens in their army.

So Monsieur Brisson decided he'd come to America. He'd been here on several business trips in connection with his Anglo-American talent agency. But this time he was crossing the Atlantic on a liner that spent much of its time dodging submarines. The trip took sixteen days, people wore their life jackets the entire time, and the only movie on board—*The Women*—was played and replayed endlessly.

The ship was sinking with passengers, Freddie shared a stateroom with six other men, so he spent a lot of time on deck. And wherever he sat, on any deck, he heard the soundtrack of *The Women*, and particularly my voice. "Screaming and carrying on," as he tenderly puts it.

After a couple of weeks he surrendered to the inevitable. He went inside to see what he'd been hearing. He remembers thinking, I will try to live through this picture. And when I came on the screen in the fight scene, he laughed, and he claims he said, "I'm either gonna kill that girl, or I'm gonna marry her."

Back Door to *The Front Page,* or How I Was Everybody's Fifteenth Choice

APPILY INNOCENT of the foreigner's intentions toward me, I was resting up after *The Women.* I'd taken myself off to Fairfield, Connecticut, where the Duchess and her husband lived. The Duchess' house was full of guests, and we were about to sit down to dinner when I got a call from Benny Thau at Metro. "Come back," he said, "get your makeup kit and go over to Columbia."

I was used to being loaned out, so I didn't take it too big. "What for?" I said.

"Well," Benny said, "you're gonna do a picture with Cary Grant; they want you right away."

I told the Duchess, and she told the other dinner guests. "Rosalind's going to work with Cary Grant, isn't it mahvelous?" she cried, and they were thrilled and agreed. "Oh, how mahvelous," they said, echoing my sister.

The next morning, going into New York on the train with my brother-in-law, Chet La Roche, and most of the people who had been at dinner the night before, everyone had his own copy of the *New York Times,* and we were all reading, and it said in the *New York Times* that Rosalind Russell was to play this part in a picture called

His Girl Friday. Then it said the names of all the women who'd turned the part down. Howard Hawks, who would be directing, had tried to get Ginger Rogers, Irene Dunne, Jean Arthur; he'd asked every leading woman in town before Harry Cohn had stuck him with me. (I was told later that Cohn had asked Hawks to go up to Grauman's Chinese Theatre and take a look at *The Women,* but I don't think he ever went.)

Anyway, coming down from Fairfield, I didn't dare look up from the paper. I kept thinking about all these people saying "Oh, how mahvelous."

I arrived back in California in a bad mood, and California was in the middle of a heat wave. I'd built my first swimming pool, a salt-water pool (you just dumped salt in, but you had to have special pipes), and it was about a hundred and seven degrees outside, and I was supposed to go down and see Hawks, but I kept brooding about being humiliated in the *New York Times,* and before I went to Columbia, I jumped in the pool, got my dress and hair all wet, and then went and sat in Hawks' outer office.

I was always so sassy, it seems to me, so unattractive, now that I think about it.

Hawks came out, did a triple take, and ushered me inside.

"You didn't want me for this, did you?" I said. (Besides being sassy, I was forever assaulting some guy—Bill Powell, Howard Hawks —with the news that he really hadn't wanted me.)

"It'll be all right," Hawks said. "You'll be fine. Now go to Wardrobe and tell them I'd like you in a suit with stripes, rather flashy-looking."

"Okay, Mr. Hawks, goodbye," I said. "I'll see you later."

His Girl Friday was to be a remake of *The Front Page,* a story about the newspaper business. Columbia had bought the property from Howard Hughes, who'd already made it once with Pat O'Brien and Lee Tracy as the reporter and his editor. It had been Hawks' idea to change the Hildy Johnson character into a woman.

We'd been shooting two days when I began to wonder if his instructing me that my suit should be kind of hard-boiled-looking was the only advice I was going to get from Mr. Hawks.

He sprawled in a chair, way down on the end of his spine, and his eyes were like two blue cubes of ice, and he just looked at me.

After the second day I went to Cary Grant. "What is it with this guy? Am I doing what he wants?"

"Oh, sure, Ross," Cary said. (All the English call me Ross.) "If he didn't like it, he'd tell you."

"I can't work that way," I said. I went over to where Hawks was sitting. "Mr. Hawks," I said, "I have to know whether this is all right. Do you want it faster? Slower? What would you like?"

Unwinding himself like a snake, he rose from his chair. "You just keep pushin' him around the way you're doin,' " he said. I could hardly hear him but I could see those cubes of eyes beginning to twinkle.

He'd been watching Cary and me for two days, and I'd thrown a handbag at Cary, which was my own idea, and missed hitting him, and Cary had said, "You used to be better than that," and Hawks left it all in. It's a good director who sees what an actor can do, studies his cast, learns about them personally, knows how to get the best out of them. You play the fiddle and he conducts. I think filming the scene is the easiest thing. It's preparing for it, rehearsing with it, trying to get at the guts of it, trying to give it meaning and freshness so that the other actor will relate to you and think of you as his mother or his wife or his sister, rather than just reciting lines, that's the actor's real work. A good director knows how to help you with it.

A good director also knows when *not* to direct. Nobody ever tried to direct Gable. They let Gable be Gable. I don't mean that he wouldn't take direction, but when he walked in with the gun and the uniform, and he'd just been over the top, what more could anybody do about that? Gable was the same sitting on the sidelines as he was when he got up and played the scene, and nobody wanted him to be anything else. People like Gable, Wayne, they're personalities, and a personality is an asset, you don't destroy it or mess with it.

Grant was different; he wasn't just a personality, he could immediately go off into a spin and become any character that was called for. He was terrific to work with because he's a true comic, in the sense that comedy is in the mind, the brain, the cortex. (Every actor you play with helps you or hurts you, there's no in between. It's like tennis, you can't play alone or with a dead ball; and a lot of pictures fail right on the set, not in the script, where they say it starts.

((88))

A group of actors and a director can wreck a good script; I've seen it happen.)

Cary loved to ad lib. He'd be standing there, leaning over, practically parallel to the ground, eyes flashing, extemporizing as he went, but he was in with another ad-libber; I enjoyed working that way too. So in *His Girl Friday* we went wild, overlapped our dialogue, waited for no man. And Hawks got a big kick out of it.

Then I started worrying that all this noisiness and newsroom high spirits might seem too chaotic to a watcher, and one night after we were finished I again went to Hawks. "I'm afraid," I said, "that audiences won't follow us."

"You're forgetting the scene you're gonna play with the criminal," Hawks said. "It's gonna be so quiet, so silent. You'll just whisper to him, you'll whisper, 'Did you kill that guy?' and your whispering will change the rhythm. But when we're with Grant, we don't change it. You just rivet in on him all the time."

Everybody in the world talks to me about that picture, though it happened in 1940 and they couldn't get another actress to do it. I've had so many indifferent directors, the kind who didn't prepare, didn't do their homework, faked their way through (and the actor is really the victim of the director), but I've been good with good directors, and for me to get Cukor and Hawks in rapid succession was terrific.

(That an actor needs not only decent direction, but decent material goes without saying. You're home free if you get material that holds you up. George Burns, who won the Academy Award for his part in *The Sunshine Boys*, told me it didn't even feel like work, playing that Neil Simon script—"The stuff is so funny, the words he uses, the way he puts it together." Being given good material is like being assigned to bake a cake—I might as well add baking to the other similes, tennis, violin playing, I've hauled in here—and having the batter made for you. It's all there, you only have to pour it in the pan, get the oven going at 350 degrees, and you're home free, everybody says you're a master cook.)

Hawks was a terrific director; he encouraged us and let us go. Once he told Cary, "Next time give her a bigger shove onto the couch," and Cary said, "Well, I don't want to kill the woman," and

Hawks thought about that for a second. Then he said, "Try killin' 'er."

And once Cary looked straight out of a scene and said to Hawks (about something I was trying), "Is she going to do that?" and Hawks left the moment in the picture—Cary's right there on film, asking an unseen director about my plans.

Cary was fascinated with certain contributions I was making to the picture, and that's another story. When I'd first read the script I'd had reservations. I knew *The Front Page* had been a hit play and a hit movie, and that the playwrights, Hecht and MacArthur, were wizards, but it seemed to me that this version, now called *His Girl Friday*, could stand some improving. My brother-in-law, Chet La Roche, was staying at my house at the time. He was president and chairman of the Board of Young and Rubicam, the advertising firm, and he was in California on business. Young and Rubicam had a million and one radio shows emanating from out here, with people like Jack Benny, Fred Allen, Burns and Allen.

So I was pacing around, and Chet asked me what was the matter and I told him this script had me troubled. "Why don't you fix it?" he said.

"What?"

"Why don't you get a comedy writer and fix it?"

I said, "Chet, let me tell you something. On these lots they have a big building, it says Writers' Building, see, and the people in that building are the ones who fix it."

"Well," he said, "*we* have a lot of writers."

It stuck in my head. I wound up hiring one of his writers and paying him a couple of hundred dollars a week to help me with the script. (I've never done it again—just as I never called in sick again after *The Women*—though many times I've wished I had.)

This writer nipped, and he used to come to my house for dinner every night, but he wouldn't eat, he just drank. I was doing over my library, and all the library furniture was in the dining room, so we sat in the living room in front of the fireplace. And he drank. And he worked. He would work a couple of days in advance of what we were shooting. I'd say, "Listen to me, don't change the construction, just add lines." And he did. He added laughs, some of them for Grant. Just little things. In one place where Cary said someday he'd make a girl real happy, this guy added, "Slap-happy." He gave me pieces of business too. There's a restaurant scene where Grant is mocking me because Ralph Bellamy and I are about to entrain for Albany with Ralph's mother. "You're going to Albany with Mother?" Cary says, and all I do is take my hand, which I'm holding clasped up against my mouth, and unfurl a couple of fingers and thumb my nose. Huge laugh, courtesy of that tippling script fixer.

It got so every morning when I went in to work, Cary would meet me, asking, "What have you got today?" Nobody at Columbia knew I was paying this writer, but in the long run, Cary found out. He was suspicious all the time anyway.

(Years afterward I was arguing about a different script with Harry Cohn, and he said, "You don't know what you're talking about. You thought *His Girl Friday* was in trouble and it turned out to be a smash hit."

"Harry," I said, "you aggravate me. Send for the original script of *His Girl Friday.*"

He did, and it came and I went around his desk and said, "Now we're going over this, line for line." I started spouting cracks from the finished picture. "Where does it say that in this script? And where is such-and-such in this script? And where is so-and-so? I hired a writer to put in those laughs."

Cohn digested the information. Then: "Who was that writer?" he said, and I told him, and *he* hired him.)

During the making of *His Girl Friday*, Cary and I would occasionally go out to dinner and to dance. He'd call up and ask would I like to go jigging, and I'd spend three days getting ready, piling on everything Elizabeth Arden had to offer and then some. Cary was between girls then, and a lot of fun, but toward the end of the picture he suddenly started talking about this Freddie Brisson. Every day he'd come on the set and say, "Do you know Freddie Brisson?" and I'd say, "No, what is that, a sandwich?" and he'd say, "No, no, this guy, Freddie Brisson," and I'd say, "You asked me that yesterday and the day before. There's something wrong with you."

Cary never told me that Freddie was his house guest, but Freddie, who'd come off a transatlantic liner after total immersion in *The Women,* only to find his host making a picture with me, had begun to believe that fate was trying to tell him something. "I want to meet that woman," Freddie said, and Cary said sure, he'd fix it.

Then came those endless questions about did I know Freddie Brisson. When this roundabout approach didn't accomplish anything, Cary took more direct action. One night he and I had a date to go dancing, and when I went to the door to let him in, he was standing there with another man.

Who the hell is this? I thought, but I said, "Hi," and Cary looked sheepish. "This," he said, "is Freddie Brisson."

I invited them in to have a drink, we all sat down, and soon Cary and I were screaming and laughing, and every now and then I would turn to this character and say, "Isn't that so?" or "What do you think?" and he would just sort of smile.

We went to Ciro's, had dinner, and Cary and I were dancing away, and to my despair this klunk, this foreigner, kept cutting in all the time.

For nine months straight he phoned me. I'd bellow, so he could hear it, "Tell him I'm not at home," but he persisted.

Finally I felt sorry for him, that's all it amounted to, and I invited him to take me to the races one afternoon. He tried to hold my hand, but I pushed him away. Then some friends who owned a boat invited me to sail down to Catalina for the weekend, and said to bring somebody, and Freddie called at just the right time, so I took him.

In 1940 the Catalina Casino was *the* dance place to go, so when my friends dropped anchor off Catalina, Freddie and I got into a rowboat and set out for the island. Tommy Dorsey's orchestra was playing at the Casino, and he had this new singer, Frank Sinatra, who was a sensation, and Freddie and I sat in the balcony to hear him. There were a bunch of autograph hunters running around (*The Women* was in release then), and Frank, who looked about twelve years old when he got up to sing, did "I'll Never Smile Again" (which became our song) straight to Freddie and me. Later, Frank came over and introduced himself, and our friendship with him dates back to that long-ago summer.

The Dorsey band was fine, Freddie and I danced our feet off, and then, back on my friends' big boat, we had fun too. It's strange to remember, because on the trip back home we heard that France had fallen.

I saw more of Freddie after the Catalina safari, but I still didn't take him—or his suit—seriously. Until the night that John McClain called and asked me to a party that was being given for British War Relief in the ballroom of the Hotel Ambassador. (There were a lot of those parties for the English. I remember one where Highland pipes were playing, and all the English actors—Ronnie Colman, David Niven, Errol Flynn—performed as a chorus line; you never saw anything so good-looking as that line-up of men in your life.)

I sat there, John McClain on the other end of the phone, and I heard myself saying, "No, John, I can't go, I'm going with Freddie Brisson." And as I hung up I realized I'd told a lie, and I thought, That's very interesting. Why did I do that?

Somewhere in the night, Freddie Brisson, whether he knew it or not, was having the last laugh.

Freddie

I HAVE a picture of Freddie, aged ten, about to be sent off to an English public school, which is like our American prep school. He's wearing a silk top hat so big it's fallen way down over his forehead; only the tips of his ears are holding it up. His parents had bought that hat big enough to last the whole eight years Freddie was away being educated. They weren't going to spring for two or three toppers.

Carl Brisson, Freddie's father, was one of Great Britain's most famous musical-comedy stars, terribly handsome, a self-educated man with enormous charisma; in his youth he was the lightweight boxing champion of Europe. Freddie's mother had been a performer who gave up her career for marriage, and Freddie, an only child, adored both of them. (Though he complains that he spent years being introduced as Carl Brisson's brother—because it didn't suit Carl's romantic image on stage or screen to have a full-grown son—only to break free, marry me, and spend years being introduced as Rosalind's Russell's husband.)

When his parents brought him from Denmark to England, Freddie didn't speak a word of English. He was enrolled at Rossall, which is a North of England college facing the Irish Sea. Rossall has produced several members of Parliament and at least one prime minister, and is very snobbish about the excellent scholastic product it turns out, but Freddie's tales of life there are shocking.

The older boys beat up the littler boys (Freddie says he couldn't wait to be a senior so he could beat somebody up), the ancient buildings were full of turrets and drafts, cold winds blew in off the water, and toughening up the boys was the name of the game. (An ice-cold bath every morning was the rule of the day.) If a boy put anything warm on underneath his football or rugger shirt, he was whipped for it.

Freddie also got the hell knocked out of him for being a Hun —to the other kids, in the years after World War I, a Dane was the same as a German—and on Sundays he had to go to church three times: twice to Episcopal service, which was required, and once, since he was a Catholic, to Mass.

After he'd been graduated from Rossall, Freddie toured as an advance publicity man for Moss Empires, Ltd., which owned all the legitimate theatres in England. He learned show business the hard way. He traveled ahead—always by car—and set up newspaper interviews, commercial tie-ups, arranged the advertising, booked the "digs" for the stars and the company. He got to know the British Isles from Inverness down to Land's End. He's familiar with every theatre, pub and hotel. He says he spent his youth either bogged down by blizzards or pushing his little MG through heavy Lancashire fogs.

Before he came to work in America, he'd visited Hollywood with his parents. (Carl had a contract with Paramount Pictures; he introduced "Cocktails for Two" in the musical *Murder at the Vanities*.) Freddie always had an eye for the ladies, and once, when he was very young and his mother and father thought he was safely shut up in the Beverly Wilshire Hotel, he sneaked down the backstairs to keep a date with Ida Lupino.

Later, in London, he became a film producer (persuading the world-famous pianist Paderewski to do the one and only film he ever made, *Moonlight Sonata*), after which Freddie decided to start an Anglo-American talent agency, bringing established stars, writers and directors from America into the newly expanding British film industry. He was so successful that by the time he arrived in Hollywood to stay, in late 1939, he represented a good many English actors and writers of top quality. He became a junior partner of Frank W. Vincent, a very elegant gentleman who, with his white hair and florid face, looked more like a senator than he did a theatrical agent. Between them, they had some of the most talented clients in Hollywood.

Frank was crazy about Freddie and wanted him to take over the business when Frank retired. I remember a bad night, after the war, at our house when Freddie had to tell him no. "Look, I'm married," Freddie said. "I have a son, and I just can't see myself twenty years from now running around trying to sell actors. I want to get into production and hire actors." Frank was heartbroken.

Freddie was a very good agent (he drew tough deals for his clients) and I think he's a very good motion picture producer too. But he always wanted to crack Broadway, and in 1954 he made it. Since then he's produced twenty-three New York shows. He belongs in the theatre.

Separations are tough; I miss him terribly when he's in New York and I'm here, but I understand that he needs that kind of action. Our son, who's one of these backwoodsmen, a real outdoor type, still can't get it through his head that Freddie's a city fellow who doesn't give a hoot about mountains and lakes, except when they're painted on scenery. "It's a shame," Lance tells me every once in a while, "that Dad can't just give up and go fishing, he'd get a lot more relaxation." "No, dear," I say, "don't worry about him, Lance. Your father gets his relaxation at the Ritz-Carlton and the Shubert Theatre in Boston. He's much happier there, in the melee of a production."

During the early stages of each new Broadway venture, when Freddie calls me on the phone from New York, I know his monologue by heart. All the time he's talking, I read the newspaper and the mail. "And this son of a bitch, he double-crossed me on this deal, and so-and-so threatened to walk out," he'll say, and every now and then I'll go, "Oh, oh my God, you poor thing," or "Oh, darling, I feel for you." Meantime I've checked out the editorial, looked at the funny papers, and written a note to someone.

About three weeks later I get the call that explains everything's been straightened out. "It's been a lot of hard work, believe me, but I can see my way clear now." It's like a phonograph record, it's so predictable.

I laugh, but I'm proud of Freddie. The man has done wonderful plays. He was the first producer to bring the work of Harold Pinter (The Caretaker) to Broadway, the first to bring Peter Shaffer (Five-Finger Exercise), the first to bring Bill Naughton (Alfie). I once said to him, "How can you put on a piece like Under the Yum Yum Tree?" He said, "So I can make enough money to do Pinter." And he was right; Under the Yum Yum Tree earned enormous profits.

Freddie has done beautiful, difficult plays, and often he's been burned for his efforts.

Everybody knows about the movie of *Alfie;* not so many people know about the play. Freddie brought it to the Morosco Theatre, importing the British actor Terence Stamp to play the lead. And Stamp walked out on the stage, opening night in New York, and gave a rather indifferent performance. I knew something was wrong by Freddie's voice, the minute he said hello over the telephone. "He lost the audience," Freddie said.

That was that. *Alfie* went out the window, which was a heartbreak for someone who'd seen its possibilities.

Those opening nights can kill you. They're just too terrible to live through, because they're so important. Everything has to work— the bloody scenery, the lighting; the entire cast has to be up and remember what they're doing, and not overplay and still have confidence and charm. It's just too much to expect.

But Freddie's been through a lot of opening nights, and he'll go through some more. Because he loves the excitement of hearing a live audience. I couldn't live in New York now, my health wouldn't permit it, and Freddie wouldn't want me to, so we spend a lot of time commuting, and sometimes I say wistfully that there are more plays being done on the West Coast now and maybe he ought to open something out here. He disagrees. "New York is where the theatre is," he says.

Why Freddie doesn't get discouraged, I'll never know. A producer has to fight every inch of the way, straighten out every writer, go over every costume, every set, fight with everybody, and when people lose the fight and quit, go after them and bring them back. And then people will tell you a producer doesn't do or mean a thing, he's just the guy who goes and gets the money and that's the end of it. The producer is the most maligned human being in show business. I'm talking about real working producers, not the ones who are called in at the last moment and bring fifty thousand dollars and get billing.

I'll brag about Freddie, professionally and personally. Often I wonder how I lucked into this guy. (Why do they say lucked out? I lucked in.) He's been a steadying influence on me—he's helped me keep my balance—and he's always been the boss of the family, too. (Because he adores me, I'm a little spoiled, which is nice, but I can't get away with total murder.)

Whenever we were home together, in the old days, and I had no early studio call the next day, we danced in our hall after dinner. We'd get right up from the table, put on Guy Lombardo records, and we'd twirl. I'd be saying, "Bend me back, don't drop me," and Freddie would be saying, "Ah, the sweetest music this side of heaven." The help thought we were crazy.

He's a funny man, though you'll never realize he's funny unless he knows you well enough to show it, and he's also one of the few people I've ever met who doesn't care what other people think. Sometimes I warn him against a kind of reckless candor—"That person you're talking to might be a future star or investor"—and you've never seen a blanker, stupider look on anyone's face as he wrestles with the warning, trying to understand it. He doesn't care what people think about how he dresses, either. I've picked him up off the plane from New York when he's had his Russian Sol Hurok fur hat on, way over to one side of his head, and the earflaps hanging down, looking like something off the pickle boat, and I've said, "Please, for heaven's sake, take that thing off, people are staring at you," and he's just beamed. "Well, it's very cold where I came from."

Freddie loves atmosphere—when he has a drink before lunch on Sundays, it has to be laid out with the lemons and the orange peels and the bowl of ice and the proper bar tools and linens—but he isn't stuffy.

There's an old Irish saying that a bad marriage is better than no marriage at all—I think it must mean that marriage is better than spinsterhood, better than never knowing, never feeling, never experiencing. Not that you should remain married to a total alcoholic or something—but I also think a good marriage may be indescribable.

Freddie and I argue like crazy, mostly about politics—I'll say, "Well, read about this character first before we get into what you think of him"—and sometimes we disagree about scripts, but we've never had a serious problem, and we don't fight. Anger frightens me. I must admit that I run from it. And anyway, Freddie would rather laugh than quarrel, and so would I. I once tried to make him admit that he could be jealous if I gave him reason, and he did nothing but laugh. Finally he said, "Okay, yes, if that'll make you feel better and stop harping at me, yes, I'd be jealous." So then I said, "Do you mean that or not?"

"Yeah, yeah, yeah," he said. "Whatever you want." And then I laughed.

Women have always liked Freddie, and I haven't minded that, because who wants somebody nobody else finds attractive? But lucky is the word I come back to. I got lucky. He's a thoughtful man. He was wonderful to his father, he was wonderful to his mother—he used to call her, send her interesting clippings with little notes attached—he's wonderful to me. He keeps track of my schedule—I'm sure he has it engraved in granite up till 1983—makes my reservations, orders my tickets, piles me onto planes with so many magazines and books and candy bars and chewing gum ("Don't forget to chew going up and coming down; you're supposed to crack your ears, you know") I can't carry them all; he acts as a secretary, sweetheart, dancing partner. And he plans things for me. That's a nice quality. He makes everything fun.

Like most Danes, Freddie's father was Lutheran, but his mother was Catholic. He was reared a Catholic, and he has a very deep faith. It's a typical male kind of faith, unadorned, direct, he doesn't need all the statues. Women go through the saints—"St. Anthony will help me find my hairpins," "St. Christopher will keep me safe," "St. Thérèse will get me this or that," but when a man has faith, it seems to me he goes straight to the person in charge; he talks to God.

Freddie's a believer, a good person, and I've never known him to hurt anybody. I worry about him more than I used to, and I wish I knew how I could keep him from overworking and getting too excited.

And he worries about me, to the extent that he saved my life last year. I'd had a cold—we thought it was a cold—and my doctor had said sleep was the best thing for me, and I seemed to be sleeping, but Freddie, who'd just got home from New York, didn't like the flush on my face. He called his own doctor and asked him to come over. His doctor said he couldn't interfere with my treatment, it wouldn't be professional, and Freddie did a little swearing, got a quick decision, the doctor came, took one look at me and called an ambulance.

I wasn't sleeping, I was in a coma. The medicine I'd been taking for my arthritis had concealed the symptoms—steroids do mask symptoms—of pneumonia.

They put me in a hospital room—call it 408—and my doctor came to see me. I was still unconscious, and later on, an old man who'd been using a respirator died across the hall, and the authorities grabbed the respirator out of his mouth and slammed it into mine and took me down to the intensive-care unit.

For some reason the man who'd died was moved into room 408 while I was out of it, and when my doctor came back a couple of hours later, there, lying on the bed under a sheet, was obviously someone who'd gone to the great beyond. My doctor sank down on a chair to contemplate the grim sight. "I sat there and thought about what a good woman you'd been," he told me later. "And how sorry I was to lose you."

After ten or fifteen minutes he got up to go attend to some livelier patients, but first he wanted to bid me farewell. "I was just going to kiss your brow," he said. And he went over to the bed and pulled down the sheet and stared into the face of this ninety-five-year-old man. It really threw him. "You know, Rosalind," he said querulously, "they're not supposed to do that. They're not supposed to take bodies and put them in other rooms."

Because of Freddie, I was still around to laugh about that. I've laughed so much with Freddie; it's been thirty-five years and it seems like twenty minutes. Maybe it's because we haven't been together a great deal that we've had to make days with each other count, but I do know we've never bogged down where we were sitting. Twice he was offered jobs out here, heading up production for movie studios, and once he almost said yes. That time I had hopes that the crazy juggling of our schedules might be over, but it didn't happen. "I hope you won't mind," he said when he came home after the big meeting, "but I just couldn't sign. You know I'd be on the phone at six-thirty every morning, which would be nine-thirty in New York, with somebody screaming at me how wrong I'd been about a decision yesterday."

"Besides," I said, "you love the theatre."

I always feel I don't know Freddie yet, that someday I'm going to have enough time with him to really get to know him well.

Back in 1940, of course, I had no idea I'd chosen such a treasure as my life's companion. I only knew that I was in love, that I was going to get married and have babies, and that in order to carry out this plan, I was going to have to leave MGM.

The Road
to the Church Was
Through a Field

METRO wanted me to stay.

I'd been around for seven years, and they'd grown accustomed to my face and my big mouth. Which had gradually got somewhat smaller. For a long time I'd butted into discussions about scripts and told directors and producers where they'd gone wrong, and then I had a discussion with Eddie Mannix. In the late thirties Eddie Mannix was second in command at Metro; he was an Irishman who'd been a bouncer at the Palisades Amusement Park in New York and had come up along with the Schenck brothers, Joe and Nick. Eddie dealt with Metro's labor problems, which had become more and more complex as the industry had grown.

One night I'd marched into his office to tell him about a problem I was having with a producer. We used to call Eddie "Yes or No" because he'd always give you a yes or no answer. "Can I go to New York?" you'd say, and he'd tell you yes or no, he didn't waste words. But this time, after I'd laid out my story and said, "Eddie, just answer me one thing, am I right or wrong?" he made an entire speech.

"You're right, Rosalind," he said. "But you're wrong. This guy has made a mistake, but no producer wants to be told by an actress that he's made this kind of mistake. He won't like you for telling him, and he won't forgive you, so you're right, but you're very wrong, and you've got to learn that."

It's taken me a lifetime; it's a very hard lesson. An inability to suffer in silence was always my great flaw, but Mannix was right, of course—the people whose errors you point out never fall in love with you.

Even so, Metro was offering a new contract, very generous in terms of money, and Mr. Mayer couldn't understand why I wouldn't sign. I might have cleared the whole thing up by explaining that I was engaged to be married, and that I wanted to free-lance, fitting an occasional picture into the space between babies, but I didn't feel I should make any kind of statement until my mother had put the announcement in our local paper back in Waterbury.

My mother did her part—the Waterbury *Republican* and *American* carried the news of Rosalind Russell's betrothal, the wire services picked it up, and finally Mr. Mayer realized why I hadn't wanted to tie myself down to another seven-year deal.

He couldn't have been nicer. He and the other Metro producers I'd worked for sent me as a wedding gift enough silver flatware to stock a hotel. Free again, I made a deal for one picture a year at Columbia so I'd have some security, and then I turned my attention to personal matters.

I remember a night out in Joan Bennett's garden with John McClain. "Rosebud," John said, "I hear you're thinking of marrying this guy, and he's not for you. I'm for you." But John was always asking girls to marry him (he was much more a beau of Joan's than he was of mine), so I didn't have to worry about breaking his heart. He and Freddie became fast friends. At our twenty-fifth anniversary party McClain swore that he'd looked up the records and Freddie and I had never been married. For his part, Freddie always referred to John as "one of Rosalind's lovers."

A few years ago, when John was very ill (he died of cancer), I called him in New York and told him he should come stay with us after he got out of the hospital. "You can go into the guesthouse, use the pool, be on your own . . ."

Three or four months later Freddie and I were planning a trip East when the phone rang and it was John. "I'd like to accept your invitation to come out," he said.

I knew he'd been sick, though I didn't know how sick, so I couldn't say we were leaving town. I told him to come along, we'd be happy to have him. Then I told Freddie that he must go ahead.

"I'll join you when I can." Freddie agreed. "And don't put him in the guesthouse," he said. "If he's not well, it's better to have him in the house. That way, you can give him some extra attention. Put him in my room."

The morning John arrived I wasn't quite ready for him. I was on my way to his room—Freddie's room—with a bowl of flowers, and I'd got halfway up the stairs, to the landing, when the maid opened the front door and there stood John, with a suitcase in one hand and a typewriter in the other. At the same instant Freddie was coming down with two suitcases and his hat on, because he didn't have any hands left to carry the hat. John stood there in the hall, looked up the stairs, and said, "Freddie, if you had any real style, you would have left early this morning."

We told him he'd be staying right in the house, and Freddie grabbed his suitcase and we took him up. He looked around the room. He'd been there before, but a long time ago, after the war. He walked over to the bed, leaned down and tested the mattress with his hand —you have to remember, he was the theatre critic for the New York *Journal-American*—and a look of rapture crossed his face. "Freddie," he said, "your next play's going to be a big hit."

If anybody ever died laughing—or making other people laugh —it was John McClain.

Back in 1941, though, none of us was thinking about dying. America's entry into the war was only months away, but young people plan for life, not death, and every Sunday (because I did not want a Hollywood wedding) Freddie and I went out to hunt for the ideal spot in which to be married.

The great site search started while I was still at Metro, and went on and on. Freddie's mother and father had by this time taken up residence in Beverly Hills, and I began to worry that they'd think it was funny the way we disappeared every weekend.

We'd take an airplane up to Carmel and we'd look around there, or we'd drive down to San Juan Capistrano and examine the mission. I'd made up my mind I wanted to be married in one of the missions Father Serra founded, and there are twenty-one of them in California, so all by themselves they could account for five months of Sundays.

The year before, I'd been maid of honor for my sister Mary

Jane in the East, so I knew I couldn't get married at home, because the crush of friends and fans at Mary Jane's wedding had been overwhelming, to the point where nearly everything was ruined. I'd planned the whole thing, had a pavilion built out in the garden behind my mother's house in Waterbury. When the church ceremony was over, my brother Jim had had to call the police for security so we could have the reception.

I was at the height of my movie career, and the fans cut the awning into the church with big butcher knives in order to peer through, and you could hear them saying, "There she is, there's Roz" —and they tore all the decorations off the church walls and they brought in food and ate it. It was a shambles. I almost passed out. I thought, I've destroyed Mary Jane's wedding.

The irony was that Ken Beirn and Mary Jane had wanted to elope. But quite soon after our father died, the Duchess had got married to a fellow named Jack Best; it had been a very small wedding. That marriage had ended in divorce, and later the Duchess married Chet La Roche in the Yale Divinity Chapel, again with very few people in attendance. So twice Clara had done Mother out of a big white wedding, and brother Jim, now head of the family, thought it would be nice if Mary Jane behaved properly. "I would like to take you down the aisle on my arm," he told her. "And Mother would like that too."

Mary Jane was working on *Life* magazine at the time, and not big on making plans. Her idea of a wedding was that she and Ken would go and talk to the priest, and she wanted the ceremony to happen at three o'clock in the afternoon because she didn't see how she could get her friends up from New York any earlier.

She loved everything I arranged—the tent, the flowers, the big silver trays: "It was as though a fairy queen had come in and put the whole thing on in twenty minutes," she said—but the wedding itself was something else again. She'd suffered such stage fright the night before, she'd almost called the whole thing off, and next day Ken went to the wrong church, and by the time he found the right one, he was dead-white and looked about to faint.

The fans were lined up along the streets with their picnic baskets, the cars could scarcely get through, and as I walked up the church steps Mother said nervously, "Watch Mary Jane's veil; now straighten her veil before she comes up the aisle," and when I stuck my nose inside the church to see what was happening, they started to play "Here Comes the Bride," so we all had to go.

What a procession. From her seat on the aisle the Duchess, furious because she couldn't as a divorced woman be in the wedding, hissed a warning in my ear, "If you steal this show from Mary Jane today, I'll never speak to you again. It's *her* wedding," and I hissed back, "I know it," and during her entire walk to the altar Mary Jane was muttering to our brothers George and John, who were ushering, "George, you get all these people right out of this church! John, I want a *little* wedding, get 'em out, get 'em out!"

I walked by myself, and stumbled three times—once I went all the way down on one knee, Jolson style—and the priest was so nervous Mary Jane couldn't hear him. "Would you please repeat that?" she said once. It was a warm day in September, and there was a fly buzzing around the priest's nose, occasionally landing on it, and the good man kept sneaking looks at me, the so-called movie star from Sodom by the sea, and in the end he was such a wreck he never asked the witnesses to sign the marriage agreement, so Mary Jane brags that all her children are illegitimate.

She's always very sweet about my having "given her" the wedding, but it had its nightmarish aspects, and not wanting a repeat, I dragged Freddie up and down the coast of California, peering at out-of-the-way chapels. We finally explained to his mother and father what we'd been doing, and his father asked if we'd ever been to Solvang. I didn't know what he was talking about. "It's a Danish community—a village," he said.

Naturally, I thought. They're Danish. And I'm not going to get married there just because they want me to. But Freddie and I agreed to go take a look at Solvang, which is forty miles north of Santa Barbara. Even so, we wouldn't let Carl come with us. I didn't want to have to say no and hurt his feelings if I didn't like the place.

We took Freddie's mother along on the hundred-and-fifty mile drive, and when we got up to Buellton we saw a sign that said Solvang, and we turned down a country lane, which happened to be a back road into the village. We passed a picnic park with lovely tall trees, benches, tables, a waterfall, a tiny dance floor, and I started thinking what a great place that would be to have a wedding reception, right out in the open.

I was half sold even before we got to Solvang proper. And in those days Solvang was out of this world. Unspoiled. Everybody spoke Danish—the village was settled by thirteen hundred Danes who came from the farm country of Denmark to settle in the glorious Santa Ynez valley—and the church, three miles off the main drag, was Father Serra's oldest mission.

Carl was right, it was a heavenly place.

And that was some wedding. It went on for three days. We took over an inn and two big hotels out on the highway (they were the only accommodations available); we had fifty guests and seventy-five in help. A wonderful man named Murphy, who owned a company with awnings, tables and chairs you rent for parties, drove up from Los Angeles four times the day before the wedding, bringing little things he'd forgotten. To help us, he covered twelve hundred miles in twenty-four hours.

I allocated all the guests' rooms myself and placed name cards on the doors. I filled the rooms with flowers, the *New York Times* and every kind of drink from Danish akvavit to Russian vodka. We even brought our own dance orchestra with us.

We were married at three o'clock in the afternoon. The road to the church was through a field, and all the little children of the town—dressed in their Danish costumes and waving small American and Danish flags, their blond hair shining—stood and watched as we drove by. I wore a Danish wedding dress that Valentina had designed, and I'd gathered wild flowers and tied bunches of them to the church pews on either side of the aisle. My family was there, and my oldest brother, James, gave me away. The ceremony was beautiful, simple and sweet, and then we all went to the picnic park for the reception.

Before the wedding I'd gone over there and set the tables, again with bunches of field flowers. We had lots of caviar and champagne, and Bill Powell was there, Myrna Loy, Barbara Hutton, who later was to marry Cary, and oh, it was lovely. I'd hung Japanese lanterns around the dance platform, and when my sister Mary Jane saw them, she hooted. "I might have known you'd have those damn lanterns," she said. (As a kid back home I was always putting on tent shows and Indian dances and whatnot on the lawn, and always, my Japanese lanterns—half of them broken—had to go up between the trees.)

It was late fall and it got dark around five P.M., and the only light we had in the picnic park was from dozens of wood fires, little heaps of scrap wood that we'd gathered and piled up. They gave off a lovely soft glow as they burned.

(There was a shack where the park's caretaker lived—with no electricity, only kerosene lanterns—in two rooms, a kitchen and a bedroom, and Freddie and I each changed in one of these rooms, while Hazel and Blanche quarreled about which of them was going to dress me. Blanche had worked for Jean Harlow—she came to me after Hazel left to go into her own leather-working business, but they were both on hand for the wedding.)

The receiving line was between the American and Danish flags; we had a Danish wedding cake topped by the groom and an American cake with the bride on it.

Before Freddie and I took off I had planned the evening's entertainment for the guests—where they were to eat, where they were to dance—since they wouldn't be leaving Solvang until the following afternoon.

October 25, 1941. It seems like yesterday.

On our honeymoon Freddie and I drove to New Orleans (stopping at the Arizona Biltmore and then going on through Texas). In New Orleans we sent the car home and took a banana boat to Cuba. Batista was still in power there, and we met him. (At one Cuban dinner party the host—an old friend of mine—introduced Freddie not simply as Mr. Russell, but as Mr. *Rosalind* Russell. Fortunately, the mistake amused the bridegroom.) We came home by way of Florida and New York, and war was declared on Sunday of the week we got back.

After that, Freddie was gone for five years.

"You Took Me in
Your Bathroom, Harry…"

O N Sunday, December 7, Freddie received a phone call from the Danish Ambassador in Washington, D. C., asking him if he could come to Washington immediately. Freddie had already taken out first papers and he'd had two years' waiting time waived because of being married to an American, so by the early spring of 1942 he was a citizen and a first lieutenant in the United States Army Air Forces. (My three brothers had also joined the armed services.)

In Hollywood we were all very gung ho, and the day after Pearl Harbor, December 8, I was up in City Hall rolling bandages.

Actors and film executives formed the Hollywood Victory Committee, which turned into the USO, and we had our first meeting on Beverly Drive, over a delicatessen, with everybody screaming and interrupting everybody else. We knew what to do with the musical people, they could be sent directly to army camps to entertain the boys—"Ginger Rogers can go, she can tap-dance," and Fred Astaire would obviously be in demand, and Joan Crawford, "She sings, yes, she can do songs"—but nobody knew what to do with the straight actors, people like Irene Dunne, Claudette Colbert, Loretta Young and me. And all through the meeting one penny-pinching guy kept getting up and saying, "Remember, we're doing this for nothing, we're not getting paid here."

It was George Murphy who suggested the routine I wound up doing all over the country. He gave me a couple of jokes, advised me to build a Gracie Allen-style act around an invented brother who joins the army and is a total idiot, does everything wrong. I did, and it worked fine; I'd never thought of myself as a stand-up comic, and Bob Hope I wasn't, but soldiers are generous audiences.

The first time I landed in Brownsville, Texas, it was four o'clock in the morning—I thought I'd never get out of Texas; they had such enormous military installations you could have made the rounds for months—and I was met by an officer, a very nice, rather heavy-set man who turned out to have been Mary Martin's first husband. High-ranking officers—after a while they were all generals —always met us, and early on, we learned to explain that we weren't there to entertain officers, or go to the officers' clubs, or meet the officers' wives, that we'd come for the GIs. We also offered to go into psychiatric wards, and when that was permitted, guards with guns came along just in case some poor disturbed patient flew at us.

I was by now involved in my new contract with Columbia Pictures. Harry Cohn, head of the studio, was a man about whom controversy raged, but I had a lot of fun with him. He had innate taste, quite remarkable taste. He once came back from Europe, walked on a set, and closed down the whole production. "This is the most garish, lousy-looking stuff I've ever seen in my life," he said, and had everything changed. He was right. And he knew clothes. He never wanted his actresses overdressed; he was always sending word: "Take those ruffles off," "Too many beads on her," "I don't like those long earrings hanging down."

Over the years Metro had loaned me out to him so much (for *Craig's Wife, His Girl Friday, This Thing Called Love*) that he'd grown fond of me. I'd had good luck at Columbia and got along well with Cohn, so his one-picture-a-year deal appealed to me. At first we'd bickered about three points I was holding out for, but he finally gave in on all of them, and the day came for me to sign the contract. I walked into his office and there were photographers at the ready, and some executive handed me a silver pen. Suddenly an imp possessed me. I put the pen down. "I can't do it," I said.

Harry exploded. "What's the matter with you? I gave in on your three points. What do you want, the buildings? My kids?"

"I gotta tell you something, Harry," I said. "Years ago I was in here one night" (you always saw him at six o'clock at night) "and you took me in your bathroom."

"I took you in my bathroom?" he howled. *"I took you in my bathroom?"*

"You had a big cabinet in there," I said, pressing on. "It went from the floor to the ceiling and it was filled with French perfume. You showed me all that perfume you'd brought back from Paris and you didn't offer me a single bottle. I gotta have perfume before I can sign this contract."

"I haven't got it any more," he said. "I gave it all away."

"Get some," I said.

"They've got a war over there," he said. "There's no French perfume around any more."

"There's plenty," I said. "We just gotta dig it up. I want a big bottle of Arpege."

Cohn turned to the photographers, secretaries, assorted bystanders. "This girl is crazy," he said.

Two days later he got the perfume and I signed.

I used to try to think up things to bug him. He was famous for his foul mouth, but I never allowed him to use profanity in front of me. Once I said "damn" and he caught me up on it. "I thought you didn't swear." "You see?" I said. "You see how mad you make me? Because of you, I've begun to use bad language."

In the long run he always laughed at me. "She's a demon," he'd say, but he thought I was funny.

Harry and Louis B. Mayer had been friendly for years—though I think they finally had some fight—in a business where rival studio heads rarely cooperated. Even after I signed with Harry, he didn't want me to come straight from Metro to Columbia. "I can't do that to Mayer," he said. "You go someplace else first, make one picture, and then we'll start."

I liked working for Harry, I like those good tough businessmen who get on with it and do their jobs. I found his bark worse than his bite, and I also thought he was attractive, rather nice-looking. He was good to me, he built me a beautiful dressing room, had it all paneled in mahogany, gave me anything I wanted. When he died they buried him from the studio. We all came and sat on a big barn of a stage, and Danny Kaye got up and said, "These stages were his cathedral."

Because of Harry's *délicatesse* in the matter of Louis B.

Mayer's feelings, the first picture I made after Freddie and I were married was *Take a Letter, Darling* at Paramount. I played an advertising woman who hires Fred MacMurray as her secretary. It was a funny idea—turning the tables, having the lady order the guy around, "Stand up, not bad, go get a fitting for a tuxedo." After that I played a whole gang of career women. If you want to lie down on a table, I can operate on you.

It was during this period that the National Federation of Businesswomen invited me to make a speech at a convention which was being held at the Cow Palace in San Francisco. Those women scared the daylights out of me. They were all college deans and women judges and politicians with the Ph.D.s falling off them, and they were having four speakers, one of whom was Clare Boothe Luce. I figured she'd tell them how to run the government, but what was *I* going to talk about?

I finally decided to stick to what I knew, and explained to my sister executives how superior the on-screen life of a career woman was as compared to the real life of a career woman. "How many phones do you have on your desks?" I asked them. "Two? Three? Four? Well, I have at least twelve.

"When I play a newspaper editor, I tear up the front page twice every edition. When I play a lawyer, I win every case. Every picture I'm in begins with eight or ten men sitting around me, begging me to speak, to tell them what to do, how to think. And there's always one with a hat down over his eyes, and he says, 'Verry interesting, M.J., verry interesting,' and I say, 'Who are you? Have you been sitting here during this entire meeting?' and he saunters out, still murmuring, 'Verry interesting.'

"I give more orders in one morning than you girls give in a month. Then I go to lunch with my hat on and my sables over my arm. After lunch I usually have a fitting, and then it's the weekend and I go to my country place. If my country place is in the mountains, I need snow boots, but if it's on Long Island, a skirt and sweater will do. Sometimes the studio fools me and puts me on a boat and I go to Europe. But I *never* go back to the office after lunch."

The businesswomen had a good time, and so did I, once I'd heard the first laughs. I told them I could order the clothes for my pictures in my sleep. I'd say to Jean Louis, Adrian, Irene or Travis

Banton, "Make me a plaid suit, a striped suit, a grey flannel, and a negligee for the scene in the bedroom when I cry." I even did the dialogue from a typical love scene for them. The guy saying to me, "Underneath it all, you're very feminine," and my saying to him, "Please, Richard, I must go on with my work, so many depend on me."

"But don't envy me," I told the businesswomen, "because in the end I always give the whole thing up, marry the guy with the hat down over his eyes, move to New Jersey and live in a mosquito-ridden cottage with a picket fence and a baby carriage outside. Why, I'll never know. Except that they pay me well."

I don't think the career women I played would be acceptable today. Doris Day came along and made the same kind of picture, but by then they were able to put in more sex, more bedroom stuff. We sometimes indicated a bed, but the camera would go over it very fast (one post, a part of a headboard) and we seldom got into one. If we *did* get into one, we had on more clothes than you'd need for the North Pole.

I'm often asked my opinion about the new permissiveness in film, the pornography, the totally naked people. I think the pendulum has swung so far in that direction as a violent reaction to the kind of ridiculous censorship we had to put up with. I made a film in which I was married to Walter Pidgeon, and for one scene I was in bed in a nightgown (which nobody could see because it was covered by a maribou bed jacket, hotter than the hinges of hell), and I had a bed tray in front of me piled with breakfast dishes and a newspaper. There were eight lights streaming down on me, so I was sweating, suffocating, having to be mopped by the makeup man every few minutes. And along came Walter in his business suit with a briefcase under one arm, and he reached over to kiss me goodbye, and they wouldn't allow it. Because I was in bed.

That's how severe and unrealistic the code was in the forties.

After *Take a Letter, Darling,* I went to Columbia for *My Sister Eileen.* Janet Blair, the girl who was cast as Eileen, started out trying to upstage me. She was new and nervous, the same way I'd been when I started, so I invited her into my dressing room and delivered a short speech about the inadvisability of the course she'd embarked on.

"Look," I said, "you're not going to steal the picture from me because I've got the better part, the sympathy comes to me. And you're not going to get anyplace with what you're doing. I know all those old tricks. When you upstage me, all I do is turn my back on the camera, and then they have to come around on me full-face for my close-up."

I said I'd teach her these things if she wanted to learn them. "When I pass out on the floor, you be the first to hold my head, to say, 'Oh, Ruth.' Don't stand back, or the audience is going to hate you for being mean to me."

She gaped. "How wonderful you are to do this!"

"I'm not doing it because I like you," I said. "I don't know anything about you. I'm doing it to get a good picture."

"It's just I was terrified," she said, "and I was warned you'd grab every scene—"

"That's right," I said. "I'm here to steal those scenes as fast as I can, but I love anybody that's trying with me, and I'll lose some. I've been known to lose some. It's very hard to steal a scene from Cary Grant. I mean I've worked like a dog to stay ahead of him, or alongside of him, or in his shadow. So fight me for it, but don't ruin your character because of it. Work with me, don't work against me. We've got to be sisters. Eileen is so selfish (she's always saying, 'Open the window, turn the bed down, give me the food') that the audience won't like her if she's not adorable. They have to feel you love Ruth, that you didn't mean to do anything bad to her, that she's your darling sister, and how could you have made such a dreadful mistake."

Janet's told this tale so often, I finally had to ask her to forget it. "Please, no more," I said. "I've had enough of that story, let's find a new one."

"Sweetheart of the Super Sixth"

NINETEEN FORTY-TWO was a fantastically busy year for me. Besides making pictures and traveling for the USO, I spent such weekends as the government would allow with my husband, and we bought a new house. Also, in the summer of '42 we discovered that I was pregnant. (The pregnancy didn't interfere with my camp travels among the GIs—I kept on going right up until the time Lance was born—but it did mean I couldn't go overseas.)

We got our house, the same one we still live in, partly because when I'd made *The Women*, I'd become friendly with Mary Boland. One day, out of a clear blue sky, she said to me, "Why aren't you married?" I mumbled something about Mr. Right not having breezed around the corner yet, and Mary looked disapproving. "Don't do what I did," she said. "Don't go through life without someone."

She asked me how much my career meant to me. "It means a lot," I said, "but not that much." She told me she'd been in love with John Drew, but her mother had broken up the romance. The mother hadn't wanted Mary to marry; Mary was too good a meal ticket. During the filming of *The Women*, Mary was having a house built, and she used to ask me to go past and take a look at it, so one morning on my way to work I drove that way. You couldn't see anything, just a bunch of guys pouring concrete, but I assured her that I'd been over there and everything was going to be just beautiful.

The house was finished in 1940. Mary lived in it for a year and then she put it on the market. Poor soul, she was lonely.

Well, I had a cute bachelor house when I married Freddie, but he wouldn't live in it. He wanted his own place. "I'm the male, I'm the boss." He gave me all the money he had—I tell everybody it was four dollars, but it was really quite a nice sum—and said, "Go buy a house."

I went and looked at Mary's house and offered the money Freddie'd given me, and the real estate agent just laughed.

Then one Sunday my mother and I were sitting around (she was out here waiting for me to have Lance) and the real estate agent dropped by. "Did you tell me you could pay cash?"

I said yes.

"Stay right here," he said, "and I'll be back." Sure enough, he came back and told us Miss Boland would sell. It took all of Freddie's money, but he got his house. I walked my mother over to see it, and Mary was there and she said, "How about this? A year and a half ago we were talking, and since then you've married and now I see you're going to have a baby . . ."

Before I left I asked her if she'd sell me her washing machine. She said no, she was sorry. "You know we can't get washing machines with the war on."

I said I understood.

When I moved into the house, there was the washing machine with a note attached to it. The note said: "Knowing you're going to have a little one, I think you'll need this more than I do. Love, Mary."

If civilians were going without washing machines, such inconveniences didn't seem very important compared to the miseries the soldiers were enduring.

My brother George was in the tanks. He'd been sent out to California to train with General Patton's Sixth Armored Division in the desert. The base was to hell and gone south, about a hundred and twenty-five miles outside of Indio, near the Arizona border, and one day I decided to drive down there.

After hours of searching I found my brother sitting on the ground, eating off a tin plate that held a mixture of meat and grease and sand. He was looking up at me and talking and chewing on sand, and the wind was blowing bitter cold.

The second time I came to visit, George wasn't even in camp, he was away on bivouac, and I went to his commanding officer and said I'd like to give a Christmas party for the men. The officer said okay, he was really more concerned about a problem they were having with George. "The boy has two college degrees, he's a lawyer. We want him to go to Officers' Training School, but he won't do it."

I went back to Beverly Hills bearing lists of phone numbers of army officers through whom various things had to be coordinated for the Christmas party, and I set about fund-raising. Overnight I got the money I needed, by going to the heads of all the departments at RKO (I was working there by then, making *Flight for Freedom*, the Amelia Earhart story); people were happy to do something for the boys in one of Patton's battalions.

When I think of the logistics involved in that party, I shudder. I was even more nuts than I generally am, because you *are* more nuts when you're carrying a child. I hired buses. I enlisted hundreds of women—starlets, secretaries, stenographers, pals.

We had a meeting on an RKO sound stage, and I told the girls what I wanted them to wear. Flat heels and warm clothes. Not one of them paid any attention; they came with the tall spike heels and the short flimsy dresses and nearly froze to death.

We had to figure out where the buses could stop so the girls could use the "facilities," and we loaded the buses with coffee and Danish pastries. We sent a truck ahead with a portable dance floor and a Christmas tree. We took a whole show with us, orchestra and all. (Red Skelton came and played Santa Claus.)

I'd first talked to General Woods, Patton's Executive Officer (his was one of my most important phone numbers), about the party, and I'd said, "These boys, first of all they want women, then they want booze and maybe some money."

"No booze," the general had said. (I think we were allowed beer, but no hard liquor.) I said I thought we'd give away prizes, and the general said he had a dilemma. "We have another division on this base. We can't invite one division and not the other." "Invite the other," I told him.

Not only did brother George's outfit .come to the party, but the Fourth Armored came too. Ironic footnote to the affair was that George wasn't even there any more. He'd finally been convinced that it was his patriotic duty to go to Officers' Training School in Fort Knox, Kentucky, and he'd said a reluctant goodbye to his men—he was a top sergeant—just before Christmas and left.

Arriving at the base, we got out of our buses and beheld an

astonishing sight. The dance floor had been put down, and it was surrounded by great M-4 tanks. The soldiers were studded on the tanks like flies on flypaper. (We took some pictures and I sent them to be developed and never got them back till the war was over. We didn't know we weren't supposed to photograph those tanks.)

We roped off the dance floor and gave the boys tickets, like movie tickets. Each fellow had four or five, good for a dance apiece. The girls all stood in the middle of the dance floor, and three or four hundred soldiers were allowed on at one time, and they and the girls jitterbugged together. Then those boys would go off and three or four hundred more boys would come on. The girls really had to dance, and they were absolutely wonderful. The boys were, too. We didn't have a single untoward incident. I'd been very worried that if we got some dingalings in there, we'd be hearing screams from underneath the cactuses, but nothing like that happened.

Then there was food—the army helped us with the food, I have to say that—and the boys and girls all ate together, and then we had the show.

I was the M.C. (I wore a fur coat, partly because it got so cold in the desert at night, partly because I was trying to cover my pregnancy). We had brought spotlights with us, and in the spillover from the lights you could pick out boys sitting all over the dance floor, and other boys piled up on those tanks. Some chairs had been set down in front for the brass, and before General Woods took his, he called for a lot of the soldiers who were stuck way in back to come closer. I remember a boy plumped down right in front of him. There was the general sitting, watching the show, and this kid leaned his head right back against the general's knees. It was very sweet, and I thought, Only in the good old U.S.A. A kid couldn't lean against Hermann Goering's knees in Nazi Germany, he'd get killed.

Later Santa Claus handed out surprises, and there was more music. It was a great party.

On the way home we fed the girls again, at about three o'clock in the morning, in Palm Springs. They'd worked for forty-eight hours without an ounce of sleep. And those boys had been so glad to see something dainty and pretty. They were on their way overseas, and one knew that some of them would never come home again.

(In 1974 I was named "Sweetheart of the Super Sixth" and invited to a reunion that was being held down in Disneyland. I went, and there in the convention hall I looked around at all the men with their bald heads and their paunches and their wives, and it struck me with a shock that the Christmas party had been thirty years ago. If a young man had gone into the army at thirty, he'd be sixty now; if he'd gone in at twenty-five, he'd be fifty-five.

Freddie was in New York, so my son, who hadn't even been born the last time I'd met these men, had driven me down here to Anaheim, and many of the old soldiers had brought their children too. It was summer, vacation time combined with a chance to visit Disney land.

When it was my turn to speak, I addressed myself to the young people. There were a great many wonderful-looking boys of nineteen and twenty in the audience. "I want to tell you about your fathers," I said. "You've probably heard some stories from them, but I want to tell you how they really lived."

I tried to describe the sand, the cold, the chiggers that covered the GIs head to toe from sleeping out in the open because General Patton had wanted them toughened up. "You get so tough you're ready to kill anything, even each other," my brother George had said. George had never come back to the Sixth Armored; he'd been reassigned to the Fifth, which was called the Victory Division. He'd coped with the training—"You're a class of three hundred; exactly twenty-six of you will graduate," the fledgling officers had been told —gone overseas and lived through the Battle of the Bulge, and wound up his war in the woods near Berlin, with General Patton doing his great sweeps and General Bradley chasing him, begging him to slow down.

Now the children of Patton's army smiled up at me with their shiny, untroubled faces. I told them that they must think about some of the men who hadn't come back, but I knew there was no way for them to feel what I was feeling.)

Our son Lance was born on May 7th, 1943.

Unromantic as it sounds, I found his name in a gas station. I had picked up a pamphlet which identified what kinds of presents you should give on wedding anniversaries—the tenth is tin, the twelfth is wood, all that business—and the pamphlet also had lists of suggested baby names. I was reading them and I came to Lance. Derived from the Scots, it meant honor.

"If we have a boy, I want him to be called Lance," I told Freddie later. "Because if he has honor, he'll have everything."

Lance was a week late getting himself delivered. Freddie, who was in advanced training school at Marfa Field in Texas, got a lift home with a guy who wasn't exactly an experienced flyer, never having flown cross-country. The pilot didn't seem to know if he was headed east or west, north or south, and Freddie was sitting in this open cockpit training plane, in the instructor's seat, and he vows that the guy would swoop down into a valley, circle around, say, "I think this is Albuquerque, just hang on, we'll take a look," or, "Just a second, which mountains are these? Don't worry, can you find a pass? Please check the map." They managed to land at Burbank airport, somehow or other.

Freddie had expected to go straight to the hospital, but there I was, standing at the airport, big as a house. "My God," he said, "you still haven't had that baby yet?"

I was as frantic as he, because his plane was hours overdue, and my mother, who'd come to Burbank with me, tried to calm both of us down.

Next day she and I were shopping, and I went into labor and didn't know it. I remember saying to a saleslady, "Would you like me —ooh—to have this baby in the store window?" The ooh was in response to a labor pain, but I hadn't recognized it, I was waiting for something much worse. You hear such terrible stories, I figured I'd be in agony for twenty hours.

By the time we got home from shopping, the pains were getting closer. I rushed into the kitchen, made sandwiches, poured tea and coffee into thermoses, and then Freddie dragged me into the car, along with my mother and the sandwiches. "What are these for?" he asked. "For you," I said. "You may have to sit all night and all day waiting."

We arrived at the hospital around midnight, and Lance was born at eight minutes to four. The way Freddie tells the rest of the story, the doctor came out and said, "You're the father of a nine-pound boy, blue eyes, blond hair. Would you like to look at him?"

"I can't wait," Freddie said. He left my mother sitting with all the sandwiches; nobody'd touched them yet.

"I go to look at the kid," Freddie recalls, "and when I come back, the doctor's eaten *all* the sandwiches. He says, 'What do you think of him?' and I say, 'Where are my sandwiches?' "

That's my Freddie. At peak moments he can rise to those lyrical heights.

Three months after the baby came I went right back to the army camps—the baby was left with his nurse—and having been pregnant, didn't own much in the way of wardrobe. I went to Harry Cohn to try and buy some costumes. (This story was told in the book *King Cohn*, but it's good enough to repeat.)

We used to be able to get clothes we'd worn in the movies for half price, and the dresses I had in mind were perfect for entertaining soldiers. One was white lace over nude crepe, very sexy, but perfectly decent. Harry Cohn said no. "No clothes. There's a war on. We can't get the materials. Jean Arthur wants clothes, Irene Dunne wants clothes, nobody's getting any. We don't sell clothes here."

It was a Saturday night—we still worked six days a week—and I said, "Harry, I'm starting out on a camp tour Monday, and you know I'm going to get those clothes."

"I don't know any such thing," he said, and he beat on his desk with a shillelagh he kept close at hand. He liked to beat on his desk. "We need these fabrics in the wardrobe department."

"Okay, Harry," I said. "I guess I'll have to call the *Hollywood Reporter*, *Variety* and the newspapers and say you have prevented me from entertaining the armed forces of the United States."

"You wouldn't," he said.

"I would," I said. "And I will."

"You're so smart," he said, "I'll tell you something. You can have the clothes. For full price. You want to pay six hundred dollars for a suit, you can have it."

Six hundred dollars was a fortune in those days, but I said okay, and told him which things I wanted—the white lace, the black lace, a certain grey suit.

He was flipping up keys on his intercom, talking to wardrobe, putting me on the phone to give my order, and when the clothes were brought into the office, he added everything up and said, "That will be three thousand four hundred dollars."

"Have you got any checks here?" I asked.

"Of course we've got checks." He handed me a book of blanks. All around us dervishes are whirling. "Does she get the beads with the black one?" somebody's asking, and Harry's nodding his head. "As long as she pays, as long as she pays."

"What do I make this out to?" I said.

He looked disgusted. "To Columbia Pictures Corporation," he said. "You know that. You don't make it out to me, it's not personal income to me."

I handed him a check for $3,400, and he took it. "All right," he said, "if you want to spend your money like that—"

"Don't put the checkbook away, Harry," I said. "Now you owe *me* a little money."

"I owe *you* money?" he screeched. "Don't you have an agent who comes over here every Thursday and picks up a very good check for you? How can I owe you money?"

"I'm going to tell you," I said. "Do you know who Mr. Hoffman is?"

"No," he said, "who the hell is Mr. Hoffman?"

"Mr. Hoffman," I said, "is the furrier that Joan Perry goes to. You've bought two or three fur coats from him."

Joan Perry was Harry's new wife, and he clearly did not understand why her fur coats were any of my business. He waited.

"Well, I bought my fur coat from Mr. Hoffman," I said, "and then I wore it for twenty-seven days in your picture, and I just called him up and asked him what he would charge to rent out such a fur coat, and he said a hundred dollars a day. So you owe me twenty-seven hundred dollars, Harry, and the difference is exactly what I intended to pay for the clothes. Now you make the check out to Rosalind Russell."

Again there was a great flurry and much hollering. "Why didn't somebody tell me about this?" Harry demanded, and one of his assistants tried to explain. "We'd have had to pay the same rental on any fur, and this was a beautiful new coat."

He had to write me the check. I took it, draped the clothes

over my arm, walked the whole length of his great big office, stopped at the door and said sweetly, "Goodnight, Harry."

His face was bright red, but through clenched teeth he managed to force the last word. "Jew!" he said.

"For We Walk by Faith, Not by Sight..."

I HAVE one more story about the war years. It's a queer story, and it began when Freddie became friends with another Dane who'd also joined the Air Force, a man named Hans Christian Adamson.

The great American flying ace Eddie Rickenbacker was about to emplane on one of the special missions (to the South Pacific) in which his career abounded, and Freddie and Hans Adamson were scheduled to be part of his crew.

Freddie's orders were canceled, but by the time the cancellation came through, he and the others had already been sent from Washington to California, so he brought Hans Adamson to our house for dinner.

During the meal (I was sitting at the head of the table, Hans Adamson on one side of me, Freddie on the other) Adamson reached into the pocket where he kept his change and brought out a shiny disc. "Here, Freddie," he said, "I bought this medal for you in the PX." He started to pass the medal across the table in front of me, and my hand shot out and stopped him. "Don't," I said.

Freddie looked shocked. "Rosalind!"

"No, no," I said. "I mean you keep it and you give it to Freddie later on."

Embarrassed, Adamson shrugged. "But I don't believe in what Freddie believes in. I mean, I don't believe in anything much, and Freddie's religious, and this is the new medal for flyers—"

"Keep it," I said again. "Bring it home to him."

He kept it.

Late that night Rickenbacker phoned, and Hans left to meet him because they were due to take off from an airfield outside of San Francisco very early the next morning.

When Freddie and I went up to bed he was still questioning my lack of graciousness. "What got into you? It was terrible. If people offer you a piece of *Kleenex*, you accept it."

"I don't know," I said. "I don't know what happened."

At the crack of dawn the phone rang. Freddie had already left for Washington, and whether or not I was supposed to go to work that day, I can't remember, but I know I was alone and it was horrendously early. Hans Adamson's voice spoke into my ear. It was the middle of the night in Washington, where his wife Helen was living. "Will you call her for me later?" he said. "And tell her I love her? I don't know, I'm apprehensive about this trip."

I was sleepy, I wanted to get rid of him, so I said the first thing that came into my head. "Hans, you remember that medal you tried to give Freddie last night? Well, nothing's going to happen to you, but if it does, you take that medal out and you hold it in your right hand, and you'll be all right."

"Okay," he said, humoring me. "Okay, but please call Helen."

Well, the Rickenbacker outfit took off, and their plane went down. Twenty-two days later nobody'd heard a word. I talked to Freddie on the phone. He said he still had faith that they'd be found. "Be reasonable," I said. "It's very sad, but Rickenbacker has gone, and so have Hans and the rest of them."

I was wrong, as anyone who read the book *Seven Came Back* can attest to.

It was a tremendous story. The trouble had begun after takeoff from Honolulu. There had been some kind of accident to the first plane, the crew had got out, gone back to some general's house, had a drink, repacked all their equipment into another plane, and started out again. But some of the equipment, the altimeter, I think it was, had been badly shaken up in the accident. At least that's what they figured out later. Once they were aloft in the second plane, Rickenbacker went forward to the captain and said, "We have a terrific tailwind." The captain said yes, it was about thirty miles an hour.

"No," Rickenbacker said, "this wind is at least sixty-five miles an hour."

The plane overshot its target, ran out of gas, and Rickenbacker told the men they were going to have to ditch. They were sure they were going to the bottom of the ocean, but just on the chance that they might make a landing, they took positions on the plane's floor and braced themselves against its sides. The captain saved their lives; he set down in the water, and then the men got busy with previously assigned emergency tasks. Three rubber boats were thrown out of the plane and inflated, but the guy who was supposed to unload the food and the drinking water from the damaged aircraft never did it. And as the others were asking him, "Where is the stuff?" the abandoned plane sank into the sea. Whether that one man had just panicked, I don't know.

Twenty-two days they were in the Pacific. The ones who took their shoes off saw their feet swell into giant blisters; they drank their own urine; they found a bird but couldn't eat it because it was phosphorescent; they finally caught some rain in Rickenbacker's hat —his famous hat—and in their clothing, and that kept them alive. At first they talked non-stop about the stars, they told stories, they had a Bible and they read from that. After a while Rickenbacker cut out the conversation. He said they had to save their energy.

By the time they were found, the men were no longer friends. And they never did come together again, that group. They were even sent to different camps to be phased out of the Air Force. Too many accusations and counter-accusations had passed among them, and though they knew they'd have a better chance to be spotted, and therefore rescued, if they stayed together and formed the largest possible target, the bad feeling was so virulent they finally cut the lines that held the three rafts together. The ironic part of it was that after they separated into smaller groups, they were too weak to go anyplace. When they were found, the rafts had drifted maybe a hundred yards away from one another.

As I've drifted, in this morass of background, away from the Hans Adamson story I started to tell.

By the time salvation arrived, Hans, who'd become diabetic, was dying. But he and the others were flown in a rescue plane—Rickenbacker had himself strapped to a wing; there was no more room inside—to a Pacific island, where the doctor who was on hand to take care of them happened to be himself a victim of diabetes. He had insulin with him, and Hans survived.

It took quite a lot of time to get the men strong enough even to make the trip home. Adamson was in particularly bad shape; he'd snapped his back in the crash landing.

But they did come back, seven of them. I received word that I should go to Lockheed Airport in Burbank to meet Rickenbacker and Adamson, and I went. When I got there I saw a fence around the field, and a lot of people standing behind it. The Rickenbacker plane, a B-24, straight from the war zone and all camouflaged, sat inside the fence. And there, too, waited Rickenbacker's mother, a woman in her eighties, and Rickenbacker's brother. I didn't know then it was his brother; he was just a man in a civilian suit with Mrs. Rickenbacker.

To get in or out of one of those B-24s you had to climb an iron ladder, and while I was watching, Eddie Rickenbacker, all alone, came out of the airplane and started down those steps. When he got to the bottom he stood and looked at his mother, and she at him. They didn't say one word, not a word. He walked slowly toward her, and she just stood, she couldn't move, and he put his arms around her. Still they didn't speak. But you had to turn away from the expression, moving and terrible, on that mother's face. Because for her, he'd died so many times.

Now I was called, and directed up the iron ladder into the stripped-down plane. There were no seats inside, just two beds, and Adamson was in one of them. A navy nurse and a doctor were attending him.

I sat down at the foot of his bed and said the usual things. "You look great, Hans, and now you'll be going on to Washington to see Helen." He said yes, he'd already talked to her on the phone. Then he called the nurse, and when she came over he waved his right hand, which was all bandaged. "You can take this off now," he said.

She brought a scissors and cut through the bindings, and then

((127))

she began unwrapping and unwrapping and unwrapping the gauze, and when she finally got to the bare skin, Hans' fingers were curled into a claw. He pried them open with his other hand. There in his palm, all green, was the medal he'd bought for Freddie.

"Can I give it to him now?" he said.

Lance

YOU NEVER KNOW why you're chosen to be an instrument. There was no reason for me to have stopped Hans from giving Freddie that medal, yet I'd been impelled to do so. Afterward Hans told me that when he was lying half-conscious, the only thing he was able to feel was the metal in his hand. He would turn it, and know he was alive.

They took him to a Washington hospital, and Freddie and I sent him a raincoat. He said it helped him get well because it meant we believed he'd be up and around and needing civilian clothes.

Which was more than Freddie needed. Christmas of 1945 came and went, and Freddie was still in uniform, though our son was already two and a half years old.

Lance was to have been the first of a crowd of babies, but it didn't work out that way.

When Freddie and I returned from Cuba at the end of November, 1941, we stopped in New York to see Mary Jane, who was by then eight and a half months pregnant. Because of her condition, she hadn't been able to travel to California for our wedding, and the young Beirns were living in a duplex on 81st Street. Mary Jane, wanting to make a good impression on her new brother-in-law, had started a fire in the fireplace without bothering to open the draft, so all we saw when she opened her front door was a cloud of smoke. After that cleared away, my sister appeared, preceded by her absolutely magnificent stomach. I grabbed Freddie's arm. "See?" I said. "That's the way I want to look."

"What kind of bride is *that?*" said Mary Jane primly, and led Freddie over to the sofa in front of which she had set out her silver tea service.

As time went on, I grew even more outspoken. Eighteen

months we were married, and I hadn't conceived. I began to worry. Finally I made Freddie go to a doctor. "There's nothing wrong with *me*," I said. "I'm one of seven. Must be you. Get yourself straightened out."

He came back from the examination looking smug. "The doctor says I'm perfectly all right."

Still I was suspicious. "It can't be me."

It wasn't either of us, as Lance's arrival proved, but after his birth I had a thyroid problem, and by the time that was taken care of, six or seven years had passed. I never did get pregnant again.

It was a sadness to us; we'd wanted a gang of children, and I always felt I could have them easily. I wasn't young when we married, but I wasn't old either, and I was pure Irish peasant stock; Lance's birth had been trouble-free.

I think it's hard to be an only child; you carry too much of the weight of your parents' hopes and expectations. With Lance we worried too much about marks and Latin and the right education. If I had it to do over again, I wouldn't have sent him off to prep school at all. I'd have kept him at home, and had the neighborhood kids running in and out, and been up to my kneecaps in dirty sneakers and smelly socks. It's something I missed, partly because I was terrified of having a spoiled child. I'd seen so many Hollywood kids and the bad things that happened to them, and I was Miss Know It All, Miss Has All the Answers. Then, too, Lance was a boy, and I thought life is tough, he's got to get started, learn to meet the challenges. But I'd do it differently today; I'd keep him close till he was eighteen, *then* throw him out into the world.

Until fifth grade he went to the Beverly Hills Catholic School, but when I came East to do *Wonderful Town*, we transferred him to Buckley, in New York, so he could be near us. Later he chose to go to Hotchkiss, an Eastern prep school, where he became involved with and helped run the school paper. Summers he worked as a newspaper boy for the Los Angeles *Times*. He used to take the bus downtown from Beverly Hills every day to solicit more exciting employment; he bugged the editors until they finally gave him a job as a copy boy. At nineteen he'd already had a by-line on the front page, and the *Times* influenced his choice of college. He stayed on the

West Coast, went to UCLA and USC, so he could go on working for the paper.

I can't say that Freddie and I were smart enough to see what an excellent newsman he was going to be; a Lance Brisson editorial in the *Hotchkiss Record* would begin on page one, instruct the reader to turn to page four, you'd read through page four and then it would say turn to page six. Lance would be theorizing endlessly about Nazism, or some other grave social problem, and I'd say to Freddie, "This kid is going to have to learn to edit himself."

A teacher at Hotchkiss told me that Lance sometimes stayed up all night getting the paper to bed. "Yes," I said, "his Greek mark shows it," but the teacher thought I was putting my emphasis in the wrong place. "We ought to pay that boy to come to school," he said. "Lance has what most people don't have, and that's enthusiasm."

It's true, but Freddie and I were always after him to get better grades so he'd make it into a top college. When I look back, it just hits me that he didn't have much childhood. It was all over by the time he left Hotchkiss, at eighteen. And what he'd had there wasn't much—no girls, no cigarettes, only the *Hotchkiss Record*.

He's never complained, he's never given Freddie and me any serious problem, and his name turned out to fit him perfectly. He has honor, he doesn't know how to lie, he hates all the crooked stuff in government—he switched from investigative reporting to politics; at thirty-three he's deputy public administrator of Los Angeles County, the most populous county in the world—and he really thinks you can fight the bad guys and win, straighten everything out. Before he changed jobs he had his face all torn up covering some riots for a television news show in San Francisco, but his father and I never knew that; he hid it from us.

Maybe he was trained to hide things too well. He learned early on to fend for himself. When the Duchess lived in Fairfield, she had acres of land, and on weekends away from school, Lance liked to go off by himself to a little island on her property, take a pan and some bacon, build a fire, lie beside a stream.

I think he's had mixed feelings about my being an actress. He's proud of me, but it was tough for him at Hotchkiss when I was playing *Auntie Mame;* he took lots of ribbing.

When he was very small, of course, he was exposed to the motion picture drill because I wanted him to know it was hard work. He came home from the park one day and asked me if I was a "movin' pitcher star." I asked him where he'd heard that, and he said from another kid. At dinner I told Freddie. "It's time we straightened him out," I said. "From now on, every time I do a picture I'll have him come on the set for at least one day."

A couple of weeks later I hauled him to work with me at five A.M. He sat for hours, watching take after take after take of the same scene. It was dull, but the lesson was learned. You can come home and tell a kid, "Mummy's exhausted," but it isn't like letting him share the drudgery.

Same thing in the theatre. When I was in *Wonderful Town* he came to the theatre with me every Friday night. He was allowed to help out in the box office. If a man named McCarthy stopped by to pick up his seats, Lance would be permitted to go to the Mc box, pull the tickets, hand them up to the cashier. He was so small nobody outside the box office could see him. He learned how to make up a balance sheet—the general manager gave him one, and he figured it out—and he used to go downstairs and help the stagehands run the winch. But even when he was in the wings, he never got in the way (sometimes an actor has a fast entrance, and he doesn't want to fall over some kid's feet); Lance learned without bothering anybody. One night, during the run of *Wonderful Town,* he was up in the light booth, and later he told me he'd run the lights. We had an electrician named Charlie who was being handsomely paid to run the lights, so I wasn't enchanted with this information.

"*You* were running the lights?" I said.

He nodded. "When you were doin' 'A Hundred Easy Ways,' I was followin' you with the spot."

"What was Charlie doing?" I said.

"Readin' the comic book," Lance said happily.

I think Lance was able to put my career in perspective, not let it throw him, because Freddie was always the boss in our family. Lance and I would talk problems out, but I'd warn him, "Be careful, because in the long run, the old man will make the decision, I won't."

At Hotchkiss, while skiing, Lance had a bad fall. It left him with a knee injury, thank God. The knee kept him from going to

Vietnam. He'd never told me he'd been hurt, I discovered it by accident on a summer morning. I was out watering the garden and he was in the swimming pool, and I kept squirting him with water from the hose. He jumped out of the pool, leaped some hedges to chase me, and fell. I didn't think anything of it, he'd landed on the grass, until I saw he couldn't get up. We had the leg x-rayed, he went back to school, but when he came home again at Christmas, he said he had to have an operation.

I was down with the flu, but I called up an orthopedist about whom I'd heard good things, and Lance went off to the hospital in a taxicab.

Next day I dragged myself down there. They wouldn't let me near him, they didn't want me to give him the flu, but they let me peer into the recovery room. All I could see was four or five lumps all covered with blankets.

"Which lump is mine?" I said.

The doctor pointed to a body. "That's Lance."

"Is he all right?"

"He's fine," the doctor said. "The cartilage was badly torn, but he'll have total recovery. He won't even know he's had trouble in that knee until he's forty."

Eventually Lance tried to enlist in the army, but he flunked his physical. The medic took a look at that knobby hockey stick of a knee and decided here was a free-loader who figured he'd sneak in for a couple of weeks, and spend the rest of his life on a government pension. "Naughty, naughty," he said, and turned Lance down.

Lance was not happy, but I was. I didn't want my only son going off to that crazy war. For what? But that's what everything hangs by, when you think of it, accident.

Lance skis now, but he also knows when it's going to rain.

My son's first bachelor apartment, shared with a UCLA classmate, was out near the Ventura freeway. The boys took me to look at it. It had a little patio with a fountain, and a living room, kitchen and bedroom. They tossed for the bedroom, and the other guy won; Lance drew the couch. Proudly he showed me a closet into which you couldn't have got three hangers, and a linen cabinet with one shelf. He was thrilled with his new status.

The day he moved his clothes out of our house, I stopped him as he was leaving. "Here, dear," I said, "here are three bottles of soda water and three Coca-Colas I want you to have."

We did his laundry at home. I charged him two dollars a week —it was an excuse to get him back every few days so I could take a look at him—and he left us this big canvas sack of wash that said "Brisson's Laundry" on it.

About eight months later he showed up at our house and asked if I minded if he came back home. "It's to protect my life," he said. "This man and his wife live over us, and they fight all the time, and the plaster keeps coming down on my head while I'm trying to sleep. And the other day there was such a brawl, she came to our door screaming for help and we took her in and were patching her up— she was lying on the bed—when the husband came bursting through the place and threatened to kill us."

"What else was going on with you boys and that wife?" I asked.

He denied the implication, inference, insinuation—whatever it was, he denied it—and moved himself into our guesthouse. By now he was not only going to school, he'd also become a cub reporter assigned to homicide. As I understand it, all cub reporters have to go on the homicide detail for a few months. Lance adored it. "There's a five-oh-nine at West End," or "There's a six-eight-two," he'd cry, rushing into the driveway with me calling after him, "What's a five-oh-nine?" His answer would waft back on the breeze he stirred up as he fled: "A man with a gun!"—and my mother's heart would sink into my shoes.

In the spring of 1975 Lance married Patricia Morrow—and am I glad about that. He had a couple of flames Mumsy didn't care for. The trouble was, I spoke up. One of them in particular he'd have dropped a long time earlier if I hadn't written him a letter. "It won't come as any surprise to you that your father and I do not approve of so-and-so," I informed him, and Lance phoned his father. "What's Mother talking about? She's gone bananas."

Freddie, who's smarter about things like that, set me straight. "Don't criticize," he said. "Don't say a word, or you'll pay a terrible price for it. What you're doing is questioning the boy's taste, his ability to choose, and that will just make him hang on till he can prove to you that the girl is a living doll."

I suppose all parents live through the fear that their children will pick the wrong partners. To me, marriage is teamwork—do you make a good team, or don't you? I look at Jules and Doris Stein, and I think, They're a team, that's what built that empire, MCA, Universal, all those big buildings over there. Jules is a great financial genius, and Doris is very aware of his thinking, respects him, is a wonderful hostess for him. In every marriage I've seen that is good, the couple works together, and I think that's fun. Even those marriages where there's an arrangement, and the guy leaves the reservation a little bit now and then, the team still comes first.

And humor helps a marriage. And religion. Not necessarily the Catholic religion, but any faith which helps to stabilize you. Evelyn Waugh, who was known for his unpleasant personality, once said, "You have no idea how much nastier I would be if I was not a Catholic. Without supernatural aid, I would hardly be a human being." Lance was brought up a Catholic, but there was a time when he didn't do much about it. The summer before we went to Hotchkiss, I took up the question with him. I offered him a choice. "Do you want me to talk to you for five minutes a day until you go away, or would you prefer a single hour-long lecture?"

"I'll take the hour," he said. "You could never stop talking at the end of five minutes."

"I'm being serious," I said. "Now, first of all, when you go away, you're going to lose your religion."

"What does that mean?" he said.

I shifted ground slightly. "I'll tell you what I want you to do," I said. "I want you to think of God as your friend. You can't neglect your friends, or they won't be there when you want them, when you need them. But if you remember Him as your friend, you'll be all right."

He's told me there were many times when he thought of what I'd said. I believe it too. No matter in what form you take your comfort—I don't care if you worship the sun, the moon, a statue, a tree—there comes a time when you're alone, without your husband, your sweetheart, your children, the human relationships that sustained you, and then you have to know that something else is there.

The formalities of organized religion don't interest me much —I don't think they're so necessary—but Freddie and I were both pleased that Lance and Patricia were married in the Church.

Patricia is a petite girl, very pretty, very smart. She's already got her law degree, and I think she wants to run for Congress. As an actress, she played in *Peyton Place*, but I was not a *Peyton Place* follower, so I never saw her. I tuned in once, looking for Mia Farrow, when she was going with Frank Sinatra. That day Mia came on the screen, said, "Good morning, Mother," sat down, ate some grapefruit. Her mother said, "Aren't you going to have your eggs today?" Mia said, "No, thank you," and got up and left, so I shut off the set. I'd have been a more avid watcher if I'd known Patricia was going to become an important part of my life.

Now I'm a mother-in-law, I keep wishing I were a grandmother, but it doesn't look hopeful. I don't think they're planning on children yet. The wedding was lovely, just family, over in the San Fernando Valley at St. Charles Church, and I, being the groom's mother, wasn't allowed to do a damn thing.

But even if I'd been the bride's mother, I couldn't have pulled my usual cover-every-inch-with-blooms number because you're not allowed to go crazy during Lent, and it was a Lenten wedding; the only embellishments permitted in the church were two large vases of flowers.

What they didn't have in decorations, they made up in manpower. They worked out the ceremony themselves, and three priests officiated. Father Tang, a very handsome Chinese priest who was born in Arizona, did the actual marrying.

Freddie and I walked down the aisle together and sat on one side of the church; Patricia's parents came down and sat on the other; then the bride and groom came down together, separated, and each went and kissed his own people. Lance kissed me and Freddie and his Grandmother Brisson. Then the couple came together again, and went up to the altar.

It was a sweet ceremony; they held hands and said their vows directly to each other. (Once you've seen that, it makes absolute sense, rather than that business we did of "I, Rosalind, take thee, Frederick," while we're looking at the priest.) Then the best man, Mary Jane's son Chris, brought out the ring, and the priests blessed it, and again Lance and Patricia turned toward each other. Lance put the ring on her finger, looking straight at her, and I got this awful dryness in my mouth. When it came to the part where they say "Peace be to you," they came down from the altar and kissed their families again.

I was pretty well undone.

Nowadays young couples are different from the way we were, and some of the differences seem sensible. Take the case of our newlyweds. Enclosed with the wedding announcement was the following card:

> *Patricia and Lance*
> *will not be accepting any gifts*
> *except donations to:*
> *Franciscan Center for the Poor*
> *218 East 12th Street*
> *Los Angeles, California 90015*

Freddie and I love silver, we have tons of it, but Lance and Patricia won't let us give them any. They don't want to polish it, and I can't blame them. When I feel like doing something nice for them, I take my green stamps and turn them in on pots and pans and card tables. Lance and Patricia live in a tiny rented house with one of those huge case pieces that holds the stereo, the records, tapes and all that stuff. In the kitchen they've got a butcher-block table, and in the bedroom they have a king-size bed furnished with Bill Blass sheets (because the sheets have the initial B on them) and they eat off two TV tables. Patricia also has a night table, but Lance uses the window sill. When they have people over for dinner, and those people sit down, they can't get up again, they're wedged in until after coffee.

Despite the tremendous responsibility of his job for the county, Lance goes to law school three nights a week, and Patricia encouraged him to do it. "We'll save on books—I've got all the books," she said. They're dear, they're happy, they work hard, and they love and believe in each other.

Lance has been a joy to his father and me, and everywhere that we look in this house, we see him. Downstairs, in our library, there's a water color that I did of him as a little boy. He's standing at the end of the diving board, forlorn—"He wouldn't go in the goddamn pool because he didn't like to be cold," Freddie says—and always the sketch reminds me of what a water rat he ultimately came to be. And in our upstairs sitting room, where we keep books and trophies and plants, there's a sort of primitive painting (not by me, by a real painter) of a man coming home from work dog-tired and being met by an eager kid who's holding out a baseball. Every time I pass that picture, I think, Oh, I have to give that to Lance, he's always wanted it.

He and I both love baseball. The years go by, and you lose those summer afternoons when you sat behind home plate with your little boy and watched the quick-footed Dodgers double steal from first and third, but a bit of their glow hangs like smoke in the memory, softening the winters which come after.

Our wedding reception. October 25, 1941.

Freddie, about ten years old, at
Rossall. His parents bought that hat
big enough to last the entire eight years
he was away being educated.

Me,
age two.

Outside the church.
Charlotte Wynters
MacLane, my matron
of honor, is on the left
and Cary Grant on the
right.

Freddie, flanked by best man
Cary Grant and his father Carl.

With my mother.

Honeymooners—
off to New York,
Florida, Havana.

First Lieutenant Freddie in the United States Air Force, 1942.

On the set of *Flight for Freedom*, 1942, with Freddie and, at left, Colonel Hans Adamson, who flew a special mission with ace Eddie Rickenbacker.

Camp Bowie, 1942. Brother George is standing at left, watching me clown around.

Lance's birth, Good Samaritan Hospital,
Los Angeles, May 1943.

Lance in 1948,
five years old.

Photo by Coburn.
Courtesy Columbia Pictures

Lance in 1956 after a performance of *Auntie Mame*.
He's thirteen and taller than I am.

With Lance on the *Queen Elizabeth*, 1958.

March 15, 1975.
The wedding was lovely.

1976. Lance knew I didn't like
the mustache, so after he shaved it off
he gave me this picture.

Mourning Becomes Electra, with Kirk Douglas, 1947. After *Sister Kenny,* I wanted to do a comedy, but I owed Dudley Nichols a favor.

With Charles Laughton, doing radio, 1944

(Permission granted by copyright proprietor Sheldon Abend.)

Humphrey Bogart visiting me on the set of
The Guilt of Janet Ames at Columbia. I'd have loved
to make a picture with him, but it never happened.

(From The Guilt of Janet Ames. *Copyright 1947 by Columbia Pictures.)*

1946 Golden Globe Awards. Anne Baxter and Gregory Peck won too. I got mine for *Sister Kenny*.

With Sister Elizabeth Kenny. Sister always wore that Aussie hat and a black dress. She was a great teacher. She had a sad life, but a rewarding one.

(Copyright RKO Radio Pictures.)

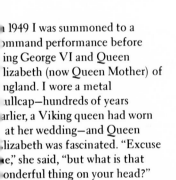

In 1949 I was summoned to a command performance before King George VI and Queen Elizabeth (now Queen Mother) of England. I wore a metal skullcap—hundreds of years earlier, a Viking queen had worn at her wedding—and Queen Elizabeth was fascinated. "Excuse me," she said, "but what is that wonderful thing on your head?"

Three years before I appeared on the cover of *Time*, we used this imaginary *Time* cover in *A Woman of Distinction*, 1950.

BENTON'S MIDDLECOTT
No Room for Romance . . .
See Education

Courtesy Robert Fryer.

"WONDERFUL TOWN"

Occupying most of this picture is Rosalind Russell, who also dominates the musical version of "My Sister Eileen," at the Winter Garden. The girl in the print dress is Edith Adams, as Eileen, and the incidental decorations are a contingent from the Brazilian Navy and assorted Greenwich Village types, all of whom combine to complicate the heroines' lives. Joseph Fields and Jerome Chodorov collaborated on the book, the music is the work of Leonard Bernstein, and Betty Comden and Adolph Green wrote the lyrics.

Drawing by Frueh. Copyright 1953 by The New Yorker Magazine, Inc.

Photographed by Mark Shaw. Reproduced with Special Permission from Time Incorporated.

Courtesy Robert Fryer.

In 1951 I went East to try the theatre again. I toured with John
Van Druten's *Bell, Book and Candle* (above, with William
Windom and Dorothy Sands). My character, a witch with
supernatural powers, was a good challenge. I'm not a terribly
mysterioso person and the part made demands on me.

With George Abbott and Rita Hayworth on the
Queen Elizabeth sailing to Europe in 1955.

Onstage party after opening of
Wonderful Town, the Winter Garden
Theatre, 1953. Here Franchot Tone is
holding me, while Robert Sterling and
David Wayne look over my shoulders.

With Arthur O'Connell in *Picnic*, 1955.
Rosemary, the frustrated schoolteacher,
is an awfully good part.

(From Picnic. Copyright © 1955 by Columbia Pictures.)

(From Auntie Mame courtesy of Warner Bros. Inc. Copyright © 1958.)

With Hedda Hopper during the filming of *Auntie Mame*, 1957.
I'd have stayed on Broadway with *Mame* forever, but I had
to leave after a year and a half to make the movie.
That was part of my deal with Warner.

A *Majority of One*, with Alec Guinness, 1961. Guinness' style, slightly peculiar, rather remote, totally cerebral, fascinated me.

From *The Trouble with Angels*, 1966.

Photo by John Mo

With Jack Warner during the filming of A *Majority of One*, 1961.

Natalie Wood played the title role in *Gypsy*, 1962, and I was her pushy stage mama.

(From Gypsy courtesy of Warner Bros. Inc. Copyright © 1963.)

With Mamie Eisenhower on the set of *Gypsy*. Some people said I didn't sing my own part, but that's Roz, and nobody else, as Rose on the soundtrack.

(From Gypsy courtesy of Warner Bros. Inc. Copyright © 1963.)

With Freddie and Gloria Guinness.

Whenever we went to Paris, the
Duke and Duchess of Windsor would
entertain us. He was charming,
she was bright.

Our twenty-fifth-anniversary party
in Palm Springs. Dyan Cannon Grant
(left), Cary Grant, Frank and
Mia Farrow Sinatra (right).

Nominated for Oscars four different times,
I finally got one in 1973, but not for my
acting. My old friend Frank Sinatra
gave me the Humanitarian Award.

Summer of 1941.
Freddie and I were courting.

Photo by Cronenweth.
Courtesy Columbia Pictures

Strolling the streets of Monterey,
California, 1961, during the filming
of *Five-Finger Exercise*.

Washington, 1961,
on our way to The White House
for a state dinner.

With Jan Handzlik on the stage set of *Auntie Mame*.
"Live, live, live," said Auntie Mame.
"Life is a banquet and most of you poor suckers are starving to death."

Sister Kenny
and Other Diamonds

SOMETIME after Lance was born, I got up one morning and fell in a heap. "Exhaustion" was the word the doctor used.

"Why," I said, "should this happen to me? At my age? I'm a reasonably young woman. I've gone around with Sister Kenny, I've never seen anybody work the way she works, put in the hours she puts in, yet she's still on her feet."

"Well, I don't know her," the doctor said, "but I can tell you this much. She eats well, or she sleeps well, or both."

He was right. Sister Kenny ate like a horse; to see her tear into a piece of roast beef was to be filled with awe. She also had the capacity to go sound asleep in a chair for three minutes, or for ten minutes; she'd just excuse herself and flake out.

I'd lived on no sleep, I never napped, I answered my own telephone, and if there was a discussion in the street, I'd be out there in the middle of it. An exponent of black humor once scrawled on the wall of a New York subway station: "Death is nature's way of telling us to slow down." I think nature does warn you. I'd abused my health, and nature had clunked me on the head.

In the early years of the war it was hard *not* to overdo, one wanted so much to be useful. Freddie claims that the reason somebody in the Roosevelt White House called me about the March of Dimes was because I'd been the first actress to go to the army camps. "And you didn't care how you looked" (a reference to my pregnancy) "or whether you could sing or whether you could dance, you just did it." That may sound a left-handed compliment; I settle for what I can get.

The White House's "calling" is something I've never taken too big. I was in show biz, and every modern President seems to have liked rubbing shoulders with show-business characters. But President Roosevelt's birthday fete was different.

The party always took place on the twenty-second of January. For many years I'd been invited, and hadn't gone. Finally we went to war, I was asked again (Freddie was also summoned), and this time we felt we ought to go.

We took the train to Washington, and Mike Romanoff, that famous pseudo prince (he was a real prince in everything but blood lines, a dreamy man), had brought special meals on board for us from his restaurant. He set up a bar, made martinis, and we ate and drank until Chicago. Then somewhere in the middle of Ohio, Mike pulled the emergency cord, stopped the train, got off and rented a car, so he could beat us to Washington, D. C. When we arrived at the hotel, he'd already put long-stemmed roses in our suite. Freddie asked him where he was staying, and Mike admitted he didn't have a place. "All reservations are gone, so, ol' boy, I'm changing and shaving down in the men's room," he said cheerily.

President Roosevelt's birthday guests were entertained at luncheon and at dinner at the White House. We, in turn, entertained at various Washington theatres and hotel dining rooms, to raise money for the March of Dimes.

When we first came into the White House for the luncheon, we were shown a seating chart. The President's seat was marked with an X. The President was already in place in his wheelchair, and each of us from Hollywood—Pat O'Brien, Joan Crawford, Jimmy Stewart —went up to him and shook hands. To each person, he said something warm—"I'll see you later, don't go too far from me"—and as you left him, he followed you with his eyes until you were out of his vision. The great leonine head was the head of his photographs, but his charm was never caught by any camera. That went for Mrs. Roosevelt, too. After three minutes you stopped thinking about her funny teeth; you were convinced she was beautiful. I remember she rose to make a speech, and he said, "How long are you going to be at this?" and she said, "Not very long, Franklin." "Well, see to that," he said.

Between lunch and dinner Mrs. Roosevelt showed us through

the White House living quarters. In one of the rooms her knitting bag was hanging over a chair, the knitting half out, very cozy-looking. It was typical of her to take us around when she could have asked an equerry to do it.

After the tour we returned to our hotels, got into evening clothes, went back for the big White House banquet, then started on our theatre rounds. We'd put on a show at one place, rush out, get into limousines, speed to the next hall, do the same show again. We covered eight or nine places. Pat O'Brien went on just ahead of me, did some Irish songs and a jig—he was darn good at both—and I told my jokes about my mythical brother-who-insulted-generals, and wound up with a Cockney song taught me by Cary Grant. "Good bye-ee, don't cry-ee, wipe a tear, baby dear, from your eye-ee," it began.

We raised a lot of money for polio research; we were glad to do it, but I guess the point I'm getting at is that I didn't see anything unusual about playing eight or nine shows that night. Energy, as I keep repeating, had been mine in abundance, along with a strong body developed back in the days when my parents were demanding that we exercise, probably to keep the sex out of us.

Because there was no time, there was time enough. Somehow, during the war years, we could get it all done. Back in Hollywood, at the El Capitan Theatre, several of us put on Noël Coward's *Tonight at 8:30*, a group of short plays, again to raise money for British War Relief. We ran for a week, and I was the only American in the cast (except for Douglas Fairbanks, Jr., who was more English than the English). Herbert Marshall and I did the piece called "Still Life," and Coward himself—he was staying with Clifton Webb—came in and rehearsed us the day before we opened. The war bruised everyone, but a good play could lift the spirit.

So there were plays, and there were parties too. Evalyn Walsh McLean, the famous Washington hostess of the thirties and forties, a remarkable woman whose money came from gold mines and who owned the supposedly accursed Hope diamond, entertained lavishly at her home in Virginia. One night, while her guest Senator Harry Truman sat playing the piano—nobody dreamed he was going to be President; nobody even dreamed he was going to be Vice-President—Evalyn sent one of her butlers down to the train station to search for soldiers who looked hungry or lost and to give them enough money so they could get home.

She never let anybody she liked touch the Hope diamond. For herself, it didn't matter. She'd had so much bad luck—a welt of a scar from an automobile accident ran from the top of her head clear down to her big toe—she believed she was impervious to further destruction. I can hear her raspy voice saying, "Rozzie, Rozzie, you can look, but you cannot touch." I once saw Margaret Sullavan grab at the great blue stone, and Evalyn got really upset.

Often I went with the McLean entourage to the soldiers' hospitals. Evalyn brought music—she hired an orchestra—and we'd all dance, the actors, the nurses, the patients who were able. Evalyn was also permitted to supply beer to certain wards. She spent most of her time with the cancer patients. She let those men touch the Hope diamond. She took it off—it hung on a chain around her neck —and the cancer patients played with it, throwing it into the air, tossing it to one another, trying it on themselves, filling the wards with rowdy laughter. They were only boys, most of them, but they had nothing left to lose; Evalyn knew it, they knew it, there was no need to talk about it.

So it went. War work. Film work. In 1942, for *My Sister Eileen*, I'd got my first Academy Award nomination. (Four times nominated, I've never won.) Glad as I was about it, the honor put me under heavy pressure. It means too much to the studios to have their people win; I still can't think about the tension surrounding those races without breaking into a sweat. In 1943 I had the baby. I grabbed for some time with him. And then one day in 1944, like Humpty Dumpty, I fell down. I landed in the hospital, uncertain what had hit me. Freddie, by now a major, was sent for.

I rested. I read. I walked the tiled corridors that smelled of carbolic acid, building up my strength and my red corpuscles. The doctors tinkered with my thyroid gland, and friends kept my room filled with flowers.

One night a nurse was taking the blooms out into the hall— they used to do that so the patient wouldn't be robbed of oxygen in his sleep—and I saw something dangling from the back of a huge bouquet. "Is that a card?" I said. The nurse looked. "No," she said, "it's a box."

She worked it loose and handed it to me. Inside, there was a gold bracelet three inches wide, solid with diamonds, along with a letter begging me to get well. The letter and the bracelet were from Barbara Hutton, the Woolworth heiress then married to Cary Grant. I phoned her.

"Barbara," I said, "there's no way in the world I can accept this gift. The flowers were exquisite, your note best of all, and that's what I want to keep."

"But you can't send the bracelet back!" she said. "It's all done in diamonds and gold. I picked it out to match your wedding ring!"

My wedding ring had probably cost forty dollars. Barbara was like that.

(Freddie and I once brought her and Cary back together after a separation. They wound up sleeping in Freddie's room at our house, and Freddie moved in with me. Next morning Freddie went back to his room to get a pair of socks, and saw Barbara alone in bed. Then he went into his bathroom, and there was Cary asleep on the floor. Stepping over him, Freddie picked up a toothbrush and came back to me. "I think we've got trouble again," he said.)

Before I'd taken sick, it had been announced that I was going to make a movie about Sister Kenny, the Australian who had evolved a method of treating polio victims. During my recuperation I continued to be obsessed by the project.

I had met Sister Kenny in 1940. For those who don't remember her, she was not a nun; Sister is the title the British give to a nurse. Years ago a reporter quoted me as saying, "She looked like an M-4 tank, but her eyes were the loneliest and the loveliest I've ever seen." I'll stand by that description.

When I first came West, I worked with crippled children at Orthopedic Hospital—this harked back to my Dad's having asked each of his children to give time to a charity—and after a while some other women and I formed an organization with a terrible name, The League for Crippled Children. A woman who knew I was connected with the League, and who'd read an article in the *Reader's Digest* about Sister Kenny, telephoned me. "Sister Kenny is coming to California," she said. "Wouldn't you like to meet her?"

We went to the airport, and Sister stepped off the plane wearing that Aussie hat and a sad-looking black dress, which was half of her wardrobe. I brought her home and ensconced her in our guesthouse. I came to know and admire her as I traveled with her and watched her work. I believe if she hadn't gone stamping through the world, stirring people up, we'd have been a whole lot longer getting the Salk vaccine.

Sister was a great teacher, and she was great with children. She knew anatomy, she knew the inside of the muscle, not just the shape of it, but where it belonged, where it sat. She hadn't, of course, recognized polio as polio when she'd seen it in the Australian bush; she'd just tried to relieve the spasms, as she called them, in the muscles.

"But it's a systemic disease," she would say, "and they are going to have to go after it as a systemic disease. My treatment is nothing; the heat, the hot packs, the massage, they just make the patient a little more comfortable. But doctors *must* develop a vaccine."

The Hearst press took up Sister Kenny, not out of altruism, but because she made good copy. She worked in two polio epidemics in Minneapolis, treating thousands of patients. I stayed out there through one of them, observing her.

She never seemed to sleep, except for those cat naps, and she dragged me from my bed at six o'clock in the mornings to go with her on her hospital rounds. I'd stand back until she'd say, "Rosalind, come over here, look at this, the way it's pulling," and there would be some poor soul with his head twisted to one side, and all you could do for him was give him the cigarette he wanted.

In the long run, good doctors liked Sister Kenny, but some medical men were jealous of her, some were suspicious, some considered her a freak, some even tried to trick her. Once a pair of residents brought her a sailor on a litter, his body hidden by a sheet. Sister didn't even need to pull the sheet down, she could tell by his neck. The sailor had muscular dystrophy, not polio. She looked up at them, blood in her eye. "That's not nice," she said. "Remove this patient."

Another time she asked a patient, a twenty-year-old man, how long it had been since he'd walked. "Nine months," he said.

"I'm going to tell you something," she said. "You can walk, and walk perfectly."

"You're wrong," he said.

"No," she said, "I'm not wrong." Supporting his back with her arm, she pulled him upright on the stretcher, pulled his feet around to one side. He sat there, the color of chalk, legs hanging down. She talked to him quietly; it was like the laying on of hands. "You've been diagnosed wrong," she said, "and your muscles have become flaccid from lying in bed, but they're healthy and you can walk."

He walked. She helped him the first few steps, and then he shuffled, alone, maybe fifteen feet, to a wall. He just stood against that wall and sobbed and sobbed and sobbed. It was terrible. I told her never to do that in front of me again. My heart wouldn't take it.

"They make such mistakes," she said, and went to look for the man's doctors to tell them what they must do to rehabilitate his muscles.

It took me six years to get the Sister Kenny movie off the ground—we didn't shoot it until 1946—and meantime, between other commitments, I kept going around with her to learn whatever I could. I was determined to put her story on the screen, even though a film about crippled children didn't sound like box office to the movie magnates. (From their point of view, they were perfectly correct. I knew in my secret soul that "message" pictures don't do your career any good, that they can put you out of work quicker than anything, but I kept pitching.)

RKO wanted to sign me for several movies. I tried to bargain. "I'll do some for you, if you'll do one for me." Finally the head of Production agreed and the Sister Kenny film became a reality after I managed to get Dudley Nichols interested. Nichols was one of the best writers the movie industry ever had—he wrote *The Informer*— and he said he'd do the screenplay. He ended up directing, too.

I think we made a wonderful film, an accurate film—though we combined several real-life doctors into the character called Dr. Brack—but no part of it was easy. It was especially difficult to do during Sister Kenny's lifetime, even though she didn't have script approval. I studied her walk, her gestures. She had a very powerful right hand, a very feminine left hand, and she stood very straight because her mother had kept a back brace on her as a child. Educated at her mother's knee, she could recite poetry—Shelley, Keats, Macauley—like nobody I'd known since the Duchess. She seldom spoke of her father, and she was sensitive about Australia's being referred to as a former penal colony.

She'd been brought up in the bush, a place called Towumba, and at her time—the turn of the century—there were seven men to every woman in Australia. If a woman married, she was not allowed to go on working, not even as a nurse. The only man in Sister Kenny's past had owned a station, what we call a ranch, in the back country. He died while we were making the picture. He'd waited for her all their lives. First World War I had interrupted their love story—both of them had gone into service—and then her work had come to possess her. He finally understood this, but he never married anyone else.

Sister Kenny had a sad life, but a rewarding one. In France, during that first World War, seeing injured men lying on stretchers on the ground with the mud soaking through the canvas, she'd set to work and invented a stretcher that sat up on little feet. She earned a royalty from this invention; it brought her a small income. Often, in the years after we made the movie, she invited me to come to Australia. I wanted to, but never found the time. I'll go someday, but it won't do me much good to stand beside her grave in Towumba; it won't be the visit we talked about.

The Hollywood cynics had been right, of course. Nobody wanted a picture dealing with a plain middle-aged woman who'd spent her days treating victims of infantile paralysis. When they came to release it, RKO had a hard time drumming up much enthusiasm among exhibitors. Even so, it's one of my favorite movies, and God knows I went through hell to get it made.

Which was why I got so mad at Hedda Hopper. After I'd had my breakdown, Hedda, not knowing any of the details of my illness, printed an item about me and Sister Kenny. The gist of it was that I'd been getting publicity at Sister's expense and that despite the announcement that I was going to make the story of the wonderful nurse, I really had no such intention, because if I'd been sincere, I'd had plenty of time to do it.

I can't remember exactly when the item appeared; I do know that once I finished making *Sister Kenny*, Hedda began to feel guilty. She asked the costume designer, Travis Banton, to come over to my house and apologize for her. He'd been on his way to see me anyhow because he was preparing my clothes for *Mourning Becomes Electra*. We were sitting in the library discussing fabrics when suddenly he said, "Hedda sent me."

"Oh?" I said. "Is that so?"

"Well," he said, "she feels very badly that she printed that story, because not only did you get the Sister Kenny picture made, but she found out that you'd been ill . . ."

I looked at the floor. I studied the carpet for about three minutes. I could feel his eyes on me. Finally I lifted my head. "Travis," I said, "we have got to change these petticoats because they are going to make too much noise on the microphones; the taffeta will rustle."

He gaped at me, and then, as I later heard, he went back to Hedda Hopper, who asked him what I'd had to say. "Nothing," Travis reported.

Hedda was nonplused. "She must have said something."

"She said absolutely nothing."

There are times when you shouldn't speak. I taught that to Lance. "Don't yell on the phone and argue with the guy; just shut your mouth, he'll go crazy." I had cast my eyes down to think, and what I'd thought was, Don't you dare answer, or forgive Hedda at secondhand, for doing what she did.

After that, Hedda herself came around to apologize, and we were friends again.

In order to get RKO to agree to produce *Sister Kenny*, I'd had to sign for two other pictures, but when Dudley Nichols, whom I adored, called to talk about Eugene O'Neill's *Mourning Becomes Electra*, I was appalled. "Not a tragedy, I'm ready for a comedy," I said. "I've been serious long enough."

Dudley laid it on the line. "I did *Sister Kenny* for you, you have to do O'Neill for me."

"Whatever you say, Dudley," I said.

I wanted to play the mother—I was a little too young, but I could have done it—with Olivia De Havilland playing Lavinia, the daughter, but Dudley insisted I do the daughter. It was murder. Katina Paxinou screaming and yelling all over the set; Michael Redgrave, a hell of a good actor, but nervous, taking pills to calm himself; Dudley refusing to change a single line because Eugene O'Neill was his idol. We made a five-hour picture, on the sound stages where they'd shot *Gone With the Wind,* and Dudley wouldn't cut an inch, not a frame.

Three times he showed a wagon coming up the driveway of the house in which we all presumably lived, and he never used anything but a long lens on the scene. When I asked him why he shot that same angle all the time, he said, "Those are the curtains, first-, second- and third-act curtains." I wanted to say we'd better put up a sign to explain that to the movie audiences.

Well, *Electra* had its own style. If you released it today, it might find its audience. But when it came out in 1946, it was an even bigger financial disaster than *Sister Kenny.* Still, as I once told Lance, flops are a part of life's menu, and I'm never a girl to miss out on any of the courses.

One grace note in the discord of *Electra:* I received a rare, handwritten note from Eugene O'Neill telling me how he loved my performance as Lavinia. I knew he was very ill, and I was doubly touched.

My next picture, *The Velvet Touch,* a murder mystery, was produced by Freddie and our own production company, and this time, RKO struck gold. The movie made a bundle, but I was beginning to ask myself a lot of questions.

There are difficult transition periods in every acting career. You go from being an ingénue to a leading woman, or from being a leading woman to a character actress. The sex symbols who can't get over those barriers are to me the saddest people.

I was trying to move from leading lady to character acting (I know I've written that I was *always* a character woman, but I'd been pulling down a leading lady's salary for a long time) and I wasn't getting the kind of work I wanted. Harry Cohn and Louis B. Mayer and Darryl Zanuck were making the decisions of my life, saying to me, "You can't play this," or "We're not offering you that," and I was tired of it. "It is easy—terribly easy—to shake a man's faith in himself," Shaw wrote in *Candida.* "To take advantage of that to break a man's spirit is devil's work." If there were decisions to be made about my life—even *wrong* decisions—I decided I was going to make them, and Freddie was going to make them.

(There was another factor at work, not only in my own worsening situation, but in Hollywood's. Although I don't approve of making excuses, in 1947 and 1948, after the war, the bottom fell out of the film business, hit by television, which was really taking over. And Hollywood reacted badly, handled the competition amateurishly, without much thought for the future. If you were a contract player with a studio, the studio usually prevented your appearing on television—even on première nights to boost their own product. Movie big shots denigrated the new medium, referring to the idiot box and the shoebox, declaring, "It'll never last. It's only a fad.")

Freddie and I used to walk around the block after dinner. One night in 1951 we were out for our stroll when, out of the blue, I said, "I'm going to New York tomorrow."

"You are?" he said. "What on earth for?"

"I have to go East to find out if I can still act," I said. "Because if I can't, then I should quit, try something else."

He was sweet about it. "Fine, if that's the way you feel, only what will you do when you get to New York?"

I didn't know, I hadn't any idea. But the same way I had known I needed to get out of Waterbury, I now knew I needed to head back East.

There was a paradox in my situation. Acting was important to me, but if it had been all-consuming, I couldn't have done what I was preparing to do. I'd have agonized over my professional decline, I'd have got a new agent and dyed my hair and had my face lifted and broken my heart. As it was, I simply wanted to know whether or not I should continue in the acting field.

The answer was waiting for me at 61st Street and Fifth Avenue, in the Pierre Hotel.

"New York, New York, It's a Wonderful Town…"

IRENE SELZNICK's Broadway production of *Bell, Book and Candle* had been optioned by Shephard Traube, who hoped to send out a touring company of the play. A few hours after I arrived in New York, a script with my name on it was left at the front desk of the Pierre.

I'd seen the show with Rex Harrison and Lilli Palmer, and I was eager to go on the road, get the feel of an audience again, so it didn't take me long to make up my mind. I phoned Traube. "Come over," I said. "I'm going to do your play. Do we need a contract?"

He was pleased, if somewhat surprised, by the speed of my decision, and we were both pleased when the play's author, John Van Druten, agreed to direct the new company.

Van Druten was rather unforgiving about Rex and Lilli because they'd left at the end of a season, even though they'd never played to an empty seat. During rehearsals we talked about his feeling that star performers owed it to management, if not to themselves, to help keep a hit running. Particularly since they might one day wish they could find another. "If a performer is lucky," Van Druten said, "he gets one great hit—maybe two—in his life. No more. Think about Katharine Cornell and you think of *The Barretts of Wimpole Street* and, possibly, *The Green Hat.* Think about Helen Hayes, it's *Victoria Regina.*"

I can't prove or disprove Van Druten's theory, but I do know the big hit—like I had in *Auntie Mame,* the thing people remember you for—happens rarely. It's the same in movies. People remember

Errol Flynn for *Captain Blood;* Gable for *Gone With the Wind.*

I went on tour with *Bell, Book and Candle,* and in the beginning I was pretty bad. The reviews were good, but I knew better. I'd been away from the theatre for many years, stage acting is another technique, and at first I wasn't even relating to the other members of the cast the way I should have. But I kept working at it, and by the time we got to Chicago, I was all right. The character I was playing—a witch with supernatural powers—was a good challenge. I'm not a terribly *mysterioso* person, and the part made demands of me.

We played Pittsburgh, Detroit, Saint Louis, Chicago. Valentina did my clothes; she was a friend of the Duchess and she'd designed the dress I wore at my wedding. "You should wear dirrrty blue, dirrrty yellow, never pure colors," she told me. I signed for twelve weeks, played sixteen, and learned what I needed to know. People were willing to put their money down to see me. It cost Shepherd Traube $14,000 to put that show on, and in the four months I was out with it, we made $600,000.

(It's a funny thing about audience acceptance: if you don't have it, there isn't much you can do about it; if you do have it, it can nourish you. I remember talking to Judy Garland when she was playing the Palace.

"Well, Judy," I said, "you're knocking them out of their seats, isn't it great?"

"Yes," she said. "And I've found out one thing, I've found out I have an audience, and nobody can take that away from me." It was true. Even though she'd been dropped by films, she had an audience until the day she died.)

Bell, Book and Candle convinced me I still had the muscles, I just had to get them toned up again. If I hadn't gone out with that play, I would never have had the courage to tackle *Wonderful Town,* a musical, a year and a half later.

When I came home from my tour with the Van Druten comedy, Freddie and I did our second RKO picture together. It was a comedy, called *Never Wave at a WAC,* and I played a divorced Washington hostess whose father was a senator. She's an idiot, this woman, and her father arranges for her to be taken into the army because it's the only way she's going to be able to get to Paris to meet her lover. When she goes to sign up, she takes her secretary with her to fill out the forms.

We went to a real army camp in Virginia to shoot the military stuff, and I had one scene where all the time they were giving me my physical, taking blood, I was on the phone to Hattie Carnegie about making my uniform. "No, dahling," I said, "I'm starting as a captain, and I'd like those bars in gold. Well, if you feel braid would be good, Hattie, you know what to do . . ."

Another time, when I was supposed to be parading with some other WACs, I broke ranks, walked away from my fellows and straight up to a general. "Hello, General," I said, introduced myself as the senator's daughter, and while the general gaped, took out a cigarette and lit it.

It was mostly cornball stuff, very funny, and I got to wear wonderful clothes and hats and furs. Freddie and I had our hearts set on having Jean Louis design them, but Jean was at Columbia, and Harry Cohn wouldn't part with him. Jean Louis came up with an alternative idea. "Would you consider using a very nice young man I know?"

"Who?" I said.

"His name is James Galanos," Jean said.

"I can't, Jean," I said. "I can't use an unknown. This is our own picture, and I can't take a gamble on anybody that hasn't done film before." (It wasn't the first time I'd ridden that particular high horse out of the barn. In 1944, like a damn fool, I turned down *Laura*. A delegation from 20th Century-Fox came over to see me, and I scoffed, "You mean you want me to play a part in a script where I don't even enter till page sixty-eight? Ridiculous! Never! And who are these people in it? Clifton Webb? Why, he hasn't done film. I'll have none of it!")

Jean Louis persisted. "Would you just *see* Jimmy Galanos?"

"All right," I said, "all right."

Jean Louis took me down to an establishment on Robertson Boulevard, and there was Jimmy, who must have been about twenty-four years of age, with two elderly Frenchwomen.

In order to get out of this rather embarrassing situation, I made Galanos a sporting proposition. I needed fourteen outfits for the picture. "Mr. Galanos," I said, "if you are willing to sketch your ideas, and Jean Louis is willing to sketch his, without either of you signing his sketches—and if you'll make me the clothes I pick, no matter whose they turn out to be—then we can proceed."

Galanos agreed, Jean Louis agreed. And they sketched but they didn't sign.

Freddie and I always put sketches down on the library floor to look at them, so when the drawings arrived, we spread them out and I studied them. Having chosen the ones I liked best, I took them to Jean Louis. "I'm pretty clever," I said. "I picked yours, didn't I?"

"You picked one of mine," he said, "and thirteen of his." He grinned. "I wanted you to like him, but not that much."

We made *Never Wave at a WAC* in 1952. At some point during that year, Freddie and I went to a party that was dying by inches, and Mousie Powell (Bill Powell's wife) and I decided to try to liven things up by singing. Mousie never wanted to go home to bed, and neither did I. We got a piano player to hit a few chords, and I was off, and off-key as well, singing the old vaudeville numbers Cary Grant had taught me, the same ones I'd done all through the war.

Among my listeners was Joe Fields, one of the authors of *My Sister Eileen*. (Ruth McKenney wrote the original stories in *The New Yorker;* Fields and Jerry Chodorov did the play.) Joe invited me to have lunch with him the following day, and I said fine.

During the lunch he inquired about my availability to do a musical version—on Broadway—of *My Sister Eileen*. He made it sound like it would be a snap; after all, I'd already played the part in the movies.

"Joe," I said, "I hate for you to be wasting your money here at Romanoff's, but I can't do what you're asking. I mean, singing and dancing would scare me out of my skull."

Joe didn't seem to understand. "If George Abbott directed, would you do it?"

That shook me. Abbott was one of the hottest directors in the theatre. Still, he wasn't a singing teacher. "I'll think about it," I said quaveringly.

Joe Fields went to New York, and from time to time I would get a telegram. Or a phone call. Some days I'd get both.

One night I was again walking around the block with Freddie, and again I said, "I have to go to New York."

"What for this time?" he said.

"I've got to go and tell them I can't do this show."

"Have you ever heard of the Bell Telephone System?" said Freddie. "It runs clear across the country. A phone call would cost you twenty dollars; to go to New York and stay for a couple of weeks —and I know you, if you go, you'll hang around and see all your relatives—is going to cost two or three thousand."

"I have to go," I said. "I've got to talk to them in person, they've been so kind. These red roses all over the place from Bobby Fryer and Joe . . ."

Freddie knew when he was licked.

I came East, and Bobby Fryer, the producer, and Joe Fields took me to hear an audition of the music. Since I don't know one note from another, I watched Fryer's and Fields' faces. They looked despondent, so after the composer had left, I shook my head. "It wasn't very good," I said.

"You see?" Joe cried. "I knew she'd know. That music is no good!"

I smiled politely. "So I really must be excused. The music is no good, and I cannot do the play."

"Just a minute, just a minute," said Bobby. "We're going to get somebody else, another composer—"

"No," I said, "No, I have to go home."

Next day Joe called with fresh news. He'd got Leonard Bernstein. Well, I couldn't say *he* was lousy, so we had another meeting. Comden and Green had agreed to do the lyrics. The noose was tightening. We were all in my agent's office, and I phoned Freddie in Hollywood. Bobby and Joe went out in the hall to give me privacy. "I'm trapped," I wailed when Freddie came on the line. "They've had me in here all day long, and I've had nothing to eat but a soggy cheese sandwich. Get me out of this."

Freddie started laughing. "You got yourself into it, get yourself out."

I turned wifely. I said he'd miss me if I lived in New York while he was out West being a movie producer. I said we had to consider little Lance. I said I was hungry.

((154))

There was no way Freddie would advise me. "If I tell you to do it, and it's a flop, you'll say I steered you wrong. If I tell you not to do it, and it's a hit, you'll say the same thing. Make your own decision."

My decision was not to do the show.

I told Joe and Bobby I was sorry I'd cost them so much time and money. "I'd like to pay for the phone calls, the wires, even the cheese sandwich."

It was like talking to myself. Bobby and Joe were still beside me as I walked back to my hotel. Suddenly I leaned against a lamppost and to my chagrin began to cry. "I've been away from Freddie and Lance too much lately," I said. "You've put together a fabulous team for the show and I know you'll find the right star."

Joe said no. "We won't do it without you."

They followed me into the Pierre, through the lobby, and all three of us got on the elevator. When we arrived at my suite, Hazel flung open the door. "Well, where have we been?" she demanded. "We're due at a dinner party at eight, and we don't know what we're wearing, and our hair has to be done—"

"Roz," said Bobby Fryer, interrupting Hazel's monologue, "if we put this show on with you for just three months, would you do it?"

"You couldn't get your investment back on such a short run," I said.

"I think we could get it off the ground with you," he said, "and then maybe we could keep it flying with someone else, and you could go back to your family—"

I was touched. He was talking about taking a very big chance. "You're silly," I said. "And I'll do the show. And now will you guys please get the hell out of here? I have to take a bath, and there isn't room in the tub for the three of us."

Next day we began. Leonard Bernstein had an apartment in the Osborne, the big stone building diagonally across from Carnegie Hall, and we all met there, George Abbott, and Comden and Green, and the set designer, and the costume designer, and they talked while I listened, bug-eyed. I didn't know what they were saying, I'd never been around a musical before. Bernstein said he wanted to hear my voice. "As soon as the others leave."

((155))

That was my cue. When I saw George Abbott stand up and put his coat on, I fled down four flights of stairs without waiting for the elevator.

Other days, other flights. Bernstein's apartment is stamped in my mind. There were posters on the walls, a piano in every room, and once in a while we'd catch a glimpse of Felicia Bernstein with their baby boy. Sometimes, as I was sneaking out at the end of a session, I'd hear Lennie saying, "Where did Roz go?" All I could think was, He's a great musician, and I cannot let him hear this voice, this foghorn.

Toward the end of the first week he trapped me. "Roz," he said, "I have to hear your range."

"Range," I said. "Gas range, firing range, mountain range—"

He waited until I was finished. Then he sat down at a piano and riffled up and down the keys, singing, "Why, oh why, oh why oh, why did I ever leave Ohio?"

"I'm so nervous," I said, but I tried to imitate what he was doing.

"Lovely," he said. "Now we'll just change the key." He moved it up a little. We did it again. "I'll have it learned by tomorrow," I said, only wanting to get out of there.

"Oh, you don't sing that," he said.

"I don't sing that? Well, why don't we practice what I sing?"

He corrected himself. "You sing that, but you don't sing the melody, you sing the harmony—"

"The *harmony*? I'll never learn the melody, much less the harmony, what are you talking about? The harmony is what you make up as you go along, isn't it?"

Late that night I held an emergency meeting in Central Park with Josh Logan. Josh had problems of his own (he'd been on the road directing *Picnic*, the playwright Bill Inge was drinking heavily and had gone into a hospital), but he was married to my old friend Nedda, and I'm sure she'd bullied the poor man into walking around the reservoir under a full moon with a half-hysterical actress.

"My God, Josh," I said, "I don't know how to sing."

"Then whisper," he said. "If you can't sing, whisper. Listen to Walter Huston sing 'September Song.' He whispers."

All at once the foolishness of his own advice struck him. "You *can't* whisper," he said. "You don't know how to whisper. So get a lot of words. People won't pay so much attention to the music if there are lots of words. You have to have something to say."

That didn't sound too bad. Somewhat comforted, I went to my next meeting with Leonard Bernstein, who remained patient throughout our sessions. I got so I wasn't too scared of the Ohio duet with Edie Adams, who played Eileen, but when George Abbott told me I'd have to sing a ballad with the leading man, I put my foot down. "This is going to be the first show ever done where there'll be no singing with the leading man. I promise I'll do the ballad for you one matinée, and you'll see, it'll empty the theatre."

We were a hit in New Haven, good notices, big crowds. Even so, Jerry Robbins was called in to sharpen things up, and working with him was great for all of us. The chemistry, the balance among the principals was already good. I'd had it put in my contract that I had approval of the other two leads. I didn't want to play sister to some seventeen-year-old girl, and have us come on like mother and daughter. Edie Adams was then in her twenties, perfect for the part. George Gaynes was just right too.

Bit by bit, I grew bolder. One day on the road I amazed myself by making a suggestion to George Abbott. By then, we principals were rehearsing down in the toilets—the gypsies had the stage—and I said, "I want to sing 'Quiet Girl.' "

Abbott was baffled. "Quiet Girl" was George Gaynes' song, and he didn't seem to need any help with it. "She's gone mad," Abbott said to Robbins.

"No," I said, "I want to do one phrase, to show that I love this man. When he leaves the stage, I want to come out and stand in the doorway of my basement apartment and look after him and sing just those five words, 'I love a quiet girl,' that's it, but I think it will tell the audience I love him."

We tried it, and George Abbott left it in. "You were right," he said. "It does the trick."

Five words, and it cost twelve hundred dollars to get them orchestrated! And that was in 1953.

In New Haven, I got the flu, and in Boston, a chorus boy

((1 5 7))

dropped me on my back during the conga number, but the fever passed, the sprain healed, and by the time we headed for New York, I was more or less in one piece.

Success on the road means nothing. New York is all that counts. The day of our opening at the Winter Garden, Abbott kept us busy so we wouldn't have time to think. He always does that. You walk around nervous and jumpy, with your hair in curlers, and he gives you notes. "Put the tray down with less noise. Close that door right on such-and-such a line." You've done it all dozens of times; once more can't hurt.

We were about to break for dinner when a chorus kid came up to me. "Miss Russell," she said, "at the curtain, you're supposed to thank the musical director." I hadn't known that. In opera, yes, I thought, but here?

Abbott was saying a few last words. "Everybody's excused, and good luck. Have a good time tonight, and the audience will have a good time."

He started up the aisle of the theatre, and I went tearing after him. "George, can I see you a moment? George, I'm supposed to thank Lehman Engel, when do I do that?"

Abbott never bothers much with curtain calls, he just tells people to stand there and bow, but I was so anxious, he called everybody back onstage. They came tumbling down the stairs from the dressing rooms and ambling in from the wings.

"All right," Abbott said. "The first call, you're all together, and you take a bow. The next call, Roz will take George Gaynes' hand, and Edie's hand, and the three of them will come one step forward and bow." He looked at me. *"If* you get a third curtain," he said, "you step forward alone. And then you can gesture toward the conductor."

It was a tremendous opening night. It worked. I gave a performance I could never again have repeated in the wide, wide world. I just made up my mind to be that character, though I was so scared I toyed with the idea of running out the stage door instead of making my first entrance. I knew that seven critics—including the critic from the Brooklyn *Eagle*—were sitting out front, and everything depended on them. But that night I was Ruth McKenney.

And I'll never forget the bows. First the line: all of us together. The little kid who'd been dancing next to me in the final number—

we called her jail bait, she was under eighteen—was breathing like crazy, but I wasn't even perspiring. (I wouldn't do the wild hoofing because I thought there was nothing worse than an old bag trying to do things she can't do.) We stood like birds on a branch, and bowed.

Second call. I took Edie's hand and George's hand. We stepped forward. I was so glad it was over, I was rigid. The three of us bowed, then faded back into the line again.

Now the curtain went up for the third time. That was me. And I had to thank Lehman Engel. Well, I came forward in a crouch, bent over like the Hunchback of Notre Dame. I couldn't stand up, I was so embarrassed all alone out there.

The reviews all talked about it. The critics said they'd never seen such a humble performer, that it was a beautiful thing to witness, humility like mine.

The audience swarmed down into the orchestra pit, and I charged off to my dressing room to wait for my admirers. Nobody came. Not even my family. Finally, Marlene Dietrich, who never missed an opening night, appeared in my doorway. She was dressed in her diamonds and furs, and she clearly could not believe her eyes. "Roz," she said, "what are you doing here?"

"I work here," I said. "How was the show?"

"Everybody's waiting onstage for you," she said. "On opening night you're supposed to see them on the stage . . ."

That was one more thing I didn't know about the musical theatre.

Josh and Nedda Logan gave an opening-night party, and when the reviews came in, Lenny Bernstein read them aloud. They were so hyperbolic I thought he was making them up. "Now stop all that," I said, "and read what the man wrote."

It was lovely, lovely. Even a person of such rare humility as I couldn't help but get a bit puffed up. Brooks Atkinson said I should be elected President, and somebody else said he was crazy about me even though my voice sounded "like the Ambrose Lightship calling to its mate." That was my favorite notice.

We were a smash. We opened on February 25th, 1953, and a week later the box office was taking ticket orders for the following New Year's Eve.

For me, it was a whole fresh start.

"How Old *Is* She?"

ALF A LOAF can feed you (*Sister Kenny* and *Mourning Becomes Electra* had both been critical successes, bringing me two more Oscar nominations), but when you get the whole loaf, you know the difference. Not just figuratively speaking; bread in the literal—and the vernacular—sense is heaped on a hit.

In *Wonderful Town*, I was able to please not just myself, or the critics, but regular citizens out for a good time, and I was richly rewarded for my pains. Which at times were considerable; the work in a musical is killing.

I won the Tony Award, the Billboard Award, the Variety Award, the New York Drama Critics Circle Award, the Outer Circle Award, the Barter Theatre Award, the Knickerbocker Award, the Los Angeles *Times* Woman of the Year Award, and various other medals, citations, blue ribbons and gold plaques, and found myself on half a dozen national magazine covers.

That's it. The obligatory laundry list. I'm only going to do it once in these pages, because I can't stand books where actors quote all their good reviews and catalogue their honors. I just wanted to prove I could lay it on with the best of 'em, if I set my mind to it.

When I started fooling around with *Wonderful Town*, I didn't even have an agent. I'd been handling my own business for a couple of years, but it was beginning to embarrass me, and I hated going over the fine-print clauses, so I telephoned Jules Stein, who was the founder and head of MCA.

"I guess I'm going to do this show," I said, "and I'd better have some representation in New York."

Then I hired a publicity woman, not to get me space in the papers, but to keep people away, to protect me from having to pick up the phone and tell strangers I couldn't see them. I didn't want to hurt anyone's feelings, but newspapers and charity events can run you ragged. In every city you play on the road, every fashion editor wants to see you, every society editor wants to see you, every theatre editor wants to see you, and you just can't give that many interviews and still do your work. You're rehearsing, you're up all night conferring on scenes, you're performing, and your energy ought to be on the show, not on trying to charm the press.

(In Chicago, during the run of *Bell, Book and Candle,* I'd agreed to chat with Claudia Cassidy, who was then considered the most important critic in the country. It was the end of winter, and she came in and took off her galoshes while I made small talk about the sloppy streets and my suite at the Ambassador East. "You can see the lake from here," I pointed out. Miss Cassidy went home and wrote that I'd begun in pedestrian fashion, by rambling on about the weather and the lake. But what do you say when you greet someone? "Hello, and then I played . . ."? Claudia Cassidy was tough, but she wrote well. She liked the word silk. Often she said something or somebody was "fine as silk.")

I don't like to read about myself anyhow. I think for the most part the Rosalind Russell in the papers doesn't sound a bit like me. I've never been much for watching my own movies, either. Some of the films I made were pretty awful, and I can't see any reason for me to plunk down cash and go in and squirm. Most of our friends have projection rooms; I've never wanted one. In fact, when I worked in film all the time, I was glad to get away from it when I could, at night or on holidays.

I suppose if Freddie had become head of a studio, we'd have wound up having a projection room so he could run rushes or whatnot, but he didn't and we don't.

The Brisson family (Freddie went straight into theatrical production with *The Pajama Game*), temporarily transplanted to Manhattan, gratefully took root. We kept an apartment with bedrooms, kitchen, everything, in the Pierre for the next twenty years. Lance had a governess who cooked for him, and every Friday night we'd have our dinner and then Lance would accompany me to the play. He used to go out front during the intermission and count the standees. The management wasn't allowed—by law—to take in more than fifty standees, but the temptation to welcome sixty, seventy, eighty at three or four dollars a head was great; often, seatless customers were perched all over stairs, curled around pillars, leaning against side walls.

I wasn't supposed to know about this little racket, but Lance filled me in. We'd refer to the standees as "candies," and though I don't imagine our code fooled too many people, we enjoyed the game. When we were putting on our coats to go home, Lance would say, in front of the general manager, "Seventy-five candies tonight," and I'd say, "Oh, wonderful, that's nice to know; last night we had eighty-two," and then we'd exchange conspiratorial smiles and go out and get in the car.

A few minutes later we'd be sitting cozily in our apartment, drinking hot chocolate and eating toasted English muffins before going to bed.

One night, while we were being driven to the Pierre, I said, "Lancemand" (Lancemand is an affectionate Danish version of Lance), "when you're out there counting your candies, what do the people say about me in the play?"

He seemed to freeze. A desperate look crossed his face, and he stared out the window.

"Honey," I said, "did you hear me? What do the people say in the intermission? About Mother?"

Again, a terrible, suicidal expression came into his eyes.

What is this? I thought. They can't all say I stink, the show's a big hit. But he's trying to hide something. What?

"Well, Lance," I said, "I'm sure *everybody* can't like it, but have you heard somebody who didn't like it? Or who didn't like me?"

"I've only heard one thing," he burst out, "that's all I've ever heard, it's just—" He stopped, his little face red. He was getting all overheated.

"Now, darling," I said, "what is it? It can't be that bad, don't be frightened."

He erupted. It was the only way he could bring himself to tell me. "All they ever say is, 'How old *is* she?'" he cried.

After I stopped laughing I tried to tell him that it was a compliment, that my role in *Wonderful Town* was so physically demanding, people couldn't believe anyone over twenty-one could do all the bouncing. I don't know if I sold him, because I was having trouble selling myself. I was then in my early forties, but I'd been in the movies for such a long time I had a feeling audiences thought I was already well up in my seventies, and just being very damn brave about it.

I stayed with *Wonderful Town* for a year and a half, and then I went to war with Uncle Sam. Ordinarily there are three outfits I don't mess around with—the Federal government, the Vatican, or Metropolitan Life. They're too big. But when, after *Wonderful Town*, the government wanted me to pay a vast sum of money in additional taxes, I got mad. "If you pay, you're guilty." I wasn't guilty, and I wasn't going to pay. Freddie concurred and called in the lawyers.

Lawyers, you may have gathered, have played an important part in my life. Because of my father and my brother James, I've been kindly disposed toward the fraternity, and because of Freddie's business, I've been surrounded by its members. Freddie's always producing a show, only to discover that the writer or the director has the same lawyer as he does, and it's up to Freddie to go out and get another guy. Sometimes he has seven lawyers working for him on various projects, and they all send in their bills during the month of December—bills for twelve thousand dollars, bills for eight thousand dollars, bills for sixteen thousand dollars. Then Freddie spends the month of January taking these guys to lunch and telling them, "That's the most outrageous bill I've ever seen."

Last year I needed a lawyer for something, and I went to my agent, Joe Rivkin, and said, "I want the meanest, roughest man that ever lived. These elegant, polite men don't get anything done." "We've got a guy," Rivkin said, "when he comes in, the building shakes, we're so scared of him, he's so tough."

"That's the one," I said.

But let me get back to the aftermath of *Wonderful Town*. We were home again, in California, and one morning I came out into the garden to find five or six men waiting for me.

"Delightful sight," I said, "but what do you want?"

Freddie explained that these were the lawyers he'd assembled to talk over the tax matter.

I said I wanted to fight. "I've always instructed our accountant never to try to get away with anything. I wouldn't cheat for five dollars, much less five hundred, so I know I'm in the right. And, fellas,

I'll tell you what I want to do, I want to sue the government, because the fact is that the government owes *me* money."

A crusader's zeal was growing in my breast; it was like being hurtled back twenty years in time and defying my crooked landlady all over again. "I've decided to win the case," I explained to the lawyers.

They thought that was fine, but they also thought I ought to know what I was up against.

According to the government, the minute I brought Lance to New York, it became my place of residence and the house in Beverly Hills became a luxury; we could go on maintaining it if we wanted to, but we couldn't deduct a nickel of that maintenance in taxes, even though the house was fully staffed and Freddie lived in it when he was working on his films.

I thought about the huge amounts of taxes the government had taken out of my *Wonderful Town* salary every week. (I didn't have a piece of the show; I'd been on a straight salary.) And I thought about the legitimate expenses they'd disallowed. They wouldn't let me deduct the cost of the car and chauffeur that took me to the theatre daily, or the salary of my theatre maid, or hairdresser, or of my secretary, though the secretary was so busy taking care of house seats all day long that she couldn't even answer a letter for me.

(In the theatre, stars are allotted house seats. They have prestige value, but that's it. You are assigned a certain number of choice seats for every performance, and you can give them away, let friends buy them from the box office, or tear them up in little pieces and sprinkle them over the Island of Manhattan, so long as you pay for them up front.)

There is no such thing as a free ticket in the theatre. Sometimes I've said I didn't want house seats, they were such a nuisance, but then Freddie's pointed out that friends come from different parts of the country and you want to treat them—it's just part of the game. Theatre people know this, they tend to pay for their tickets—I won't ever let an actor pay when I use his house seats—but the public doesn't understand. People would never think of going to a banker to ask if he has any extra money, or to a butcher to ask for a free rib roast, but they reckon on getting theatre tickets for nothing. Naturally, the demand is greatest when you're in a hit; the general manager of

Wonderful Town said I had the biggest bill for house seats he ever heard of on Broadway.

When you've got a hot ticket, you have to expect the demands. Even my family would call me with requests, never for themselves, but because "I have a client, and it's his twenty-fifth wedding anniversary, and I hate to ask you, dear, but it would mean *everything* if he could get seats for *Wonderful Town* . . ." I'd jot down the date, and the secretary would sit there with a bunch of shirt cardboards on which she kept charts—Monday, Tuesday, Wednesday matinée, etc. —and make the phone calls.

We figured it took eight phone calls to settle a single pair of tickets. It sounds ludicrous, but it was always "I'll call you back and let you know if Thursday's all right," and then when you called back with the information about Thursday, they'd changed their minds. "Well, would *Friday* night be possible, because *that's* really his birthday?" and then the secretary would have to say, "I'll talk to Miss Russell, maybe she can get them from the box office, because according to my chart her seats for Friday night are already gone."

Fortunately, Freddie is a pack rat, and he had kept voluminous records of my *Wonderful Town* expenses. He keeps voluminous records of everything. Nothing happens in his life that he doesn't make a note of. He writes a long note if he sneezes. "Got up at eight this morning, shaved, kissed R.R." his diary will say. Before I got married I threw photos, clippings and letters out as fast as they came in, but Freddie happened along with his filing cabinets, his scrapbooks, his notebooks and his pictures, and now we have a garage and a cellar both full of memorabilia.

We sent our *Wonderful Town* documents—including all those bills for house seats—and Freddie's detailed diaries down to the government's offices in a truck. It was a little truck, but it was a truck. The government's lawyers couldn't believe their eyes; they were staggered.

"It's evidence," we said. From that day forward, the United States of America kept offering to settle. I refused. The case of Rosalind Russell versus the Federal government dragged on for a long time, but I finally got a check, plus six percent interest on the money they owed me, and Freddie and I celebrated by giving ourselves a nice boat trip to Europe.

Actually, we'd been headed for Europe anyway, because Freddie and George Abbott were going to put on *The Pajama Game* in London.

George had asked if he might travel with us, Freddie had said fine, and I'd been appalled. I thought the world and all of George, but for me, the trip wasn't business, it was pleasure, and I didn't think I needed a director on my vacation. "We're paying our own fare," I complained to Freddie. "I don't want to spend money to cross the ocean with George at my elbow telling me what to drink and when to eat and how to live."

Volumes have been written about George Abbott. He is a gifted, practical, industrious New Englander, still working in the theatre as he nears his ninetieth birthday. His virtues and his eccentricities have been chronicled by him, as well as by others. He's famous for being prompt, for being careful with a buck—in the days when coffee was a nickel, he'd call you back to the counter if you forgot to leave your own five cents—and for disapproving of alcohol.

I didn't fancy being disapproved of on my own time (though I'm no dipsomaniac, I've been known to knock back a martini before dinner), but Freddie convinced me I shouldn't borrow trouble. He and Abbott were working together, we were all friends, and I must keep cool.

Our first night out, at eight o'clock on the nose, there was a knock at our cabin door. "Abbott here," called George.

"We'll meet you upstairs, George," Freddie called back.

"But it's eight o'clock," said George.

We hustled out of the cabin, went up to the salon and had a drink. When I ordered a second, George's face clouded over. "Couldn't you have that in the dining room?"

I shook my head. "Because you've said that, George, I'm going to have the second drink, and then I'm going to have a third drink."

George is a pragmatist. He adjusted.

George is also a dancin' fool. I love to dance, but there was no way in the world I could keep up with him. Fortunately, Rita Hayworth was on board with us, and the second night out, George, who likes pretty women as well as he likes dervishes, spotted her across the crowded room. "Don't you know her?" he asked me wistfully.

Freddie knew her. Rita had been a client, back in his agenting days, so after muttering in my ear (as George and I rhumbaed past) "I'll fix it," Freddie approached her. "Rita," he said, "George Abbott, the famous New York director, is a mad dancing nut. Roz is going to call you and invite you to come and have dinner with us, but for heaven's sake, will you get up and dance with him, and get him out of our hair?"

"All done, kid," said Rita.

Next night we had dinner, the four of us, and George was like a twelve-year-old boy. We never saw him again for the rest of the voyage.

In London, in order to get me off the hook—or at least, off the hoof—we tried to supply George with different dancing partners. He wore 'em out; nobody could dance as much as he. Every night started the same way. At eight o'clock sharp there would come a bang, bang, bang on the door of our hotel suite. I'd say, "Tonight is your night to be ready, Freddie, get the damn tie on." Sure enough, at the stroke of eight, bang, bang, bang on the door. Next night it would be my turn to answer the knock, followed by the crisp announcement, "Abbott here." But at least we could sip our drinks in peace. Never again did George say, "Let's go," or "Couldn't you have that at the restaurant?"

One evening I came in from shopping, tired, my feet swollen, and Freddie told me that tonight's dancing girl had canceled.

I sank down on a couch. "You," I said, "have told me, since the day I married you, of the beautiful women you knew in London, the ones you used to go out with, the ones who wrote you those love letters. I thought I'd have to watch it, these fabulous women were going to be meeting the boat. Well, where are they?"

"I don't know," said Freddie.

"I can't do it," I said. "I can't dance any more, Freddie."

"I'll call this friend of mine at Paramount," said Freddie.

It was already six-thirty P.M. Freddie called this man at Paramount, he said yes, he knew a girl who might like to go dancing, and gave Freddie a phone number. Freddie tried the number, reached a woman—clearly the girl's mother—and went into his routine. "My name is Frederick Brisson. I am here from America to produce a play. My wife, Rosalind Russell, and Mr. George Abbott, who is a very famous Broadway director and a very nice gentleman, and I would like very much to take your daughter Katherine to dinner tonight."

What a selling job; he scarcely took time to breathe. "We're meeting at Claridge's and going to Mirabelle for dinner, and then to the Four Hundred to dance, and I assure you that I will see to it that Katherine is brought home in the car at such and such an hour . . ."

The lady on the other end listened to his whole story. When it was over, she drawled into the phone, "Freddie, you son of a bitch, how dare you call and ask for my daughter, when it's *me* you should be wining and dining?"

It was one of the old girl friends. She gave permission for her daughter's night out, but she made a condition. "You come by and fetch her, Freddie, because I want to see what you look like."

Although we went to great lengths to find twinkle-toed partners for George—I once picked up Abbe Lane in Rome on the street —the girls we provided didn't always suit him. After dinner he and the girl would get up, take to the dance floor, and he'd try her out. If he didn't like her, he'd come back to the table, dump her, then turn to me. "Come on, Roz . . ."

I'd look at Freddie, stricken, thinking, My God, he's going to kill me, and then I'd have to get up. And for the two hours I was flying around the floor with George, Freddie was stuck at the table, trying to entertain the abandoned lovely.

Some nights, of course, George fell in love with the girl. He was about sixty-five at the time, they were all twenty, but every one of them faded before he did.

That was a great trip.

A Queen
May Look at a Cap

WITH AND WITHOUT George Abbott, Freddie and I have had a lot of great trips and met a lot of fascinating people. At home or abroad, I like talking to working people the best, no matter what they work at. I spent this morning with a plumber who was explaining a job he was doing in one of our bathrooms, and why they didn't make faucets like ours any more. He was a very interesting young man. But my editor says book buyers don't want to read about my plumber, they want to read about my adventures with kings and presidents and the owners of large pleasure craft.

I've hobnobbed with those too. Partly because Freddie is such a gregarious soul and partly because, as I said before, politicians and the gentry like to surround themselves with show-business characters.

We've known the Roosevelts, the Trumans, the Eisenhowers, the Kennedys, the Johnsons and the Fords, although Freddie claims that Harry Truman was really *his*, Freddie's, friend. "He was working on me to get his daughter in the theatre. You were only let into the White House when he was there because of me."

Freddie takes credit for most of my social successes. When President Ford, after a White House dinner for Chancellor Schmidt of West Germany, invited me to come to Martinique to meet Giscard d'Estaing, I thought he was kidding. To Freddie, the invitation (which I had, regretfully, to decline) made perfect sense. "If he wanted a representative personality from America, who could he get better than Rosalind Russell? Who has a very nice husband, very well-dressed . . ."

My very nice, very well-dressed husband has shown me so

much of Europe. He speaks the languages, he has friends in England, France, Italy, Scandinavia, Spain, so he's right at home when he goes to those countries, and that's been nice. We've missed traveling to the Orient, but Freddie was always combining business with pleasure, and his business was in Europe.

Whenever we went to Paris, the Duke and Duchess of Windsor would entertain us. I don't know how she found us the first time; we weren't acquainted with her (though Freddie had played golf with the Duke), but I suppose she had a secretary, or he had a secretary, or they both had nine secretaries, who made lists of people arriving off the boats, and then called around to the Ritz, or the Meurice, or the Plaza Athenée, till they rounded up the ones they wanted. The Duchess' great drive was to supply the Duke with different faces, not to have him confronted by the same ones all the time. She'd use one guest to divert the Duke before dinner, then during dinner he'd find himself between two other ladies whom she hoped he'd find entertaining, and after dinner somebody else would be brought along to keep him interested.

He was fond of having someone with whom he could speak German, and it was also quite easy for someone like me to talk to him because he had a curiosity about the theatre.

We visited the Windsors at their Bois de Boulogne home in Paris and also at their country house, The Moulin, out past Versailles. The mill was done in exquisite taste. You came up a flight of tiny stairs into a drawing room, and beyond the windows of the drawing room was a wheat field that stretched almost as far as the eye could see. And on a table right outside these windows sat a wonderful huge vase filled with bright red canna. That red canna against that wheat—I'd never seen anything so effective in my life.

The Duchess had a weakness for porcelain vegetables and fruits—asparagus in Sèvres, grapes in Haviland china (the Duke once told her he thought she'd gone a bit too far in the matter of these unnatural provisions), but I can't think of any other area of decoration in which anyone ever suggested that she overdid.

There was a dining room in the house proper, the main section of the old mill, and then a smaller dining room—small for the Windsors, it could seat twelve, possibly fourteen—in a kind of barn. The barn had a cathedral roof, and down at one end, on an otherwise blank wall, was a map twenty feet high. It had been given to the Duke by the newspapers of London, and it was marked for him; there were dots at Birmingham, Southampton, every place in the British Isles where he'd ever made a speech.

Very handsome, the map covered the space like wallpaper. The Duke's desk, which came from Buckingham Palace, stood against that wall too, with an inkstand on it, and next to the desk, on a window sill, lay a crown. I remember thinking it was small, because the Duke himself was small. It was also very handsome, not just a rinkydink affair, but I don't know where it came from or how he'd got it. He never did go through a coronation, and anyway, I don't suppose a coronet becomes the personal property of the monarch on whose head it's placed. All his medals and orders were mounted in a case over the fireplace. The Duke was very conscious of having been a king. He'd say, "Well, that happened when I was King," or "I met so-and-so right before I became King." He seemed always to measure time that way, right to the end of his life.

The Windsors were an interesting couple; he was charming, she was bright and I liked her very much, but one often wondered, Were there ever recriminations between them? Regrets? One never knew.

Paris was the scene of many a triumph for Freddie, my social lion. He likes to tell about one of our first trips there. He'd called for a lunch reservation at the Berkeley restaurant at the Rond Point. "Of course, Monsieur Brisson," the man at the other end of the phone had said, "everything will be ready, the wine, your usual table, leave it to me." Freddie hung up, looking smug. "You see how well known I am in Paris? I'm Mr. Big. I didn't even have to use your name."

We got to the restaurant. "Monsieur Brisson," Freddie said to the maître d'.

"He hasn't arrived yet," the maître d' answered politely.

"And this is Madame Brisson," Freddie said.

"Not arrived yet," said the maître d'.

"Rosalind Russell," Freddie said.

"Monsieur Brisson ordered a table for two, sir," the maître d' said. "Do you mean that you're going to be three?"

"No," Freddie said, "no, we're going to be two."

And it looked as though we were going to be two who didn't get to sit down.

In due course, the whole business became clear. The owner and publisher of *Le Figaro*, the famous Paris newspaper, was a man named Pierre Brisson, and that was the Brisson the restaurant had expected. Pierre Brisson also turned out to be a distant relation of Freddie's. The Brissons had been a Huguenot family; in their eagerness to get out of France when the purges came, some fled to the north, some to the south, and Freddie's branch of the tribe had wound up in Denmark. We later met *Figaro's directeur*, who was delighted to rediscover a connection and who showed his delight in a very concrete way a couple of years afterward.

Figaro was a tough paper for the motion picture companies to crack. They advertised in its pages, but they couldn't get publicity for their stars. I'm not talking about a scandal, which anybody will print, I'm talking about straightforward publicity. In the thirties and forties Metro killed itself trying, but it couldn't plant Garbo, Gable, Dietrich or anybody else in *Figaro*.

Lap dissolve, as we say in Hollywood. I arrive in Europe, having just made a movie which I'm being sent over to help promote. On the voyage across the big pond, a *Figaro* reporter had interviewed me—this was unusual enough—and then said that when we got to Paris he'd like to have a photographer follow me around the city. Freddie and I first spent some time in England, then went to France, and sure enough the *Figaro* reporter contacted me again. In our hotel room, I fussed. "What a waste of time. Why should I go out with that photographer? They'll never print a damn thing."

"You're here to sell a film," Freddie said. "You did it in London, and you got marvelous press. Suppose they only print one picture? At least you'll have had one picture in *Figaro*."

Next day the photographer and I went to the Arc de Triomphe, the Place Vendôme, the Tuileries and three other locations. *Figaro* printed all six pictures on the front page.

In large letters under the masthead was a headline featuring the big *crise* of the moment, and right next to it a smaller headline which read *"Madame Brisson Arrive à Paris."* In every single caption I was identified as Madame Brisson. I don't know what MGM thought about it, but Freddie was insufferable for a week.

He also got top billing—or at least top scrutiny—the first time we met King Frederik and Queen Ingrid of Denmark. The King and Queen were on a state visit to Washington, and Count Knuth-Winterfeldt, the Danish Ambassador, gave a reception for them, and Freddie and I were invited to the Embassy to be presented to Their Majesties.

At the White House, the husband goes down the receiving line ahead of the wife, but at the Embassy, I was sent along first. I curtsied to the King and Queen, and I noticed that neither one of them looked at me at all. What with my being a great big fat enormous huge movie star (this is the way one of my friends describes all movie actors who've achieved a certain notoriety), I was rather disconcerted to be totally ignored, but not so disconcerted I couldn't take in the fact that the royal couple was staring at Freddie, who followed in the line.

That night at the White House, before a State dinner for the King and Queen, it happened again. This time, as we approached, Freddie went first, and the King, unaware that Freddie knew the language, turned to the Queen and spoke in Danish. "Here he is," he said, "that's Carl Brisson's son, the one I told you about. Here he comes now, with the wife . . ."

In equally pure Danish, Freddie said, "Good evening, Your Majesty," and the King almost fainted. And still Their Majesties never looked at me. We've got a photograph of the scene, star bowing deeply—and being cold-shouldered while the royal couple gaze at Freddie Brisson.

I *have* been gazed at by a queen, however. In 1949 I was summoned to a command performance before King George VI and Queen Elizabeth (now the Queen Mother of England). It wasn't too long after the war, and things were still very grim in Great Britain. We checked into the Savoy Hotel with several dozen cold-storage eggs, because Hazel, who had come on the trip with us, had an ulcer, and I wanted her to eat decent breakfasts. Every morning, when the room-service waiter came around, I would ask him to open a bureau drawer and take out an egg to have prepared for Hazel. One day, while I was lying in bed reading the newspaper, I heard a noise, a kind of click, click, click. "Oh, madam," the waiter said, turning from the bureau, "there are four eggs here that are broken . . ."

"That's a shame," I said. "Why don't you take them, and maybe you can make an omelet."

The English are survivors. I knew the waiter had broken the eggshells with his fingernails, hoping I'd say exactly what I'd said. That's how hungry people were there.

But about the command performance. I wore a metal skullcap. Hundreds of years earlier, a Viking queen had worn that cap to be married in. I should have worn it at my own wedding, but I was too stupid. My soon-to-be mother-in-law had told me about this lovely silver helmet that Prime Minister Stauning (he's as famous in Denmark as Disraeli was in England; he wore a stovepipe hat and died in World War II) would like to send me as a present. She kept saying silver, but I didn't figure it was like table silver (which it is); I pictured silver cloth, like that bloody bandeau of lamé that I'd had to wear to the dance at Canterbury prep. That's what I need at a country wedding, I'd thought, to be decked out in silver lamé, walking up the aisle. Valentina had already designed an apron of lightweight wool as part of my gown because I'd wanted everything very earthy, very countrified, so, sad to say, I paid no attention whatever to Freddie's mother. Was she trying to dress me for my wedding? Well, let her forget it.

Sometime after we were married, my mother-in-law showed up with the helmet. It was light as a feather, and there were little Viking wings on the sides, over each ear, and a split in the back for a bridal veil to come through, and a little chain. It was enchanting.

Sick that I'd blown the chance to show it off at my wedding, I put the cap away, but in 1949 I got it out again and took it to England. At a rehearsal for the command performance, I asked an equerry if it would be suitable to wear something on one's head when meeting the King and Queen. "Of course," he said. "When women are presented at Court, they wear the feathers, the three plumes."

I couldn't wait for the big evening. It came. I dressed, adjusted my silver helmet, told myself, "This'll kill the people," went onstage and launched into one of the Cockney songs Cary Grant had taught me.

Later, being presented to the Queen, I curtsied, and she smiled sweetly. "Where did you learn that song?"

I told her about Cary's coaching.

"It's a long time since I heard that," she said, "and you sang it very amusingly."

We actors were being presented in alphabetical order, so Walter Pidgeon had gone before me, and Jean Simmons was to come after me. As the Queen started toward Jean Simmons, King George approached and I went into another curtsy. All of a sudden the Queen was back, gesturing to me. I came up out of a half crouch, leaving the King standing there. "Yes, ma'am?" I said.

"Excuse me," said the Queen, "but what is that wonderful thing you have on your head?"

I never think of that moment without delight. It was like "Where did you buy the hat?" or "Is that diamond necklace real?"; it was such a marvelous, feminine thing.

It isn't only royalty that is fascinated by show people. An actor can hang around the straight, non-titled, rich and be wined and dined till he's too fat to play in anything but wide-screen. I was never very good at that. I used to go to Palm Beach once in a while, but the people there drove me nuts. I find obsession with lineage tedious. (One of my friends in San Francisco finessed a rich South American who was pressing her for his fellow guests' credentials—Were they really old San Francisco? Had they come around the Horn? To whom were they related?—by telling the man, "I think we should get something straight. There is no one in this room who's very far removed from the shovel, the pick or the hoe.")

Though to tell the truth, I'm rarely bored. If I win a clod as a dinner partner, I get fascinated by the challenge. I keep a little scorecard in my head. I'll ask my partner how he feels about the energy crisis. No response? I check that one off. I ask if he's political. No? I check that off too. But maybe he knows something about Aztec Indians, and once you find an area he's familiar with, you're home free. I happen to like all sorts of people, but the rich tend only to like the rich. Their interests are mostly limited to each other; they share a sort of decadence of thought and motive that makes a short time with them seem long enough.

Having generalized so boldly, I will now contradict myself. "General notions are generally wrong," wrote Lady Mary Wortley

Montagu in the year 1710. Two of the friends of whom I'm fondest are Loel and Gloria Guinness, for whom the phrase "jet-setters" might have been coined. They're very rich (when they came to Palm Springs for one of Frank Sinatra's Christmas parties, Gloria confessed to me that this was the first time they'd stayed overnight in a house they didn't own), but they're also very real.

Freddie met the Guinnesses first. In Palm Beach they used to have a house which featured a tunnel leading under the highway to the ocean. This tunnel they made into a kind of family room connecting the living room, facing the ocean, with the veranda, which faced Lake Worth. One day they called us up and invited us to come with them on a boat trip. "Of course, we'd love to. We will someday soon," I said, thanking them.

Months passed. The Guinnesses proffered another invitation, and I had a holiday coming up between pictures. Freddie and I were sitting around after dinner, and he started talking about seagoing yachts and how the owners who ran them were a dwindling breed. "We should go," he said. "You know, people will have to give up these boats, and you won't get this kind of chance again."

I remained uncertain. A boat severely limits your freedom. If you're not enjoying yourself, you can't get off in midocean.

"We should go, darling," Freddie said again. "I hear it's divine, and the Guinnesses are such fun."

I said all right. "But you tell them I'm kind of crazy, that I might drop out, dive overboard at any moment. Leave an opening for me, because it's my holiday and it's brief."

I lived to wish my holiday had been longer. I think we went to Venice that first trip. Other times we went to Spain, Sardinia, the Greek Islands. The Guinness boat was called *Calisto* and she was a beauty—teakwood decks and bright furnishings and all the comforts imaginable. (Some years later they sold *Calisto*, bought and rebuilt another boat, and called it *Sarina*. It, too, was a heavenly ship.)

Like the Duchess of Windsor, Gloria Guinness is known for her great style, her taste, her perfection as a hostess. The Guinnesses' days have not been all sunlight and sweet islands (Loel's son Patrick, who was married to Gloria's daughter Dolores, died in an automobile accident, and the loss almost killed Loel), but they are people whose grace never fails them.

On the Sardinian trip we went ashore—Freddie and I were thinking of renting a house there—and bumped into Princess Alexandra, the first cousin of the present Queen of England. "How do you get invited on that boat?" she said.

"Do you want to go on that boat?" I said.

"Oh, yes," she said, "it's divine."

"I'm sure they'd be happy to have you," I said.

"Oh, I don't think so," said the Princess.

That struck me as delicious. A royal who needed arrogance lessons. Princess Alexandra is very pretty, very natural, a hard-working do-gooder of a princess, but she had no confidence whatever that she'd be interesting to the kind of people who owned such a boat.

The time we went to Greece with the Guinnesses we flew in their private plane to Corfu, where the *Calisto* was waiting. Once aboard, we sailed to Piraeus and a number of small islands, and then through the Corinth Canal to Athens, where we met Aristotle Onassis. He was on his yacht, *Christina*, and he invited us aboard. I remember standing on the deck of the huge *Christina*, and it was one of those I-wonder-what-the-poor-people-are-doing moments. I gazed back at the *Calisto*, which was following in our wake, and I said to Freddie, "Look! I'm on this one, and I've got that one trailing me, coming up in the rear!" and we laughed like little kids, and Freddie said, "Try to behave as though we do this all the time."

Maria Callas was with Onassis on the *Christina*, and so was a Danish-Greek lawyer Freddie knew. The four of us from the *Calisto* dined with them, then sailed on to Hydra. Onassis enjoyed talking Spanish with Gloria (she's Mexican-born, and he, as a young man, had worked in South America in the cigar business). Callas was fun, and there was music and singing and dancing all the time we were aboard.

Freddie and I always got a kick out of brushing elbows with types who were larger than life. Once, when we were touring around the South of France, we met Picasso, and he invited us to drive up into the hills to visit him at home, but we weren't asked to stay for lunch, nor were we allowed to see many of his paintings. (Years later, in California, we met the painter Francoise Gilot, who had lived with

((177))

Picasso and written a book about it. Now married to Dr. Jonas Salk, the father of the polio vaccine, she's brought a touch of Paris into Salk's sober scientific world. These days he wears purple ascots.)

But of all the people Freddie and I have encountered in our travels, the most bewitching was probably the fashion designer Gabrielle Chanel.

Mademoiselle

WHILE I WAS AT METRO, Louis B. Mayer tried to buy the rights to Chanel's life story, but she wasn't interested in selling them. Time and again, between 1936 and 1940, MGM made offers to her. Chanel had been the rage of Paris since the twenties and there were all kinds of wonderful stories about her.

One was that she'd been on the docks in Marseille or some such place (the South of France, but not the fancy part) and she was cold, and a sailor had put his pea jacket around her, and that was where she'd got the idea for the Chanel suit. Another was about her coming out of a *palazzo* in Venice and falling into the canal because her heel had caught in her long skirt, and deciding then and there to wear pants in public. Still a third was that she'd cut off her hair when it had got burned on a heater. She just took scissors and chopped it off, and then she went to the opera and everybody gasped, and that was how she'd started the craze for bobbed hair.

She was one of the greats, and hers was a great story—she and the Duke of Westminster were lovers for fourteen years—and her contributions to fashion—the cardigan jacket, the little black dress, the sling-back pumps—brought her huge success.

But World War II closed the House of Chanel. Then, in 1954, after fifteen years out of the designing business, Chanel came back to work and knocked off the other top young couturiers all over again.

At that point I went to work on Freddie. "I don't understand you," I said. "Why don't *you* go after the story of Chanel? Here's a woman who's seventy-four or seventy-five years old, and instead of sitting in the shade with her cat, she's finding new worlds to conquer . . ."

He thought I was right. He spent the next fifteen years trying to put together a show about Chanel. (Meanwhile, he produced about eight other shows and a film. That's how long it took; the musical *Coco*, starring Katharine Hepburn, didn't open on Broadway until December of 1969.)

From 1954 on, every time we went to Europe, Freddie saw Chanel. I was with him when he first met her. One of the heads of *Paris Match* had arranged a dinner for six or eight of us, and Chanel talked up a storm. It was easy to follow her French, even if you weren't fluent in the language, because she made such powerful and expressive gestures. I remember that a bracelet flew off her arm and she went right on talking, and the butler reached down, picked up the bracelet in a napkin, and Chanel held out her arm, while continuing to speak, and the butler put the bracelet back on. The woman never missed a syllable. A torrent of French poured from her, a tirade, it sounded like a waterfall. Among other subjects, she was talking about the American woman. She said the American woman had no *chic*. I said I thought American women *did* have style. Chanel said such style as they had didn't count, it just didn't count.

When we left I said, *"Je suis contente de vous voir, mademoiselle,"* and she answered, in excellent English, "It's been very nice meeting you, too."

It took a couple of years before Chanel and Freddie got around to drawing up contracts, and then a friend gave Freddie a piece of information he hadn't had before. "I think you ought to see a man named Wertheimer," this fellow said.

"What for?" said Freddie. "Who is he?"

"He owns Chanel," said our friend.

Freddie wasn't buying. "Nobody owns Chanel but Chanel," declared Freddie scornfully. He was wrong. Pierre Wertheimer was the name of the man who'd put Chanel back into business and who had bought out Chanel perfumes. He ran the biggest racing stables in the world, bigger even than the Aga Khan's (or the Greystock herds of my youth, for that matter), and every day he ate lunch at Maxim's. Once Freddie knew this, he took to going to Maxim's and lurking, in the hope of drawing a glance, an encouraging word, anything. Wertheimer just let him flub around. He didn't see any reason to talk to this Brisson; he didn't want anybody to do a play or a movie about Chanel. For two years Freddie tried to get an appointment with him

—Wertheimer worked one hour a day in his office, three to four P.M., that was it—and finally he was victorious.

They had one of those long French lunches and then returned to the Wertheimer establishment. Mr. Wertheimer looked up from his desk. "There's no reason for you to sit down," he said. "You won't be here long enough. There's no way I'm going to let you do Chanel's story, so I'm sorry if you've been led up the garden path."

Wertheimer and Chanel were then at odds with each other, but she was still an enormous asset to him, and he had no intention of letting some stranger come in and cheapen her value.

Chanel, who was by now very fond of Freddie, had a flying fit when she heard Wertheimer had queered the deal, and their feud heated up. She threatened not to do her next collection. Every time she finished a collection, she threatened that she would never do another, but this time there was reason to believe she might be serious. Wertheimer had to consider her age, her temperament and the fact that she didn't need the money. She was a very rich woman, she *could* quit anytime, and she wanted to have Freddie do the musical. Freddie had talked Alan Lerner into writing the book, and while Chanel knew little about the theatre, she did know about *My Fair Lady* and that this was the man who'd done the script. Also, Alan spoke French, so they were able to communicate.

Eventually, Freddie got Wertheimer's consent. He—Freddie —came in one night about seven-thirty, looking a hundred and twelve years old, but he'd worn Wertheimer down. On the one hand, Wertheimer had Freddie talking his ear off—"I'm not going to destroy Chanel, or cheapen her"—and on the other hand, he had Chanel threatening to show him he couldn't boss her around, and Wertheimer just gave up. He said he wouldn't interfere, or sue, or make trouble, Freddie could go ahead with the show, as long as he, Wertheimer, was not portrayed in the musical. That meant Freddie had to start with a whole new set of lawyers—Wertheimer's lawyers. Sometimes I wonder why it only took fifteen years to get it all together.

The only regret I have about our relationship with Chanel is that I had to stop wearing my Chanel suits. I owned a few, but I wouldn't put them on any more because I was afraid people would think she was giving us a discount. She didn't hand out suits or give discounts. She did offer a discount to professional people, but only for films or plays. Claudette Colbert, for instance, told me she got ten percent off.

Not that Chanel was chintzy. Whenever I left her, she always made me a present, a piece of costume jewelry or a handbag. *"Le sac pour Madame, s'il vous plaît,"* she would tell an assistant, and off I'd go with a brand-new pocketbook.

The people I knew who wore her clothes all liked her, never said that she was mean, or that she charged more for a blouse, say, than she should have. I think she was quite fair about prices, as those things go.

Once, trying to help Freddie's campaign along, I said American women would love to see her life put on the stage, and she told me it wasn't important what American women thought. *"Femmes américaines, rien, rien."* I don't think she meant this as an insult, I think she was trying to say that what *was* important was getting a very French feeling into any story about her.

She was a kind person, but extremely volatile. She didn't like Charles de Gaulle, and she screamed about him through all the years we knew her. If a conversation lagged, she'd be off about de Gaulle; she tore into him every few minutes.

She was not beautiful—her nose kind of spread as she got older—yet I never introduced her to a man (she was fussy about whom she was willing to meet, so you couldn't take everybody to her) who wasn't knocked out by her.

The man and Freddie and I would leave her salon, walk down the rue de Cambon, and I'd just be quiet, and wait. Every time the man would say, "Gee, I'd have loved to have had an affair with her." They all said it in so many words.

There are women who, no matter what their age, never lose their charm for men. Mistinguette, Colette—but they're not all French, either. A woman from my hometown, Dolly O'Brien, was twenty years older than Clark Gable, and he was wild about her. Those women exist, and Chanel was certainly one of them.

The last time Freddie and I were in Paris, the manager of the House of Chanel asked us to come to the salon. "She would have liked you both to see that it's been kept as it was when she was alive," the manager said. We went, but it made us sad. Everything was still there

—the great Coromandel screens, the fabulous chandeliers, the iron deer in front of the fireplace, huge but so graceful, the books in their beautiful bindings (she knew every one of them; she was an omnivorous reader), but the personality had gone out of the place.

Chanel was the only woman I ever knew who could do things oversize, and make them work. If you were invited to lunch in her little dining room, just off the salon, the only adornment on the table was likely to be an enormous hunk of rock crystal. She sat on a couch to receive guests, and you were on time, and the table was already set, and you were offered one whiskey or a sherry. After lunch—she provided perfect meals, served perfectly, though at the end, in her eighties, she ate very little—you'd be taken back into the salon for coffee.

That's when you'd get a taste of her consummate showmanship. While you were sipping demitasse, the head *vendeuse* would come in with a model and say to Chanel, "Mademoiselle, we cannot remember the way you wanted this scarf," and Chanel would get up, adjust the scarf by giving it a kind of flip, then she'd pat the model on the behind, and model and *vendeuse* would go off.

Old Roz knew it was all staged, that Mademoiselle must have instructed the *vendeuse*, "Now, you and Véronique come into the salon at ten minutes of three," but that was part of what was so wonderful about her.

She had living quarters in the House of Chanel, but never slept there; she kept a small suite at the back of the Ritz, the garden part of the Ritz, and that's where she died. She'd been out for a long Sunday lunch, came in around four-thirty, asked someone to call a doctor, lay down on the bed, and was dead ten minutes later.

"You don't need money," she once told an interviewer. "You need richness of heart, and elegance."

She had both those things.

"Whom Unmerciful Disaster Followed Fast and Followed Faster..."

EDGAR ALLAN POE,
"The Raven"

GETTING BACK (from High Life, or How I Spent My Vacations) to the subject of work, I went from *Wonderful Town* straight into the movie version of *Picnic.*

Josh Logan, who was directing, came to me and said, "Would you like to do *Pic*—" and I said "Yes" so fast he never got the *nic* out.

Rosemary, the frustrated schoolteacher, is an awfully good part. (The way I understand it, Bill Inge had sisters who were teachers, and the play was originally written about Rosemary.)

The company went to Kansas to shoot the picture, and for the second time in my life (it hadn't happened since *The Women*) I heard that I was just too gorgeous for a role. My first scene was shot at the picnic grounds, where my sweetheart, Howard (played by Arthur O'Connell), and I were sitting in an old grandstand. My first line was "Look at that sunset, Howard." To get a sunset glow on our faces, a pink filter had been put over the camera lens, and when Harry

Cohn, back in Hollywood, got a look at the rushes, he exploded. "Tell Russell she looks too good."

There was no reason why Rosemary shouldn't have looked good in that scene—she was on her best behavior, she was wearing her best dress, and she hadn't yet touched a single drink. It was the day she hoped to coax a marriage proposal out of Howard.

I'd had every intention of going to pot when the time came, no rouge, runny mascara, lipstick smudged in the corners of the mouth—when poor Rosemary got drunk, she was going to come on messier than I had for Junior Laemmle, and she was going to be twenty years older besides—but once we'd got the word from Harry Cohn, we really went to work on my face. I was a wreck. We drew streaks under my eyes with lead pencil (not black crayon or eyebrow pencil) because lead pencil makes the lines look like veins.

The drunk scene, shot in one take, almost played itself. The woman's loneliness, her desperation, welled up in me and took over. When I asked to do the scene again, Josh said no. "You'll never get it that good again." (In 1974 I put on a one-woman show, which included film clips, at Ford's Theatre in Washington, and Henry Kissinger saw it and said he was shocked by the clip from *Picnic.* "Ooh, what a terrible drunk you are."

"Isn't any woman who's spurned?" I said.

Henry, who used to be known as a collector of women, assumed the question was rhetorical, and we went on to other matters.)

A lot of the schoolteacher's stuff was cut out of *Picnic.* It made me unhappy, but I understood the reasons. The studio was introducing Kim Novak, they thought they had a big star, they wanted to protect her. And because Bill Inge knew and wrote her so well, Rosemary is sneaky, she can take over.

Josh worked on *Picnic* with the great Chinese cameraman James Wong Howe. (I know a lovely story—it may be apocryphal, but I heard it from an actor who swears it's true—about Howe. Some years ago Howe opened a restaurant in Hollywood. Because of his fame as a cameraman, a local newspaper sent a photographer to get a picture of Howe and his staff in front of the new café. The photographer, who didn't know anything about Howe—to him this was just a run-of-the-mill assignment—lined up the fledging restaurateur and his staff, only to discover he couldn't get them all into his view finder, so he backed off the sidewalk, into the street. Wishing to save the man's life, which was being menaced by passing cars, Howe called out a suggestion: "Why don't you use a wide-angle lens?" The photographer turned surly. "Just stick to your chop suey and let me take the pictures," he said.)

Howe and Josh Logan did some beautiful things, some sweet things, in *Picnic*. One sequence at dusk stays in my mind. There were lanterns all around the picnic grounds, and the movie camera was tilted down over a brook. Then, one by one, the lanterns came on, slowly, shimmering in the water, and all at once it was night in the park.

Our company lived at a little hotel in Hutchinson, Kansas, where they took very good care of us, except in the matter of tornadoes, about which they couldn't do much. Once Josh and I landed in a ditch while the winds raged around us, and we later heard that a neighboring town had been entirely blown away.

William Holden, the leading man of *Picnic* was known for his great athletic prowess. He also took a drink from time to time, and then, when the humor was on him, did a bit of showing off.

A bunch of us were sitting in his suite one evening, making conversation, when Bill took a running leap out of the open window and hung by his fingers from the sill outside.

This wouldn't have been so amazing if he'd lived on the ground floor, but the suite was ten stories above the ground.

We all gasped and pleaded, which only encouraged the bad kid in Bill. "Look!" he crowed. "Ten fingers." He took two fingers off the sill. "Eight fingers!" He was hanging by just two fingers— "Hey, Rosie, lookit!"—when I decided something had to be done. "Let's get out of here," I said to the others. "Come into my suite, and be quiet, and we'll put the lights out as though we'd all gone to bed. If we don't pay attention to him, he'll stop this nonsense."

We crossed the hall, and were sitting in my living room, in the dark, when all of a sudden a figure streaked through the place, opened a window, and swung out. Bill had gone down to the lobby, tipped the bellboy to open up my back door, and now he was hanging from my window ledge.

He could have fallen ten flights to a sidewalk; miraculously, he didn't. He was strong as an ox, stubborn as a donkey, and luckier than anything.

Nineteen fifty-five was my year for attracting natural disasters.

Having seen the wreckage caused by tornadoes, I worked for Kansas Disaster Relief, and because of this, a promenade in Udall, Kansas, was renamed Rosalind Russell Avenue.

It took a bunch of cyclones to get my name on a street in Kansas, so I ought to have had a premonition when my hometown of Waterbury, Connecticut, said it was going to rename a theatre after me. I should have run like a thief, told them I'd sue, and suggested that a Sarah Siddons Theatre would have a pleasant sound.

But no, I was flattered. Waterbury authorities explained that I was the only motion picture star to have a theatre named for her (I don't know whether they meant in Waterbury or in the United States or in the entire world, but how could such a declaration not go to a girl's head?), and asked if I wouldn't show up for the reopening of the Rosalind Russell State Theatre on August 18th.

I showed up, and the event turned into the biggest cataclysm that ever happened. There was a flood. Before the rains came, I rode in a parade in a white satin dress that was all beaded, with a matching little thing that sat on my head, being Princess Grace all over the joint, and there was a drum and fife corps—that's very big in Connecticut; they always wear the tricorne hats—and when the manager of the theatre on East Main Street greeted me she was blind drunk, and there was a big dinner at the great snob Waterbury Club, and my brother had to make a speech, and everything was to be televised—crews had been there for a week, setting up cameras all over the Waterbury green—and then the storms washed everything away. (The bridges were washed out, and the railroad was washed out; there has been no train service whatsoever between New York and Waterbury since.) That night was absolute disaster. Fifty-five people died right in the town.

In the midst of the nightmare, I was sitting on the stage at the theatre, and I looked out into the audience, and there sat Annie Dorgan, with her red, red cheeks and her hennaed hair and a big orange hat. I ran off the stage, down the steps, through the crowd, crying, "Annie, Annie, it's Roz," as though she didn't know me, and we hung on each other's necks, Annie crooning, "Oh, God love ya."

I left town—I was supposed to do the *Ed Sullivan Show* the next day—with Hazel and a driver in a rented car. I directed the driver—"Go up this hill, go down that lane, I know this town"—because I realized if we could get to New Haven, we could get from there to New York. There was no hope of driving along the Naugatuck Valley toward Bridgeport; the Naugatuck River had overflowed. It was a terrible night, and I've never been to Waterbury since. (When the town had its tercentennial—three hundred years—I did a TV spot welcoming everybody to the theatre and telling them I hoped they'd enjoy the performance that night, but there was no way anyone could have got me back there in the flesh.)

Still, I'd proved I could survive floods and tornadoes. I was ready to tackle *Auntie Mame.*

Mame

PATRICK DENNIS, whose real name was Edward Everett Tanner, had sent his novel *Auntie Mame* to about twenty publishers before he got a nibble. He'd ship it off, it would be rejected, he'd get it back and send it out again. I'd never have had his tenacity; one of those rejection slips, or whatever you get, and I'd have said that's the end of that, and thrown both slip and manuscript into the wastebasket. But Patrick persisted, and he prevailed. Finally the book was sent to a man named Julian Muller (at Vanguard), who liked it, and he went to work with Patrick. It was Mr. Muller who suggested those *Reader's Digest*-style chapter headings.

As I said earlier on, I got the book in galley proofs, and was struck by Mame's resemblance to the Duchess. Eventually Bobby Fryer asked me if I'd play her on stage, and I didn't hesitate, even though there was no script extant. Freddie and I were on our way to Europe, but we stopped in New York long enough for me to sign a contract, and then we sailed on one of the *Queens*. The deck of that ship was a garden of those books. (*Auntie Mame* was a great hospital book, a great vacation book.) I used to walk along, and stop beside readers tucked into steamer chairs and ask if I could speak to them. Then I'd inquire about Mame. Everybody said the same thing. "Oh, I know a woman just like this." Or, "I have a cousin," or "There's a woman down the street from me who wears these crazy clothes and a lot of beads." They all seemed to have enormous enthusiasm for this kind of woman. I'd ask them why, and they'd say, "Well, she's just as good without money as she is with money."

If I'd needed further convincing that Mame would be a crowd-pleaser, I was getting it from perfect strangers with no idea that I had an ax to grind.

I was heavily involved in the play version of *Auntie Mame*

right from the start. I wanted to underwrite the whole show, but the producing team of Fryer and Carr had recently floated a disaster *(Lost Horizon)* and they said they'd get hell from their big investors if these investors weren't allowed to buy into *Auntie Mame.* Even so, I managed to purchase a good many shares. I'd learned about the benefits of ownership from *Wonderful Town.* In *Wonderful Town,* I took a lot of money, all salary, and most of it went to Uncle Sam. This time I was willing to settle for less salary, but I wanted a piece of the action.

After that, I put my mouth where my money was. I even picked the director. I didn't know Morton Da Costa—customarily called Tec—from a hot rock, but when I came out of the theatre after seeing *No Time for Sergeants,* I turned to Bobby Fryer. "What's the name of the guy who did this?"

"Morton Da Costa," said Bobby.

"That's the director I want," I said.

Bobby was startled. "Roz, you didn't even laugh—"

"I don't like toilet jokes," I said. "The toilet seats coming up eight times, that's just not my humor. But this guy took a book [*No Time for Sergeants* had also been a novel] and made it play on the stage."

Da Costa had previously directed *Plain and Fancy,* which I'd seen too. "He's knocking at the door," I told Bobby. "He's had a couple of nice hits, now he's ready for a smash, a real smash, and he'll be eager to work."

Never have I been more clever. Tec has enormous talent, enormous flair. He came to Beverly Hills, and we spent nine hours together, talking and eating—we went through two meals, lunch and dinner, without noticing how the time was passing—while we tried to decide on a writer for our script. We had grandiose notions, starting with Noël Coward, but Noël wasn't looking for assignments, and Proust was dead. Finally I said, "Now, who's really going to write this?"

Tec grinned. "You and I are," he said.

"Well," I said, "if you're willing to put in the time, we'll give it a go."

I don't mean to take anything away from Jerry Lawrence and Robert Lee. They gave us a structure, did the basic play-making, wrote the hunt, which was hilarious. But every single day Tec Da Costa and I sat at the bar off my living room and turned out material, which Tec would then take down to submit to Lawrence and Lee at the beach where they were working. I made a pact with Tec that he was never to mention my name to Lawrence and Lee. "No writer can take advice from an actress," I said, "but they'll take anything from a director."

One of my sources of treasure was Freddie's Aunt Tilde. Aunt Tilde is eccentric, not like Mame, but a bit of a dingaling all the same. She was forever sending me magazine and newspaper articles, which I'd read when I couldn't sleep. I'd pull out a bunch of them at two o'clock in the morning and find myself laughing. She'd mailed me a picture of a goblet with a flame coming out of the top—I thought it was a drink, though come to find out, after a second or third look, I realized it was an ad for a gas company—and I used that picture as a model for the flaming drinks in the play.

Aunt Tilde also sent me a picture of a woman looking over her shoulder, with a dress cut down to her coccyx and a rose on her behind. "This would be wonderful on you," Aunt Tilde had scrawled across the picture. I used a dress like that when Mame was in mourning. There she was, crying, draped in a black veil, and then she turned around to the audience, and she had a totally bare back and a rose on her behind.

I stole from everywhere. Once, in Connecticut, my brother-in-law Chet La Roche asked if he couldn't fix me a martini. "I'll make it for you like they do at the Yale Club," he said.

"What do they do at the Yale Club?" I said.

"Rinse the glass with vermouth, throw the vermouth out and throw the gin in," he told me.

That's what we had the little boy do in the play, when he mixed the cocktail for the banker. (The business only works, incidentally, when the child is very young. I wanted Jan Handzlik in the film because he was a darling, and I loved him and we'd done the play together, but he was too old by the time we made the movie. They dyed his hair, and rather than seeming innocent, he seemed precocious, as though he knew just what he was doing. There's a vast difference between a nine-year-old boy and a twelve-year-old.)

People thought all these bits were straight out of the novel, but they weren't. In fact, people would come backstage and say we'd got every page of the book into the play, though, in fact, we'd left out masses of it.

I virtually removed myself from the second act. (This astonished theatre pros. After a preview, Jerry Robbins was half admiring, half open-mouthed. "Only you would do that," he said.) I didn't want the second act. "Somebody else has to carry it," I said to Tec. "Nobody is funny enough to enthrall an audience for two and a half hours. Jack Benny is not that funny, and certainly I am not."

We discussed various broad comedic shoulders available to us, and finally decided on Gooch—the mousy secretary who winds up soused and pregnant—to bear the burden. But before you nominate me for sanctification, let me tell the entire truth. "Gooch will carry the second act," I said, "but I'll take the last scene; I'm not giving that away."

There are a couple of theatre lessons it's good to learn at the beginning of your career. One is: never be caught in dead wood. Another is: don't be a hog. Let 'em say, "Where is she? When's she coming back?"

There was a place in the second act where Gooch told her troubles. Once we got into rehearsal, everything stopped when this recitation began. It just wasn't playing. Finally I went to Tec. "The scene is junk," I said. "We can tell that story in a crossover."

Tec pointed out that to get a good crossover in a musical—where something is happening down in front of the curtain while the stagehands are shifting the scenery behind the curtain—takes a certain amount of genius.

"Well, Jerry Robbins is excellent at crossovers," I said.

"Jerry Robbins is excellent at everything," said Tec, but he agreed that we would try to help Gooch out of her morass.

We sent her—wonderfully played by Peggy Cass—across the stage, talking to the Japanese houseboy, Ito. I gave her a black fox stole—"Just drag that," I said—and Peggy took it and started walking and talking about how O'Bannion had seduced and abandoned her, and she had to find Mame, and my fur piece was hanging behind her, and Ito was following the fur piece, nodding. Audiences screamed with laughter.

The crossover also moved the show on to the next scene.

After every out-of-town performance, Tec came to my apartment in whatever hotel we were in, in whatever city, and he'd type, and I'd dictate, and we'd both yell. "That stinks," he'd say about one of my lines, "but it gives me an idea." We got along famously; we could insult each other and it never bothered either of us. We kept working until one night in Washington when he came to my dressing room and told me he'd frozen the show.

"You have no right to do that," I said. (A director has every right to do that, but I was in there fighting.)

"Roz," he said, "we've *got* to freeze it."

Freezing, for those who don't know, means setting a show, no more changes in lines or business, this is the way it's going to be, so you can all relax and learn it. "Well, look at Gooch," I said. "She's been getting terrific laughs, and now she's got that rotten finish, sitting in a chair reading letters from O'Banion. We gotta figure out a better ending for her."

We finally put Gooch on the stairs and had her lean back so the audience could see her big belly. It got a big belly laugh. (Sorry, that was irresistible.)

I enjoy working on details; for me it isn't drudgery, but pleasure. The trouble was, I'd got so engrossed in the overall show, I ran down the stairs on that opening night of *Auntie Mame* and realized I'd scarcely bothered about my own part. All the time I'd worked with Tec, my concentration had been on other things, because if everybody isn't good, if somebody's dragging the play down every other line, if the material isn't there, you're in trouble. Then, with the audience already out there waiting, I thought, I don't know what I'm doing. I knew where I was going, yes, but I really was not as good in *Auntie Mame* on opening night as I had been in *Wonderful Town*. (During *Wonderful Town* rehearsals, while experts were sweating over the ballet, the dance steps, those various pieces of the production, I'd been doing my own homework. It makes a difference.)

Still, what the audience didn't know didn't hurt them. *Auntie Mame* moved. Everything—the people, the words, the scenery (the sets by Oliver Smith were built on platforms that rolled in and out) —moved. I had an entrance down a narrow, curving staircase, and I literally never touched the steps, just kind of flew, and I was down. Months into the run, I met an old man in the Colony restaurant who said he'd seen the play eight times. "Thank you," I said, "so glad you've enjoyed it," and he said, "Oh, I don't come to see the play, I come to see you running up and down those stairs."

Although I'd based my playing of Mame on the Duchess, the character was really more biting, more crispy than my sister, yet she didn't turn anyone off. People loved her. To this day, when I walk in the streets of New York, truckdrivers lean out of their windows and yell, "Hello, Mame!"

I stayed in the show a year and a half. Lance went from Buckley to Hotchkiss (way to hell and gone up in New York State), Freddie went from *The Pajama Game* to *Damn Yankees,* but I stayed at the Broadhurst Theatre. Sometimes I was the only one of the original company who did. It's rough when you get into the second winter of a hit show; everybody gets the flu. One night I went in— every understudy but mine had been on, and tonight even the understudies were out—and Benny Stein, the general manager, told me we couldn't take the curtain up. "We don't have enough actors to do the play."

A second company, starring Connie Bennett, was getting ready to go on the road, and they were rehearsing someplace down in Greenwich Village. "Can't you get hold of those people and tell 'em to get in a taxi and come up here?" I said.

"We don't have any clothes," Benny said.

I said that didn't matter. "Just tell 'em to come up here."

We held the curtain, and a batch of actors came up, the ones who played O'Banion and the snob girl and a few others, and that was one wild performance. If the second cast had been rehearsing for any length of time, we'd have been all right, but they'd just begun, and they didn't have the foggiest notion of what they were doing. As they came on, I'd say, "Hello, dear, why don't you sit right there in that little chair? And you, you sit on the couch, dear . . ." I threw in a few extra "Ooh, how mahvelous-es," and filled in all the other parts, and kept talking.

That second *Auntie Mame* winter I had the flu three times myself, took antibiotics like popcorn, and kept going. Even the little boy, Jan, got sick; we had to use two different understudies for him.

When we'd started doing the show, Jan dressed in the basement. Those basements aren't too hot. Or sometimes they're plenty hot. He'd run around down there in his costume, and by the time he came up to go onstage, he'd be filthy. Finally I had him report to me in my dressing room. I gave him his own little area, and a square piece of soap and his own soap dish and his own nailbrush. Also, the language he heard around me was better than he'd been hearing in the basement. (We were a big cast, almost as big as a musical, and in big casts, actors and stagehands tend to sit around basements playing cards and expressing themselves in colorful fashion.)

I worried about Jan. Once in a while I'd ask him what he'd had for dinner, and he'd tell me a strawberry ice cream soda. His mother was an out-of-work singer, and I talked to Freddie, who got her a job in the chorus of *Damn Yankees*. Before that, Jan used to travel home to New Jersey by himself. It had me crazy. I'd drive him to the boat, and watch him go, with my heart in my mouth. "It's only three blocks, and when I get off the ferry, I run all the way," he'd tell me, trying to be reassuring. His mother later died, and his grandparents finished bringing him up. It's strange to think he's a grown man —over thirty years old—now.

One Sunday night, when we were dark, I was invited to dinner by Pat Dennis. Dennis (or Tanner) wasn't poor to begin with, he came from a wealthy Chicago family, and of course his income had been augmented by *Auntie Mame*, so I wasn't surprised to find that his town house on East 82nd Street was very chic. There were two Tanner children, lovely children, a boy and a girl (they'll be grown now, too), and Mrs. Tanner, and just three guests besides me—Anita Loos, who wrote *Gentlemen Prefer Blondes*, and one other man and his wife.

The living room was on the ground floor; the kitchen and dining area upstairs. "Come in and have a drink and some hors d'oeuvres," Patrick had said, greeting his company at the front door, but we'd no sooner sat down and started studying the canapé tray than a very loud voice came pealing down from an overhanging balcony. "Dinner is served!" shouted a huge black woman in an apparent fury.

Embarrassed for the Tanners, I abandoned the hors d'oeuvres and got to my feet. "This way, Patrick?"

"Yes," he said, "right this way, please."

We all filed upstairs and sat down again. Now a second black woman appeared, and these two maids, or waitresses or whatever they were, served dinner. Meticulously, but wrong. The forks were on the right, the knives on the left. Surreptitiously, I shifted my silverware, dragging it across my lap so nobody would see me doing it. Glasses were in the wrong place, and the women served us from the wrong side. I felt so sorry for the Tanners, I didn't know what to do. Obviously, they were trying to put on the dog for me, and they'd hired this help for the occasion and it wasn't working out well.

The more mistakes were made, the more I talked and the faster I talked. Nervously, I introduced subject after subject, trying to cover the gaffes, hoping I was reassuring my host and hostess, hoping they could tell this kind of thing didn't bother me.

The servants came and went, botching everything under their hands. I remember thinking, Oh, this tall one is really ridiculous, but that's help today, and what can you do? I suppose the Tanners are paying twenty-five or thirty or thirty-five dollars for this night, so I'll just get through it.

The food was perfectly good—the Tanners had their own cook in the kitchen—but as these maids spilled gravy on the table-cloth, the floor and a couple of the guests, my misery became acute. Why hadn't our hosts just put out some comestibles, buffet style, and let us help ourselves? The hell with all this chi-chi and two maids who couldn't have served Alpo to a hound unless the dog had opened the can himself. But neither Patrick nor his wife ever looked up as if to acknowledge that they'd made a mistake, and if they were determined to ignore the mess, I knew I had to ignore it too.

The horrendous meal over, we all went back down to the living room. Demitasse was poured. I accepted mine and went over and sat on a love seat near the fireplace. All of a sudden, the tall maid came over and plunked down next to me with her coffee cup. She was holding her pinkie finger high and sipping her espresso with avidity.

Again I didn't know what to do. I wanted to die for my host and hostess. Would it be better for me to move, or just to ignore this whole development? I launched into a new cascade of talk. I got worse and worse and phonier and phonier, and in the middle of my perora-tion, everybody burst out laughing.

The maid sitting beside me was Cris Alexander. He was an actor and an artist who was six feet two inches tall. (I knew him well; he'd painted Lance's picture.) He also had blue eyes, which should have clued me that something was amiss, except that I'd resolutely refrained from staring at him while he'd made all those mistakes. He and Patrick had gone to Bloomingdale's and bought lady's shoes and a wig and a maid's uniform, and Cris had made up black, just to play this joke on me. Even when he sat down beside me, I didn't catch on. I never would have caught on, either.

And they did it to me on my night off.

Sunday night was the only time I ever went out. I'd discovered that if I stayed up Saturday night, after playing two shows, I was so shot down Sunday, I couldn't enjoy myself; but if I went home Saturday night and rested Sunday, I could really have a nice Sunday evening. At least I could dine at nine, rather than six. Usually, Freddie and I would walk over to Voisin, at 63rd and Park Avenue, to dine, and afterward we'd stroll on to El Morocco. There was nothing going on at Morocco; Sunday was quiet. Ethel Merman might be there, and we'd sit and talk—she was married to Bob Six at the time, and working in a show called *Happy Hunting*, right next door to *Auntie Mame*. Freddie and I would have a dance, coffee, and maybe a liqueur, and end the evening by walking home to the Pierre.

Lehman Engel, who had been musical conductor of *Wonderful Town*, was conducting the Merman show, and he often used to stop by my dressing room in the Broadhurst to say hello. He was a very cheerful, upbeat man, and he kept asking me to let him give a little after-theatre supper so I could meet Dame Sybil Thorndyke, the English actress.

Week after week I refused. "You know I don't go out during the week—"

"But Dame Sybil is a violent fan of yours," Lehman said. "She adores you, she's seen the play."

Finally I got self-conscious about making such a big deal of it. "All right," I said, "a week from Thursday."

A week from Thursday came. I took off my theatrical makeup, put on fresh street makeup. I got myself decked out, told Freddie we were going to Lehman's—briefly—just to meet Dame Sybil, out of our great admiration and respect for her.

We got to Lehman's apartment building, and I took the stairs while Freddie rode the elevator, which was a very tiny one. Damning my claustrophobia and huffing and puffing all the way up four flights,

I arrived at Lehman's party. The great actress—she was elderly even then, though she only died in 1976—was sitting there. She looked like a queen on a throne, and I almost genuflected. "Dame Sybil," I said, "how wonderful to meet you, this is a great honor and a privilege."

Allowing me to take her hand, Dame Sybil went into a disquisition on how much she loved me, what a superb actress I was, how many weeks she'd been looking forward to this moment, how I'd given one of the great performances of the season, as a matter of fact, of all time. She ended by saying, "You are absolutely fabulous in *Orpheus Descending!*"

She had the wrong actress.

Here I was in the biggest hit in New York—*Orpheus Descending* was *not* the biggest hit—and she didn't know who I was. I gave Lehman Engel a look that should have killed him. I laugh about it now, but I didn't laugh then. If I'd had a snake, I'd have hurled it at Dame Sybil's neck.

(The mis-identification that happens every now and then is a great ego-leveler. I came out of the stage door at *Wonderful Town* one night, and was signing autographs—there was always a nice friendly crowd waiting—and was rejected by a woman who looked at my signature and said, "That isn't what I wanted."

"Why not?" I said.

"I wanted *Jane* Russell," she told me, "the one with the big . . ."

Well, yes.

And once, years earlier, at a hotel cocktail party given by Metro to sell one of my pictures, I talked to a white-haired woman who said she'd been surprised to be asked to this gathering but that she'd been glad to come. In order to make conversation, I ruminated on the weather. "There's a tremendous difference in climate between here and the West Coast. I always try to remember that one should bring clothes to keep oneself warm here." Now, since the party invitations had gone out asking the guests to come meet Miss Rosalind Russell, I'd assumed this woman knew whom she was talking to, but after a while she said, "You live on the West Coast?" "Yes," I said, "it's my home now." "Well," she said, "what store do you work in?"

"I. Magnin," I said, without batting an eye.

She nodded. "I knew you were connected with clothes."
Keeps you humble. Makes you mad.)

I'd have stayed on Broadway with *Auntie Mame* forever, but I had to leave to make the film version; that was part of our deal with Warner's. Afterward, when *Mame* was turned into a musical, the producers came to see me, and we talked a long time, but I said no. "It's not for me any more. I've done it, I have to move along."

Angela Lansbury got the part; she worked like a dog, and I've heard she was fine. I believe it, she's a good actress, but I didn't go to see her. I never look back, just forward. Turn the page. Go on.

1958-1968: A Mixed Bag

Nineteen fifty-eight started out well, with the making of the *Auntie Mame* movie, but the summer brought sadness. Carl Brisson was dying in Denmark, and even as Freddie, Lance and I packed to go to him, my own mother lay ill.

I told Mary Jane I was unhappy about leaving.

"Don't be unhappy, Roz," Mary Jane said. "Mother doesn't recognize any of us. And she's comfortable, she has wonderful care, nurses around the clock, there's nothing we can do that isn't being done."

On August the eleventh, while I was still in Copenhagen, my mother died. She was eighty-three years old. My brother James telephoned to tell me not to come home. "Stay with Freddie, because you can help him, you can help his mother."

I stayed. I found an English priest in a Danish Catholic church, and asked if I could have a memorial service for my mother. The priest said a mass in English, at the same time they were holding my mother's funeral in the United States. She'd been such an active, funny woman that it was right for her to go when her life had become meaningless to her. But it was hard for me. I adored my mother, and I've always had a little nagging pain because I wasn't there to say goodbye.

In 1959 my foot and hand prints were embedded in concrete in the forecourt of Grauman's Chinese Theatre, in recognition of my "contributions to the motion picture industry." It had taken me twenty-five years to get there.

New challenges came with the early sixties. (This is beginning to sound like a *March of Time* short subject.) I did a bunch of movies that had first been Broadway plays. I was trying to get away from the image of Mame. (Even in all those career-women pictures I'd been

Mame, so when I finally played her, it was nothing new to me, she was the same character, only a bit more exaggerated and with a little boy instead of a leading man for a foil.)

A lot of people thought I was making a big mistake, abandoning a sure winner. "You're nuts," Bob Hope told me. "What's wrong with playing Mame? I play myself. I go out there and make those bum jokes . . ."

"I want to use other muscles," I said. "I'm tired of 'Oooh, dahling!' "

My muscles were put to the test when Jack Warner asked me to play the lead in *A Majority of One*.

"You've been drinking," I said. "What would I be doing playing this Jewish lady from Brooklyn? I'm a little Irish girl from Waterbury, Connecticut. Use Gertrude Berg, it's her part—"

"We'll never use Gertrude Berg," said Warner. "She made a picture over at Paramount years ago, and it was a disaster."

"But that has nothing to do with this," I said. "You'd be crazy to put me in that part, and I'd be crazy to take it."

Jack Warner knew how to make an offer irresistible. "Would you play it with Sir Alec Guinness?"

"Well, that's another cup of chicken soup," I said. "I'll think about that little item."

I reached Guinness by telephone at the Haymarket Theatre in London. He was starring in a play about Lawrence of Arabia, called *Ross*.

I asked if he might really be coming to America to play the Japanese gentleman Mr. Asano.

"I want the dollars," he said, "so if you'll do it, I'll do it."

"I want to work with you," I said, "so if you'll do it, I'll do it."

Warner Brothers gave Guinness a trip to Japan, where he stayed for ten days studying manners and mannerisms, and then he came to Hollywood, and Wardrobe did him up in a Japanese outfit and Makeup pulled his blue eyes way back in a slant, and he still made a pretty funny-looking Japanese.

It was enthralling to see him in action. He worked like a precision watch. If he did a scene twenty times, he'd be the same twenty times. He admitted that he practiced in front of a mirror. His style, slightly peculiar, rather remote, totally cerebral, fascinated me.

After that, Jack Warner hired me again, this time to play Rose, the mother in *Gypsy*. Why hadn't Ethel Merman been cast in the movie role, after she'd been such a great Rose on the stage? It was the Gertrude Berg story all over again. Merman had starred in the movie version of her musical *Call Me Madam*, and the results hadn't come up to the producer's expectations. I felt she should have got the part in *Gypsy*, it belonged to her. But I'd learned from Myrna Loy, early on: "Grab 'em if they come up."

At first I was only to act the part; Rose's singing was dubbed by a professional with a big trained voice. When I heard it, I got sick. "It isn't me," I said. "I'm bad, but I can't stand to hear that. Everybody knows I don't sing operatically, it throws the balance off."

Warner Brothers agreed and rescored the picture, and I sang my own part. People still say I didn't, but that's Roz, and nobody else, as Rose on the soundtrack of *Gypsy*. (People also say that Freddie went around buying up other actresses' hits in order to provide his wife with starring vehicles. That's nonsense. It would have been a nice husbandly act if he'd done it, but he hadn't. The facts about *Gypsy* and *A Majority of One* are as I've stated them, and nobody's ever accused me of being married to Jack Warner. I did star in the movie of *Five-Finger Exercise*, which Freddie produced in 1962, but that was because he'd originally brought the Peter Shaffer play to Broadway. When nobody else wanted to buy it for pictures, Freddie bought it outright and we filmed it for our independent company at Columbia.)

In 1964 the *Harvard Lampoon* named me Woman of the Year. I went to Harvard to receive my award—a chamber pot—and looked out at the sea of young men and said, "Boys, when I think that you could have invited some cute young thing, I don't know what I'm doing here, unless you all miss your mothers." The boys loved that.

In 1966 I was voted into the fashion Hall of Fame, and *I* loved *that*. It struck me as hilarious, because the first time I ever made the Best Dressed List (three times on the list and you're in the Hall of Fame) I was pregnant, and my style left something to be desired.

In later (less pregnant) years I suppose I did get more interested in clothes. I started taking Galanos clothes from Freddie, rather than jewelry, after we were robbed in the Pierre Hotel.

I've mentioned that when my father went abroad to check up

on his younger brother, who was studying medicine in Vienna, he always brought a pretty bauble home to my mother. After Mother passed away, her jewelry was divided among her daughters. The handsomest piece I inherited was a diamond sunburst Dad had given Mother for an engagement present—it wasn't large but the stones were beautifully matched, and everybody who saw it admired it.

Well, Freddie and I were about to take off on one of our transatlantic jaunts, and I decided to carry all of Mother's bits and pieces with me. I would go to Bulgari, on Capri, and have everything reset. I didn't know exactly what I wanted done, so I threw everything I owned—clips, dinner rings, a diamond watch, little brooches with sapphires in them, even things which hadn't belonged to Mother, stuff I'd collected—into a bag and brought it East from California.

Before we sailed we were going to spend a few days in our apartment at the Pierre. The night of the robbery Mary Jane and her husband, Ken, and Freddie and I were going to the theatre to see *How to Succeed in Business*, and I tried to make Mary Jane borrow some earrings to wear the following night. (Elsie Woodward, who's always referred to as "the grande dame of New York society" was giving a farewell party for Freddie and me, and she'd invited the Duke and Duchess of Windsor, who were staying at the Waldorf Towers, and there was going to be a nice dinner dance, and Mary Jane was invited.) I had diamond earrings shaped like snowdrops, perfect for a fancy bash. "They'd be beautiful with your new dress," I said.

Mary Jane said no, she didn't care to be responsible for the snowdrops, but she would borrow a more modest pair of earrings, gold with a few diamonds in them. Thank heaven, she did; I still have those, anyway, along with one good bracelet I was wearing when we left for the theatre.

But I'm getting ahead of my story. Freddie and I came home from *How to Succeed,* and there was a box of flowers balanced across the arms of a chair in our living room. I opened the box, and the flowers were dead. "They've been around for a week," Freddie said, puzzled.

I love flowers, so I took them into the bathroom and broke the stems and laid them in the tub to try to revive them. After that I went to a bureau to put away the jewelry I'd been wearing, and as soon as I opened the top drawer, I knew somebody had been in there.

By now Freddie was in his pajamas and already in bed, reading.

"Freddie," I said, "I've been robbed."

"Stop your nonsense," said Freddie. "Get undressed and come to bed and stop fussing with those flowers. I've got a big day tomorrow, and there's Elsie's party tomorrow night—"

"No," I said. "I've been robbed."

He put down his book. "Are you serious?"

I said yes. "I think my jewelry's gone."

"Call Blanche," Freddie said.

"I hate to get her up."

"You have to," he said.

Again I checked through the two top drawers. My gloves were all over the place, scarfs and handkerchiefs disarranged, and I knew Blanche always put things away neatly. I rang her room, and she answered, her voice sleepy.

"Did you take the jewel box downstairs?" I said.

She said, "No, I didn't, Miss R.," and three seconds later she was in our apartment. I don't know how she got dressed that fast.

We called the house detective. We'd been renting this apartment at the Pierre for twenty years, but when the detective showed up, we'd never seen him before. He was new; he'd only been on the job about three months.

"I've been robbed," I told him.

"What of?" said he.

"Well, my jewel box is gone," I said, "and in it was everything I owned except this bracelet and these earrings I had on tonight."

"Well, now," said the detective, "let's just take it easy."

"About what?" I said.

"Let's just stop and think," he said. "You sure you didn't leave your jewel box in Hollywood?"

"Yes, I'm sure," I said. "I gave my sister some earrings tonight, and we were going through all the jewelry. I'm positive of that."

He thought for a few seconds. "Well, now," he said again, "let me make another suggestion to you."

"What is that?" I said.

Freddie, listening intently, was beginning to boil. I could see the color rising in his neck.

"Do you know Hedy Lamarr?" asked the detective.

I said yes, I knew Hedy Lamarr. "What's that got to do with it?"

"Well, now," he said, "you know she claimed she was robbed out on Long Island a few weeks ago, do you remember that?"

"Yes," I said.

"And then she came back to New York," he went on, "and there was her jewelry in her apartment in New York. Couldn't that have happened to you?"

Freddie came to sudden, rude life. "One more crack out of you," he told the surprised security officer, "and I'm going to toss you right out of this thirty-eighth-floor window."

The man backed off, edging toward the door. Freddie went after him. "You see that bracelet my wife had on, the one she was showing you? That's what her box was filled with—jewelry like that!"

(It wasn't quite true. I had had one other fabulous bracelet, made for me by David Webb out of my wedding earrings and some other earrings. But what grieved me most was losing my mother's things. Nothing was insured, either; I'd been going to have the pieces insured after they'd been reset.)

The detective, by now a bit wary of Freddie, allowed that we ought to call the police, which we did. A couple of detectives from the Seventeenth Precinct came over. They looked exactly like detectives in the movies. They wore grey felt hats and thick-soled shoes, and one of them was fractured, bombed half out of his mind.

"Wha's missin' here?" he said. "If's over fifty thousan' dollars, we gotta call 'ee FBI."

We discussed the value of my jewelry, and the FBI was called.

The more sober of the two newcomers spotted the empty flower box and asked me what time the flowers had arrived.

"They were here when we came home," I said.

"Ah," he said, like Peter Sellers playing Inspector Clouseau, "who let that box in?"

"I assure you I didn't," I said.

The detectives questioned people on the desk downstairs (they didn't know anything about the flower box) and bellboys (they didn't know anything about the flower box), and then they stared at the dead flowers in the bathtub and talked about how foolish it was for the FBI to be brought in. "It's the biggest ring of master jewel thieves in the world works these hotels," confided one of New York's finest. "By six o'clock in the morning all your stones will have been punched out. They just throw the gold away, keep the loose stones—and you can't prove anything with loose stones."

The cops were right. The thieves weren't caught, and I've never since had any interest in jewelry. I just lost it when I lost my mother's things.

Now, at Christmas, Freddie gives me a lemon tree for the garden, or a dress. I get an outfit for our anniversary and a coat on my birthday. Freddie thinks he's ahead because even Jimmy Galanos' costumes don't cost as much as emeralds and rubies.

I have a pretty good collection of Galanos' clothes. If he makes me a day dress, I always tell him to give me a big deep hem. Once he saw me in one of his creations that had been shortened to suit the mode of the moment, and he burst out laughing. "If that isn't the funniest thing! Is that a twelve-inch hem you've got there? Why don't you make a bandeau out of it, or something."

"No, no," I said. "It'll go down again. They go up, they go down, they go over . . ."

I've given away a lot of clothes (plenty of friends get a crack at my Galanos'), but it always tickles me to think I'm in that Best Dressed Hall of Fame, because I can't bear to shop and only do it twice a year. And if I ask for brown suede pumps, the salesman had better not bring me black. I think shopping is barbaric—all those people pushing stuff on you that you don't want or need. Twice a year is enough. In the old days, when I had to travel, I'd buy three suits —that's a lot of suits—and two sweaters and three blouses, and I'd try to get a topcoat that would go with at least two of the suits, and then a fur coat if I was going to Europe in the winter. You kind of have to organize it. I like clothes, but I don't believe in devoting a great deal of time to them.

Today I think you can buy wonderful things and look attractive without spending a lot of money, but you have to stay very skinny to do it. The layered look, the bulky look, with scarfs hanging off you and shawls, the huge peasant skirts, those don't work if you're carrying any weight. You've got to be built like an unfed bird.

Despite my loathing of shopping, I used to do the wifely thing every Christmas and take care of Freddie's gift list for him. He'd be in the middle of production meetings or cutting a picture, and he'd say to me, "Now, I want you to get a little thought for So-and-So," and I'd go out and get some trinket and bring it home and show it to him, and he'd be horrified. "Oh, no, I have to give her at least a very nice handbag."

"A nice handbag," I'd say, "is seventy-five to one hundred and ten dollars, it's not a little thought."

"It's gotta be a handbag," he'd say.

"Well, then, tell me that at the beginning," I'd say. "Don't tell me it's just a little thought."

When I think of the pages of names he's pressed on me over the years, every one of them due for a "little thought."

One time it was a matter of hundreds of gifts; the list was so long it was ludicrous. I was at Saks in Beverly Hills, and I finally sent for Freddie's secretary to come down and help me. (He's a real entrepreneur, my husband, staffs on both coasts.) I'd been writing addresses on the gift cards, as well as the envelopes (I always do that because if the card falls on the floor and the store picks it up and finds a message which says, "Merry Christmas, Bill, and lots of love," the store has to wonder, "Bill who?"), so now I gave Freddie's secretary the envelopes I had left. "Here, you address these while I finish the cards."

I'd been at the job for so long, my hair was hanging in my eyes and I was half dead. After about an hour Freddie's secretary put down her pen. "I wouldn't go through this for anybody," she said. "How on earth do you do it?"

I was tired enough so I wanted to tell her she gave me a pain. Instead, I asked her a question. "How long have you been with Mr. Brisson?"

"Nine and a half years," she said.

"Let's see," I said, "Christmas is a week from Wednesday. I want to know how you'd feel, after nine and a half years, if Mr. Brisson walked in a week from Tuesday without something in his hand for you."

"I suppose I would be hurt," she said.

"Then address those envelopes," I said. "I don't want to hear another word about them."

I've had Christmas shopping. I can't do it any more.

And I can't—or at least I won't—smoke any more, either. I

put down cigarettes about ten years ago. I'd puffed like a chimney, though never in the morning (for some reason, I thought if I didn't start till afternoon, it wasn't so bad), and Mary Jane and Freddie swear I used to have two cigarettes going at a time. I'd ask Freddie for a light, and he'd say, "For the one in your hand or the one in your mouth, Roz?" But in 1967 Freddie made an appointment for me to go to a doctor about a sore throat, and after I'd been checked, the doctor told me I was coming along fine. "Just get a little extra rest." Then, as I was leaving, he looked up at me. "Oh, by the way," he said, "you'd add ten to twenty years to your life if you'd quit smoking."

He'd never seen me before, but he could tell. That's all he said. He turned back to whatever he was doing, and I walked out of the office and went down in the elevator, and when I got out into the street I passed a trash basket, opened my bag, took out a pack of cigarettes, threw them away, and never lit up again.

Which isn't to say I'm viceless. Ask the two guys I met in a hotel outside of Philadelphia. I'll bet they still think I'm a disgrace to church, country and American womanhood.

My encounter with these gentlemen was accidental. No sooner had I made it into the Fashion Hall of Fame than I was cast as the Mother Superior in a movie called *The Trouble with Angels,* where I got nothing to wear but a nun's habit.

We were shooting in the East, mostly in a school in a town called Ambler, about forty minutes from Philadelphia, so my brother James and my sister Mary Jane decided to come from Connecticut to visit.

Our company was living in the Hotel Marriott, and there were a couple of days when we worked in Philadelphia proper, near some of the famous public buildings. On those days I got into my nun's habit in my hotel room so that I could hop right out of the lobby into a company car and be driven to the Liberty Bell and play the scene without worrying about where I was going to find a changing room.

The night before Mary Jane and James arrived, I booked them rooms close to mine, stocked the rooms with magazines and bowls of daisies from a nearby florist, and surveyed my handiwork. Anything missing? Yes, indeed. Mary Jane and James would surely like to have a drink before dinner. I went out and bought liquor.

Next morning I dressed as a nun, put on my makeup base—

that's really all we wore as nuns, just a base—and being a little behind schedule, went tearing out of my room. I had to drop off the hooch, then make tracks for the limousine that would be waiting downstairs.

I put a bottle of Scotch in James' room, came out into the corridor, ran along for a bit, darted through another open door waving a pint of bourbon, and came face to face with two men in shirt sleeves sitting on a sofa having a discussion.

It was six A. M.

"Excuse me," I said, "pardon me, I'm so sorry." I fled, found the right room, dumped Mary Jane's bourbon, and when I came back into the hallway the two shirt-sleeved men were standing there watching me.

Somebody from the camera crew was holding the elevator and yelling, "Come on, come on," and I raced past those men, whose mouths stayed open even as the elevator doors closed behind me.

I went from playing a nun to playing a man-eater in *Oh Dad, Poor Dad, Mamma's Hung You in the Closet and I'm Feeling So Sad*, a picture which should have been great, but wasn't. After that I made *Rosie*, in which we tried to mix comedy and tragedy, and all we managed to do was confuse the audiences. I did a sequel *(Where Angels Go . . . Trouble Follows)* to the nun picture. The first film had been good; the second wasn't.

But by the close of 1968 more was coming to an end than a string of disappointing Rosalind Russell pictures. Bobby Kennedy and Martin Luther King, Jr., had been assassinated, the war in Vietnam continued to tear the country apart, My Lai cost many of us our innocence. More than ever I found myself being grateful for Freddie, for Lance, for the good hard work which had filled the forty years since I had appeared as Mrs. Cheyney on the stage of the American Academy.

Katherine Anne Porter once wrote that she agreed with E. M. Forster "that there are only two possibilities for any real order: in art and in religion. All political history is a vile mess, varying only in degrees of vileness from one epoch to another, and only the work of saints and artists gives us any reason to believe that the human race is worth belonging to."

She also wrote that while the voice of the individual artist might seem "perhaps of no more consequence than the whirring of a cricket in the grass," the arts survived the civilizations that produced them, and could not be destroyed because "they are what we find again when the ruins are cleared away."

I have been lucky enough to work in the arts—even though acting is more ephemeral than painting or poetry—and the voice you hear in this book is the whirring of one much-obliged cricket.

"Acting Is Standing Up Naked and Turning Around Very Slowly"

ONCE I'D DECIDED to go ahead with this book, Freddie hauled home from his office a load of letters, clippings, pictures, posters, memorabilia of my public life. I tried to wade through it all, as well as through the relics we've got stored in the garage, but I just couldn't do it.

(The reason we keep prizes, photographs, etc., in the garage is that I don't like them around the house. But last year I found my favorite trophy out there and brought it back to my bedroom. It wasn't won by me, it was won by Lance for being Best Newsboy in California one long-ago summer. It's the worst-looking thing, pure plastic, but it warms a mother's heart.)

I've always contended that a successful actor gets two things —service and a scrapbook. And the time comes when you don't get the service any more, when the headwaiters and the salesgirls no longer recognize you, so you wind up with the scrapbook as you sit in the rocking chair out at the actors' home.

But an actor, on his way through the world, also accrues opinions about his craft. (Jack Lemmon once asked me what I thought acting was. I said, "Acting is standing up naked and turning around very slowly.") So this is going to be a kind of nuts-and-bolts chapter for those readers who are curious to share a few of my observations, prejudices and convictions as they apply to my profession. Anything I've neglected to say before about working in Hollywood, I'll try to say here.

It's a cliché that film is the director's medium. It's a cliché because it's true. The director has total artistic control; he's the creator. That's why the minute a director has a success in New York, he starts thinking about Hollywood. Look at Michael Bennett. He had a smash hit with *A Chorus Line*, and he started packing his suitcases, he was on his way out here before the ink dried on the notices.

The theatre is equally exciting, but in the theatre, the writer is the creator and has the final word, while the director has to fight for the lighting, scream about the sets, practically make the costumes. Out here the director is king. You press a button and send for platoons of help. Set designers and builders arrive. The Wardrobe people come, dragging bolts of materials with them. Costume designers make sketches, and redo them at your whim. Seamstresses turn out gowns with ruffles, pleats, paillettes, and you can just sit there with your big fat cigar and say, "No, I think I'll have a few more of the blue sequins on that skirt." (Naturally, I'm talking about big-budget productions, not quickies made in the backyard by two kids from UCLA who have their grandma holding the microphone.)

A good director shoots his picture knowing exactly how he's going to cut it, splice it together. He tries to get his cameraman put on salary a couple of weeks before the shooting begins, as the sets are being built, so the two of them can come in before the cast and the rest of the crew and start planning.

It's duck soup to work for those guys who know what they're doing. But I've worked for plenty of the others. There are directors who shoot four hundred million feet of film (a busboy at McDonald's could come up with some kind of movie if he shot that much), do enormous numbers of retakes, have actors going through a scene thirty times. They can drive you crazy. "It doesn't look right, you standing at the table, go stand by the bar . . ."

They change everything around and around and around because they don't know what they're doing. And the actor is their victim.

But I'm oversimplifying. Despite what I said about artistic control, even a good director can turn out a bad film, because there are so many elements which have to be brought together. The amount of verbiage that goes on among the producer, the director, the set designer, the leading man is just incredible, and wreckage sometimes ensues. A director can win a battle and lose the war if he saps the confidence of the actor, who has to go out and give the performance.

In a movie you're dependent on the good sense of many specialists. Take *Auntie Mame*. It made money, won awards, pleased audiences. Even so, we had problems. Travis Banton, who had done the clothes for Broadway, died. Orry Kelly came on in a hurry and made wonderful new clothes, but the issue of the set was not so efficiently resolved.

I didn't see the set until we began shooting. Even if I'd come in sooner, I couldn't have changed much. I'd insisted that Tec Da Costa direct the picture, but he was new to film, didn't know anything about it, and the Beekman Place house he'd been presented with—and had innocently okayed—was atrocious. Instead of a narrow staircase down which Mame could fly, there were stairs perhaps twenty feet wide, and the Rockettes could have danced single file on the enormous coffee table.

This may not sound like a major mistake, but it's difficult to play comedy in a huge set. You lose the intimacy of the looks, the takes that get the giggles. Walking through a vast hall with thunder and lightning and shadows, that's for drama. Comedy needs brilliance, lighting that keeps lifting all the time, that's like changing keys every few bars in music.

Sometimes I think if I had it to do over again, I'd direct. I couldn't have made a worse job of it than some of the boobies I've labored for.

In a 1975 picture called *Hearts of the West*, a director tells some extras to "Keep it simple, but make me believe it." As far as I was concerned, that wasn't even caricature. I've had directors offer me nincompoop generalities, convinced they were useful. Once a director kept me and another actor going over and over a scene because he claimed we didn't have our lines right. "Hold it, hold it," he would cry. "Let's get the lines straight, start again." We'd start again, and he'd stop us again. "Now wait a minute, kids, let's take another crack at this . . ."

I finally went and peered at the director's script, and he'd been reading the wrong scene, a scene we'd shot four days earlier. He'd already viewed the rushes, but he didn't remember. My leading man was a famous performer, yet our director never managed to get his name right, and after a few days I had to practically sit on this actor to keep him from quitting the picture, the country, the business.

Have I worked for dopes? Yes, I have.

I worked for a dope who hired an actress whose method was to improvise, and who then explained to her that she wasn't going to be allowed to do it. She got even with him. In the two weeks before we started shooting, she gained twenty pounds and couldn't get into a single costume.

I've worked for countless dopes who didn't do their homework. (Doing your homework is a theatrical cliché right up there with film being the director's medium.) You get one of those guys who says, "Okay, we'll run through this now," and then you see him fussing with the pages, hurriedly scanning the lines we're about to shoot. "Oh, Roz," he begins, "uh, sit on the couch. And smoke a cigarette if you feel like it. And, Bob [or Sam, or Charlie], just wander the room if you feel like it."

The kind of direction that's no direction. The kind of director who has no idea what the characters are supposed to do, what the meaning of the particular scene is, or what has gone before that makes the playing of this scene inevitable.

I always resented their carelessness, yet these men who weren't prepared were the same ones who howled and took out their rage on the script girls when something went wrong.

In the old days certain directors drew their pay just for saying "Action!" and "Cut!" That was all. I don't think they could get away with it today. There's no question in my mind that the new directors are far better film-makers than the old ones, though some of the old ones, like Alfred Hitchcock, Billy Wilder, George Stevens, William Wyler (as well as Hawks and Cukor, about whom I've talked in earlier chapters), were total geniuses. As the industry grew, the need for manpower grew with it, and directors starting emerging from the cutting rooms and the prop departments. Nothing wrong with that. We got some wonderful talent, but we also got some dogs. Many a studio magnate's relative, who never should have been allowed behind a camera, was given a picture to direct.

Anita Loos, who goes back to the time of D.W. Griffith in Hollywood—she wrote the subtitles for his silent film *Intolerance*—is fierce in her judgments of MGM's first movie-makers, according to an interview she gave *Women's Wear Daily* sometime ago. "The directors were dunces," she said. "That they ever made anything good was due to Irving Thalberg. He handed them scripts that were practically foolproof. Most of the directors didn't know anything about human beings. Some of them didn't even have any common sense. One idiot insisted on spending thousands of dollars to rent a Stradivarius violin for an actress who didn't even know how to play."

I believe it.

I've known non-dopes who were dopes too, directors talented but short-sighted who, after one or two successful pictures, couldn't get their fat heads through the door. They'd turn down every new project that was offered because nothing was worthy of their talents. Vanity destroyed them. They forgot there would be next year, and the year after that, and that new geniuses come along every season, and that after a while nobody remembers your name.

I've been in movies where miscasting has caused disaster.

I've been in movies where lack of discipline has caused disaster.

I've been in movies where I worried because I didn't think we were working logically. I adored Dudley Nichols, yet it troubled me when we shot *Mourning Becomes Electra* that our set was in a huge mansion with no sign of any help, any servants. I wondered who came up with the lunch or the dinner. I thought that our isolation should have been explained, if only by the addition of a single line. Sometimes one line can do everything for you. You can say, "I hate blue," just throw it away, and then if you come on in the next scene in a blue dress, it has a meaning.

I've been in movies where my reading of the screenplay was incompatible with everybody else's. I thought *Oh Dad, Poor Dad, Mamma's Hung You in the Closet and I'm Feeling So Sad* was supposed to be a comedy, and by the time I learned we were going to do it as a tragedy, we were already in Jamaica, five thousand miles from home, and I've never walked off a set in my life. (I only called in sick that once, with *The Women*.) I still think I was right about *Oh Dad*. My clothes—designed by Jimmy Galanos, great wild outfits covered with feathers and brilliants that made me look like a predatory bird—were the only things the critics liked. I believe *Oh Dad* could have been a hit, but I can't prove it.

No matter what picture I'm doing, I try to have meetings with the director before we begin to work. *If* I can trap him. Directors are always saying, "I got a story conference, Roz, I can give you fifteen minutes." That isn't good enough. It's in those meetings that you learn if they really know the character you're going to play, have her clearly in mind. I ask them what kind of picture they want to make. I ask them what they want me to do. If they're good, you start kicking ideas around until you finally get into the bone of the story, the thing you're going to hang everything on. Getting that kind of help, that extra thing, is what counts.

Once we start shooting, I shut up and do what the director says. Somebody's got to hold the enterprise together, and to me, the director is always the boss. I do it his way, no matter how much I may disagree with him. I don't say this is the best way to behave; Brando is known for being difficult, yet when he insists on something, he's usually right. But I'm just too New England. On the set, I defer to the director. I've never had a fight, though I've seen plenty of them. All that pouting and the insults and the slamming of doors into the dressing rooms isn't my game. I don't understand how any woman does it; you come out of it a total wreck, and you haven't played the scene yet, and then you have to go on and not have a line in your face and keep your chins up and your stomach in. Anyway, I wouldn't know how to have one of those fits; I'd start to laugh.

I'm professional when I work. I remember doing a dramatic scene over at Warner Brothers. It was long, four pages of dialogue, and Warner's is a noisy lot because of its nearness to Lockheed Airport. We did forty, forty-five, forty-eight takes of that four-page scene, and I'd get right down to my last three lines—and a plane would go over. The producer came on the set and stood looking at me. He knew it wasn't my fault, but he was frantic. That was a rough day, but I've lived through a lot of them, and I've never lost my temper or started blaming the technicians. Hollywood has the best crews in the world, and you have to respect their skills.

The same way I try to confer with my directors (before the fact), I also try to confer with my fellow actors.

I've played with a lot of talented people. Robert Donat and Michael Redgrave were fine to do scenes with, they would relate to you. I've played with sex symbols and with intellectuals. (At the height of Errol Flynn's fame, in 1938, I learned I was to make a picture with him. He was so handsome, so romantic that I wondered if he would find me attractive. Not excessively, a fellow actor warned me. "On Errol's own Richter Scale, it's the French girls that rate 9.5.")

Clark Gable, Bill Powell, Cary Grant, Jimmy Stewart, Errol, Ronald Colman, Brian Aherne, Bill Holden, Alec Guinness, so many more. They were all good, and they were all nice.

And there are photographs of all of them in my garage. Along with stories about me and them which I've never read. It bores me to read about myself, and it's always upset me to look at myself on film. I never went to rushes except when I'd had a costume change, so I could make corrections. (If I had a big bow on my chest and it was too eye-catching, I'd see it and know I could pull it down smaller the next day without anybody's noticing.) Looking at rushes can really disturb you. I'm never satisfied with the work I've done, so it's always been better for me to stay away.

I'd have loved to make a Western, to play opposite Gary Cooper or John Wayne or Henry Fonda, but producers would never have dreamed of putting me with one of them. Producers think in limited terms, and they almost always saw me as a sophisticated Park Avenue creature. That was why I leaped to do *Picnic*, fought to make *Sister Kenny*, why I inclined toward character acting, where you could get ahold of something.

I say I've worked with good people, but I've come up against my share of stiffs too. When an actor won't relate to you, you try a million and one things to stimulate a response from him (or her). So much of your work is offscreen, in preparation. Say you're playing with an actor who doesn't know his script. You can tell immediately whether he's just dogging it or whether he's having a problem with the lines. Sometimes, inviting him into your dressing room, throwing everyone else out, giving him a cup of coffee, saying, "I'm having trouble with this scene, let's go over it, kick it around, see if we've got the right words here," puts the other person at ease. After a while he relaxes, and learns the scene with you. Sometimes you make little changes, and call the director and ask if he minds if you say so-and-so instead of such-and-such. This technique doesn't work with very nervous actors, but you try everything you can think of to get the job done right.

To me, the hard work in the film business is dealing with the personalities involved. When they say, "Camera!" that's easy, that's baby talk, but the other thing is hard. Mostly, though, your fate is in the hands of the director, so I get burned up when things don't go well and the movie flops, and everybody blames the actor. If the picture doesn't make money, they say you can't draw any more. They ought to look to the concept of the director, because there isn't much an actor can do in the hands of a guy determined to muck up the material.

I've often worked on the material, on movie scripts (as I did with the play version of *Auntie Mame*), but only once did I actually get screen credit as a writer. A young man named Larry Marcus and I had an idea for a story about a schoolteacher who's attacked by one of her students. We sold it to a man who later sold it to Universal, who made it with Esther Williams, who was very good in it. I had fun with Larry Marcus. So that we could concentrate without a thousand interruptions, I finally dragged him off to the Hotel Del Coronado, down at the beach, and sequestered him there until we'd finished our story. I knew we'd never get it done otherwise. We spent a week working, and I only let him go to his room to sleep. About five o'clock every afternoon I'd take him out on the beach and walk him up and down—it was winter—like he was a puppy. "This is all you get, Larry, this air," I'd say. "Breathe in a lot of it, because after dinner we start work again."

The picture was called *The Unguarded Moment.* I wish I could tell you it was *Gone With the Wind.*

Back when I left Metro, things had already started worsening for women; the good roles had begun to fall off. Greer Garson stayed on at the studio, but she didn't get any more quality parts, and Joan

Crawford finally had to quit and go to Warner's before she made *Mildred Pierce*, for which she won an Academy Award. Still, free-lancing could be risky. I was supposed to do a third picture (besides *Sister Kenny* and *Electra*) for RKO, but when Floyd Odlum sold the studio to Howard Hughes, this third picture was canceled. A little while afterward Freddie and I were in a Palm Springs nightclub when I heard a voice in my ear. "Miss Russell?"

I turned around, and standing behind me, looking nine feet tall, was Howard Hughes. There was a girl beside him.

"Yes?" I said.

"I've flown down to apologize about having to cancel the picture," he said. He had nice manners, and he thought nothing of flying around in the night, taking some nubile young beauty with him.

Nubility makes me think of the movie kids who weren't al-lowed to grow up. Judy Garland had developed a bosom they could scarcely disguise, but the studio kept her playing little girls. (As a parent, I was glad Lance never wanted to act; I'd seen too many stage mamas coaxing, "One more time, dear, play Tom Sawyer," and the kid's thirty-five years old.)

In the nun picture, *The Trouble with Angels*, I worked with Hayley Mills, another overripe adolescent, and she was a demon. She used to stick out her tongue whenever I passed (she couldn't stand me) and she was bursting at the seams with repressed sexuality. Hayley was eighteen or nineteen, but she had that baby face, so Disney kept hiring her to play children's parts. Her talent was enor-mous, but it was only a question of time until she would break out. Her parents had a fit when she went off with the old guy she later married. Hayley will be all right, though. She's bright. She'll probably end up taking Margaret Thatcher's place and start running the British government.

Hayley's out there in the garage, too, tucked away in one of the boxes, neatly labeled by Freddie: "Rosalind Russell, *Trouble* Stills."

Souvenirs of efforts past. When you look at that stuff, you really wonder what it's all about.

Frank

IN THE FOREGOING PAGES, I seem to have made two contradictory assertions:

    1) that a life in art is marvelously gratifying

    2) that the debris of a life in art sometimes make you wonder what it's all about

Both these assertions are true. And I'm as moody and full of questions as the next deep thinker. But a few things I know for certain, and one of them is that most people need some work, some love, some laughs, some friends.

Frank Sinatra is a friend. He has been a friend for close to forty years, since Freddie and I met him on Catalina when we were courting.

Because our long-standing relationship is public knowledge, promoters are forever calling me to get to Frank. I answer the phone in August, and it's a man who wants to know if I'll appear for a charity next December. After we settle that, he sneaks in the zinger. "And if you could get Frank Sinatra . . ."

"If I could get Frank Sinatra, I'd drop Freddie Brisson," I say, hoping to get off with a little joke rather than an argument.

No soap. The guy goes on. "But really, if you could get Sinatra, we could draw a huge crowd, we could take the Felt Forum or Madison Square Garden . . ."

"I would," I say. "I'd take both of 'em, and run between 'em."

The guy persists.

"Listen," I say finally, "nobody can promise Sinatra will show up any place. He doesn't show up for his own weddings."

That was before Barbara. In between wives, Frank was known for running like a rabbit if a girl dropped his name to a reporter, let alone a justice of the peace. But in July, 1976, at the Palm Springs estate of Walter Annenberg, the publisher and former Ambassador to Great Britain, about a hundred and twenty of us watched as Frank married Barbara Marx. They exchanged rings (and cars, too; she bought him a Jaguar, he bought her a Rolls-Royce), and when the judge asked the bride if she took the groom for richer or poorer, Frank whispered, "Richer, richer." At age sixty he was trying for the fourth time to get the Mr. and Mrs. business straight.

Back in 1966, ten years before, Frank had given Freddie and me our silver anniversary party. It had come about accidentally, because on our twenty-fourth anniversary a bunch of us were having such a good time that Freddie was overcome with the joys of friendship. "I'm inviting you all to our twenty-fifth anniversary, which I've decided should be celebrated in Copenhagen," he said.

"We accept," people cried. "We'll be there." "I'm running home to pack."

Having gone that far, Freddie went further. He actually wrote to the Hotel d'Angleterre in Copenhagen and gave the management dates and space requirements.

Every time we saw Frank after that, he'd heckle Freddie. "Are we booked? I'd prefer to go by boat."

Freddie was dead serious about the plan. "We'll bring the people who are already in Europe from wherever they are in Europe, and we'll organize the people from California . . ."

In due course I realized I'd have to sit him down and tell him a few blunt truths. "Freddie," I said, "you can't have people coming to Denmark on the twenty-fifth of October. It's dark at three o'clock in the afternoon in Copenhagen in October. And it's very cold. You'd have to tell the women to bring fur coats and long underwear, and they'd freeze and be uncomfortable. And the way the d'Angleterre is laid out, there are two or three good suites, and the rest are bedrooms. Very charming bedrooms, but who are you going to put in them? It wouldn't work in a million years unless we did it in the summertime, and that wouldn't be our anniversary."

He listened, but he kept right on making lists of how many rooms and how they could be arranged, until one night when Frank and a few other friends came to our house for dinner.

Everybody was sitting in the living room drinking coffee when Frank stood up. "The Dane isn't going to give any anniversary party," he said. "This bum is just a lot of gab, but he won't spend a quarter and he won't take us anyplace."

Freddie and Frank rib each other all the time, and Frank was wound up. "I'm taking over the party, and if Silent Sam is lucky, he'll get invited." (Because he talks so much, Frank nicknamed Freddie Silent Sam.)

A few of the other guests agreed that Freddie should be permitted to come for one of the courses, though certainly not for the whole evening. "Why don't you have him after dinner?" someone asked.

Next time I saw Frank, he was still enthusiastic about his idea. "We're going to do it, Roz, the twenty-fifth wedding anniversary. I mean it."

September rolled around. I was lying out by the pool when the phone rang. It was Frank, from London. "Roz, would you mind terribly if we had the party in Las Vegas?"

"Of course not," I said. "Whatever you want."

"We could handle the people better," he said. "I figure we'll have something like three hundred."

I stopped him. "Twenty-five couples for twenty-five years," I said. "That's fifty people. Fifty people, or no people at all. Because one way or the other, there are going to be hurt feelings. If we have three hundred, we have to have five hundred. If we invite five hundred, we have to invite a thousand. And it winds up with everyone who's left out saying, 'I knew her when, I made my first picture with her, I did her test,' and it's endless. This way, I'm responsible. You just blame it on me, say, 'She won't have more.' We stick by that, Frank, or there will be no party. None. Because that's the way Freddie and I would have done it at home."

Fifty was the number we kept to. I wrote the invitation, which read as follows:

Mr. and Mrs. Frank Sinatra [this was when Frank and Mia were married] *request the pleasure of your company to a Lost Weekend on the occasion of the 25th Wedding Anniversary of Silent Sam and his bride.*

Agenda:

Friday, October 21st.

6 P.M. Meet at Chez Brisson with bag and baggage. Sweet punch and salted nuts will be served. Bus leaves for airport at 6:30. Commentary on points of interest en route by driver.*

7 P.M. Leave in Howard Hughes' wooden flying boat. Dancing in the aisle to Ina Ray Hutton's band.** Free gum and kleenex.*

7:45 P.M. Arrive in Las Vegas. Straw drawing for rooms.

9 P.M. General assembly in The Leader's quarters.*** Salute to the flag. Election of den mother and father.*

10 P.M. Bed. Lights out. Correction, dinner, informal. Songs of welcome by Silent Sam.****

Saturday, October 22nd.

7 A.M. Gym class and breathing exercises

8 A.M. Relay race to Lake Mead

11 A.M. Punting competition*****

1 P.M. Death Valley lunch

3 P.M. Golf tournament

6 P.M. Prizes and Medicare registration

7 to 9 P.M. Free time. Letter writing and check cashing.

9 P.M. Dinner. Dress, black tie. Additional songs of welcome by Silent Sam. Reading of the minutes. Future business. Suggestions for party for 26th anniversary. Question

---

*   Can you imagine anything more revolting?

**   Ina Ray Hutton had an all-woman band.

***   The Leader is what his pals call Frank.

****   Freddie launches into Danish songs on almost any provocation.

*****   These 7 and 8 and 11 A.M. festivities which I had invented, thinking they were hilarious, were taken seriously by some of the guests. They were goofy enough to think we were really going to get up and run around Hoover Dam for the exercise.

((223))

and answer period. AA symposium. Lottery drawing. Main
speaker, Sonny Wisecarver. ******
    12 midnight. Singalong in Leader's quarters
Sunday, October 23rd.
    8:35 A.M. Blastoff. Union Pacific leaves for Anaheim,
Azusa and Cucamonga.

The festivities began, as planned, at our house, although
Frank was already in Las Vegas making hostly preparations. The first
group of friends arrived—the Cary Grants, Jimmy Stewarts, Dean
Martins, Kirk Douglases, Mike Romanoffs, William Goetzes, the
Vincente Minnellis, Roddy MacDowall, producer William Frye and
playwright Leonard Gershe—and Freddie and I served caviar and
champagne. Then a bus took the California contingent to the airport,
where we boarded a DC-9 that Frank had chartered. En route to Las
Vegas, there was more caviar, more booze.

In Las Vegas we were met by another bus and taken to an
Italian restaurant, where all of us who'd come from Hollywood
greeted all of those who'd come from New York—the Bennett Cerfs,
Claudette Colbert, Pat Kennedy Lawford, the Alan Jay Lerners, Mr.
and Mrs. Arthur Hornblow, Jr., the Leland Haywards, Josh Logans,
John McClain, the Denniston Slaters—and Sir James and Lady Hanson from London. Then we dined superbly.

Frank had taken over the three top floors of the Sands Hotel,
which is where he always performed in Las Vegas. I had made up
silver-colored labels with names and room numbers for everyone's
baggage, which was automatically put in their rooms.

If you wanted to play golf or tennis or go fishing, Frank
arranged for it, and then, on Saturday night, came the big party, for
which I wore a floor-length white gown with crystal and white beading. Galanos had made it specially for me.

We were in one of the Sands' private rooms, not too big a
room, and it was decorated prettily, all in white and silver. There were
several tables spaced around the dance floor, and that evening, husbands and wives sat together. I had designed the place cards, which
were silver double picture frames. In the left-hand frame was a picture

---

******Sonny Wisecarver was a local Los Angeles celebrity, a fifteen-
year-old boy who got all the girls pregnant.

of Freddie and me as bride and groom; in the right-hand frame, a picture of the guest couple. Whenever possible, I'd gotten a photo from their wedding; how I managed to do that without asking the subjects' cooperation, I'll never know.

Everyone had to go find his own picture in order to know where he was going to sit. Frank had bought silver cigarette boxes for everyone, inscribed "25th—Roz and Freddie." The ladies were given silver bags stuffed with twenty-five silver dollars for gambling. (Frank had arranged with the bank to get dollars stamped with the dates of the wedding and anniversary years, 1941 and 1966.)

Ours was a family table. Freddie and I sat there, along with Lance, who'd brought a young lady, Freddie's mother, Frank and Mia, our best man, Cary, and his wife Dyan Cannon. (I think that marriage was already on the rocks; Cary did nothing but cry all evening.)

Frank had asked one person at each table to say a few words. John McClain got up and said he'd investigated the Brisson marriage and found that we'd never even had a license, but that just before this party we'd made a quick trip to Mexico and straightened everything out. At our table, Lance made the speech. (How young he looks in the pictures, his hair so close-cropped his head seems shaved.) He was adorable, very nervous, and he drank lots of water. He talked about gratitude, the derivation of the word, what it meant to him, how he felt gratitude for his parents. Freddie and I were moved and charmed.

When it was time for me to speak, I said, "Frank, I'm afraid I'm going to be inarticulate." "That'll be the day when you can't talk," he said, so I tried. "Twenty-five years is a very long time," I said, "but it is also a very short time when you love someone." I felt throughout the entire room a feeling of love which circled back to us.

There was a good band for dancing, and after the speeches, Frank sang some of his songs, with special lyrics written by Sammy Cahn, substituting, for instance, "Roz and Freddie" for "love and marriage." He finished by singing "It's Been a Long, Long Time."

Then Dean Martin joined Frank, and they *both* sang, and there was other entertainment brought in from the hotel—at one point, fifty violinists serenaded us—and the party didn't break up until after two-thirty in the morning.

Nedda Logan summed up the evening: "I want to freeze this

((225))

night in my mind forever. I'll never get over it. I don't think any of us ever really will."

Sunday, before we called it quits, we all had a wonderful lunch together, and I thought how smart I'd been, because fifty people were manageable, whereas two or three hundred wouldn't have been. We were all glad to see one another; it was a triumph of a celebration.

I sift through the pictures in Freddie's albums now, and think about how much has changed in ten brief years. Leland Hayward is dead, so are John McClain, Bennett Cerf, Denny Slater and Freddie's mother. Frank and Mia are divorced, Cary and Dyan are divorced, Jeanne and Dean Martin are divorced.

But on that night in 1966 we were all together, and Frank had given me and Freddie something special.

He's a giver by nature, and it's hard to think of ways to reciprocate, so on the rare occasions when he asks for our help, Freddie and I hop to it. Before Christmas of 1967 we went down and worked with him to get the newest—and third—of the guest cottages in his Palm Springs compound ready for occupancy. Frank runs a meticulous and efficient household.

Palm Springs is a desert surrounded by beautiful mountains. The season starts there in October and goes until May. (Though I know some nuts who are so crazy about the heat, they go down to sunbathe when it's a hundred and twenty degrees.)

The town of Palm Springs is nothing to look at from the outside, but when you get into people's homes, and their gardens, it's glorious. It's a golfer's paradise; there are at least thirty-nine golf courses, with houses built around them.

Frank's compound is on a golf course. Years and years ago it was a dinky bachelor house, and he kept adding to it and adding to it. (He's not only called the Leader, he's also known as the Innkeeper, because he never stops building.) The compound today consists of several houses and a heliport, and you could have bought it for 1.4 million dollars before Frank and Barbara were married, but now they have rebuilt and refurbished everything. They can sleep twenty-four. Twenty-five is a crowd.

Anyway, when Francis Albert was getting ready for his 1967 Christmas party (he'd invited twenty-two friends to spend from December 18th until after New Year's), finishing up the latest, biggest guesthouse, Freddie and I worked with him. We drove down, spent a couple of days cleaning up the mess the workmen had left behind —Frank loves all that; he's up early in the morning, tearing around, supervising everything—and then we went into town to buy what was still needed for the house. Every one of Frank's guest bedrooms has two dressing rooms and two baths, so a man and his wife don't have to drip on each other, and all these baths and dressing rooms required stocking.

In the village, Freddie helped Frank to pick out glasses and soap dishes, while I chose toothbrush holders and wastebaskets and makeup mirrors. (If you visit the Innkeeper, you want for nothing. There is a Jacuzzi whirlpool bath in your tub; your medicine cabinet is filled with cotton balls and eye pads and mouthwash and shaving tackle; there are shower caps in your bureau drawers, bathing suits in your closet. There is also an old railroad freight car turned into a communal sauna.)

After the more practical purchases had been effected, Frank decided the new guesthouse needed some paintings on the walls. The three of us walked into a store, where a woman stood talking to a salesman. Frank was checking out the merchandise when the salesman, who had done a double-take, came rushing over. "Mr. Sinatra, can I help you?"

"How many paintings have you got here?" said Frank.

"I don't know," said the salesman.

Frank walked along a little further, admiring the pictures. "I'll take 'em all," he said.

"What?" said the salesman.

"I'll take 'em all," Frank said, "everything you got."

"Just a minute," said the woman who'd been there when we came in. "You're waiting on me."

"I *was* waiting on you," the salesman said, in an ungallant demonstration of cleverness about which side his bread was buttered on. "I'm now waiting on Mr. Sinatra, and the store is closed, and I'm going to Los Angeles to get some more paintings."

That afternoon, when the delivery man arrived at the Sinatra spread with a truck full of art, Frank put him to work. "You're gonna help hang 'em," he said, and for about four hours Freddie, Frank, the man off the truck and I hung pictures in the new guesthouse.

By the time the other guests arrived, every ashtray and potted plant and book and magazine Frank had acquired for the new cottage was in place. He and Mia had not been seeing each other since the Christmas invitations had gone out, but Mia came anyway, and so did Loel and Gloria Guinness. Frank had ordered little plaques made for the new bedroom doors. The plaques, which say "The Guinness Room," "The Brisson Room," and so forth, are still there, commemorating the first couples to sleep in those chambers.

A few days before Christmas, Freddie and I decided we'd give a house warming. I distributed invitations to everyone except Frank. Freddie and I went into town, found a Danish shop, bought some Christmas decorations and a Danish flag. The hors d'oeuvres consisted of wonderful Danish smoked salmon and other tidbits which we had sent down from Los Angeles. We also provided plenty of akvavit and a fully stocked bar.

We decorated the guesthouse living room, and after it got dark—we had to wait to do it so that Frank couldn't see us—we built a snowman outside the front door on the lawn. We'd hired a couple of men to go up into the mountains and bring us back garbage cans full of snow, and we made a figure that looked just like Frank. He was in a tuxedo, with a hat and a microphone.

At seven o'clock all the guests—not just our group from the new guesthouse, but the people staying in the other houses—arrived for the cocktail party, and started going through the smoked eel and the caviar like buzz saws. About fifteen minutes into the serious eating, we heard a knock. Freddie opened the front door a crack, peered out at Frank, and slammed the door shut again. "You're not invited," he yelled. Frank skulked around for a while, looking through the windows, before we took pity on him. Most of what I remember about that night was the akvavit flowing, and my thinking, No one would ever believe how much we've laughed.

Frank believed how much we laughed; what Frank didn't believe was the snowman. He just couldn't figure out how we'd gotten snow in the desert.

Next morning we woke up to see that our host had hoisted four flags above the compound. The American flag was flying, so were the Danish flag and the Italian flag, and in the midst of all of them was a flag featuring Alka-Seltzer.

We've had fun with Frank. He's an interesting man, a complex man, a very Italian man. He really doesn't like for women to smoke or drink or use bad language. I once wrote a magazine piece about him, and I said there were several Sinatras, including one nobody knew, one he kept very secret. I don't think man, woman, child or beast could pry that man loose, and that's the person Frank lives with when he's alone.

People are always asking me about him and Mia because I was one of the "chaperones" on that boat trip they took before they were married. Well, I've known Mia all her life. As a child, she used to come to Lance's birthday parties. And I've known Frank even longer, but he isn't a man to bare his feelings. All I can say is, for a while there, he was crazy about her.

Back in 1971, when Frank said he was retiring from show business, I think he really meant it. It didn't work, and it couldn't work, and nobody but Frank believed it should work. In a way, I suppose he just wanted to get everybody off his back once and for all. He'd reached the stage where the requests never stopped. Would he do this telethon? Appear for that benefit? Sign pictures for every kid in such and such a high school? Sing to people's ailing uncles, or their house plants?

He stayed away for a couple of years, and he gave house parties in the desert, until he realized he was kidding himself, that being the Elsa Maxwell of Palm Springs didn't fulfill him, that he needed to go back to work, which is his life.

The night he "retired" in 1971, I introduced him to the audience he had said would be his last. We were running a huge gala for the Motion Picture and Television Home (Gregory Peck was men's chairman, I was women's chairman) and we raised over a million dollars, $830,000 from ticket sales at $500 a pair, the rest in contributions.

Before he went on, Frank sat backstage and talked to a reporter. He said he'd first performed in public when he was a kid, for a couple of packs of cigarettes and a sandwich. "So here I am tonight, forty years later," he said, "finishing the same way I started, singing for nothing." And he smiled.

It got to be midnight. We'd been overwhelmed by four hours of entertainment. The top people in our business had contributed their services. David Niven had paid his own way from England to appear in a chorus line, backing up Pearl Bailey. Princess Grace had come from Monaco, and she and Jack Benny and Jimmy Stewart and Cary Grant and Sammy Davis and Bob Hope and Barbra Streisand and I don't know who all else acted and danced and sang.

I was fearful that the audience might be worn out by the time Frank appeared. I was fearful that I wouldn't be able to control my own voice as I took the stage to say a few words about Frank's leaving public life. "Our friend has made a decision," I began. "A decision we don't particularly like, but one which we must honor." I said something about his blue eyes, started to choke up, caught myself, and ended in a rush: "Tonight, for one last time, we have The Man, the greatest entertainer of the twentieth century."

Frank came on and did a half-hour of old favorites—"All or Nothing at All," "Nancy with the Laughing Face," "The Lady Is a Tramp," "My Way." The audience thought that "My Way" was the end, and they began to scream. He waited for them to quiet down, and then he talked, very soft, very easy. "I'm a saloon singer," he said. "And I want to go out as a saloon singer."

He launched into "Angel Eyes," a song from way back in his past, the kind of song for three o'clock in the morning, when you're sitting in a half-empty club with a half-empty glass.

Partway through the lyrics, he lit a cigarette. He was working in the dark now, except for a single spotlight, and as the spot wound down on him, he sang the last line, "Excuse me while I . . . disappear," and he walked off in the dark.

Brilliant showmanship. Brilliant. There was nothing left, just silence.

Frank didn't know his retirement would be temporary, and that night he teased me. "You'll follow me one of these days, Roz. It comes with age."

"Breakage Seems to Happen Quick"

F. SCOTT FITZGERALD,
The Crackup

W HAT CAME TO ME with age was not retirement, but rheumatoid arthritis. I hesitate to put it that way for fear of adding to the folklore about arthritis being purely an affliction of one's dotage. The doctor who diagnosed me said a lot of people in the theatrical industry had the disease but wouldn't admit to it. "They think it's a confession of old age."

"Well, isn't it?" I said.

"No," he said, "it isn't. There are dozens of kinds of arthritis. Infants develop it soon after they're born, teenagers have it, so do any number of men and women—mostly women—in their twenties, thirties and forties."

By coincidence, I'd been working for the Arthritis and Rheumatism Foundation for eighteen years, before I myself got sick, though I suppose I'd been moving toward the trouble for a long time. "Of course all life is a process of breaking down," Scott Fitzgerald wrote in 1936, "but the blows that do the dramatic side of the work —the big sudden blows that come, or seem to come, from outside— the ones you remember and blame things on and, in moments of weakness, tell your friends about, don't show their effect all at once. This breakage," said Fitzgerald, "seems to happen quick."

In 1969 I'd made a spy picture called *Mrs. Pollifax—Spy*. We were shooting in the Grand Tetons of Wyoming, eleven thousand feet up. The high altitude, the climate, the severe conditions (I had to play some scenes in icy water) were draining, but I was so arrogant about my good health that it wouldn't have occurred to me to take any special kinds of precautions. In fact, when I saw anybody in the cast or crew shivering, I pitied the poor frail creature and gave away my mittens, my shoes, my boots. (And later found myself jumping up and down to keep warm because, while I hated to admit it, I was very cold.)

From the minute we started it, that movie worried me. We were way up in the hills, and the script wasn't right, and we shot at night, and I wasn't sleeping. We had two hundred men up there, and I was scared to death that we'd lose somebody off that mountain. The company had to dig roads out of the side of the cliff in order to haul up the heavy equipment, and cauldrons of hot food were lugged up every noon, and I used to wonder who on earth had picked this place and if we would ever make it down to safety. The Grand Tetons are not only high, they're mean; wherever you glanced, you saw these peaks with what looked like sawteeth, very sharp, *arrrgh*, coming at you.

We finished the picture without apparent casualty, and I came home to the Christmas rush. Freddie was in New York getting *Coco* ready for Broadway, and I had a couple of hundred Christmas gifts to wrap, and my hands were refusing to cope with the ribbons and the bows and the knots.

I went to a doctor. "Look at my hands, they're acting very strangely." The doctor wasn't a rheumatologist and didn't know what to tell me. Probably he ought to have said, "You shouldn't go to New York, you should go to bed," but that's all ifs and maybes.

Cleo and Tilde (Freddie's mother and aunt), my maid and I got on a plane heading for New York and Freddie's opening. I was exhausted. I remember saying, "Forgive me for not sitting and chatting with you, I'm very tired," and then crawling into my own seat and putting my head up against the window and trying to sleep.

Freddie met us at the airport. He told me later that he was shocked at the way I looked. But he was frantic himself with a million last-minute *Coco* problems.

I used hot stuff—Heet, Infra-thing, whatever it was—rubbing

it on my hands, and it seemed to help. I got through the opening. Earl Blackwell gave us a big party afterward; dozens of our friends were there, and I was trying to look after everybody while Freddie was at the advertising agency, waiting for the reviews. It felt to me as though every person who shook my hand was squeezing my fingers off; I thought they were going to drop right on the floor. I tried to keep my hands behind my back, up my sleeves, under my arms; nothing worked.

The next morning I woke up with big swollen knuckles. Freddie called Floyd Odlum and asked him what doctor to see. When Floyd Odlum was fifty years old, working as a dollar-a-year man for the government during the second World War, he woke up, just as I had done, with arthritis. He was a powerful person, the president of the Atlas Corporation, and accustomed to finding assistance if he needed it. "Get me an arthritis doctor," he said to the people around him, and they came back with bad news. There was no such thing as an arthritis doctor. No specialists.

Odlum proceeded to form the Arthritis and Rheumatism Foundation. He brought in orthopedic men who knew about bones and joints, began the telethons to raise money, and when he got sicker, let himself be used as a guinea pig. The doctors gave him heavy doses of cortisone before anybody knew what side effects such dosages could have. When cortisone first came on the scene, it was hailed as the answer to arthritis, and doctors poured it into everybody. Only later did they find it was destructive to the bones, and had to be used with extreme care. (In my case, after taking it for a few years, I felt I was being poisoned. The medications can sometimes be worse than the disease.) Floyd had remissions, and carried on with his various business enterprises till the load became too heavy. (When in his eighties, he lived on a ranch in Indio, California, with his wife, the flyer, Jackie Cochran.) Floyd had been responsible for interesting a great number of good doctors in arthritis. When Freddie phoned about me, Floyd recommended Dr. Richard Freyberg at the Hospital for Special Surgery in New York. Dr. Freyberg (now retired) was an orthopedic man and a great rheumatologist.

Dr. Freyberg tested my blood, examined me thoroughly, and assessed the results. "You have an extremely high sedimentation rate," he said.

((233))

That was just medical jargon to me. "Can I beat this rap?" I asked.

He said it wasn't likely. "You are also very anemic." We sat in his office while he explained. He said sometimes arthritis just disappeared, but that I had the worst kind of rheumatoid arthritis, so I must be prepared for lesser miracles. And that I must also be prepared to rest for a long time. I was given a shot in one knee, and a choice. "We could hospitalize you here in New York," Dr. Freyberg said, "but I'm sure you'd rather be in your home."

I said I would and immediately returned to California and went to bed for three months. Then I started to heal, and began to exercise again. I got into my swimming pool, which was wonderfully helpful. And I thought about how fortunate I was to be able to have a heated pool, and about all the arthritics who weren't so fortunate. (There are therapeutic pools in most hospitals, of course, but many sufferers can't get to these hospitals.) I also thought about what Dr. Freyberg had said, that most actors were afraid to discuss their arthritis, and I made a decision. I was going to go public.

There are people who love to tell you how sick they are. Ask them how they feel, and they bore you with the details. They'll write it out for you, carve it in granite. They want the attention.

I'm not one of those people. I tend to believe Elsie Mendl was right when she said, "Never complain, never explain." Don't go on about why you didn't come to my house for dinner. You missed, you left an empty place, messed up the party, and that's that. Never mind that your old Aunt Becky was lost, or the kid tripped on his tricycle, nobody wants to hear it.

This being my philosophy, it was hard for me to do what I thought was the right thing, and talk about my arthritis. I didn't want to talk about it; I'd have liked to pretend it had never happened. I'd made a good recovery. I don't say cure, because you're not supposed to use that word, Sister Kenny taught me that. But I felt the problem of arthritis needed to be thrust in front of the public in order for us to get help, to get something done.

Millions of dollars go to scientists working with cancer and with heart disease, but arthritis research has been a stepchild. (Arthritis victims spend four hundred million dollars a year on quack cures. If we had the four hundred million, we'd lick the disease.)

Also, I thought I might be able to help other sufferers by demonstrating that you can learn to live with arthritis. I had a feeling that when something like arthritis happens to you, you either let it defeat you, or you defeat it. You're either better for it, or you're worse for it, depending on the adjustment you make.

In the last few years I have heard from literally thousands of arthritics. People send mail to Rosalind Russell, Hollywood, California, and the post office delivers it to the Screen Actors Guild, and from there it gets sent to my agent, and from there it's sent to me. You can't believe some of the letters. One of them said if I'd carry a hazelnut in my left hand, within forty-eight hours I'd wake up cured. I try to answer the people who make any sense at all. I have to be careful, because I can't give medical advice, which so many writers ask for. All I can do is tell the patient to go to a good rheumatologist. It isn't that there's anything wrong with the family physician, it's just that the family physician tends to offer warm baths and aspirin. And often he's not sufficiently knowledgeable about steroids, so that even if he prescribes them, he may fail to warn the patient that anyone on these drugs has to be constantly watched and checked.

I tell the people who write me to try to forget they have arthritis. Every case is different. If you have it above the waist, you're better off than if you have it in the hips and the knees, because you can ambulate better. If you can't ambulate well, your circulation gets bad. It happens to some people gradually. I have a friend who's a pianist, and his hands are becoming more and more painful. He moves them constantly, cracks them, clenches them, anything to keep them mobile, because they're his living.

But the main thing is to deal with your own individual problem as best you can—try to go to intelligent people for help, don't take every silly nostrum that's advertised, and work at pretending you don't have anything wrong with you. Of course you can't totally achieve this goal, but you have to try. If you're invited out, instead of saying, "No, I can't go because of my arthritis," say, "Yes, I can go." You may not be able to get into the potato race, but you can still be very much a part of life.

It's hard to get good help in any field, especially in medicine, but I think anyone with arthritis should make every effort to get to a rheumatologist he can believe in, and then do what that doctor says to do. That's more or less the way I feel about it, and pretty much all I have to give in the way of advice.

Recently I read an interview with the actor John Carradine in which he said he'd had arthritis for more than thirty years. "It's never stopped me from getting a part," he said. "Although I can't be too sure of that. I would think twice before hiring someone with hands as deformed as mine."

Well, it stopped *me* from getting parts, and I know it. Because of my talking about it, not because of my hands. When I first became ill I could have hidden it easily, since I still got around very well. I paid a price for climbing on my soapbox. The owner of one Hollywood studio told Freddie, "I would never hire Rosalind again, because of her affliction."

"She's got more energy than you and your whole studio put together," said Freddie fiercely.

"But she might have an attack while she was working," said the studio head.

This kind of stupidity was hard to swallow, but I had to accept it and go on living.

Now, several years later, my arthritis is worse. I'd be hobbled if I didn't stay on steroids—sometimes the cortisone puffs up my face, giving me chipmunk cheeks—and even with the steroids, my right hip got so bad that in August of 1976 I had to have a complete hip replacement.

I think there will be other breakthroughs (like this kind of operation) in the near future, because arthritis research is finally being taken seriously. The Federal government has come up with fifty million dollars' seed money, and it's about time. There are twenty-two million, five hundred thousand people in this country who have active arthritis, and we should have been offered more hope a long time ago.

Sister Kenny put polio on the front pages, and kept it there. I doubt if we'd have got the Salk vaccine as soon as we did if she hadn't made all those headlines. But for too long nobody got riled up enough to do anything about arthritis, and doctors thought there was no money in the rheumatology racket, so we wound up with a lot of poor old ladies wearing little shawls and sitting in the attic nursing cups of tea. That's wrong—very wrong—hence my strong personal interest in seeing research move forward faster.

When you've got arthritis, your adrenal gland doesn't work properly. Steroids stimulate the adrenal gland, which is connected with the pituitary gland, which goes to the brain. So you can get euphoric on steroids. And you can turn into a bleeder because of steroids. But at least this information is now being disseminated, and if those of us who are involved continue to raise our voices, more solutions to the problems should be forthcoming. The fifty million dollars' seed money will go toward finding some answers.

Loss of health is the worst thing that ever happens to anybody, and for me, 1975 was a terrible year. I had the pneumonia, and afterward it was hard to rebuild my strength. That summer Freddie took me on a cruise to Russia. We spent two weeks on a boat, we saw places we would never see again, and pretended we were off on a far fancier trip. Freddie cared for me like a baby, but I hate for him to be around when I'm feeling sick. I don't like him to see me that way; I pretend I'm fine.

When we came home again, I went right into meetings, some with the Arthritis Commission in Bethesda, Maryland, some with the National Endowment for the Arts in Washington, D.C. Because Lady Bird Johnson was involved in a new Arts bill, I traveled down to the LBJ ranch, and it was while I was in Austin that I knew something was very wrong with me. Two days of symposia, two nights of banquets (and being entertained by every amateur group in the State of Texas), and all I wanted was to drink water. I carried a glass wherever I went.

When I got back to California, my doctor put me into the hospital, and it was discovered that I had a couple of tumors which had been growing for years.

Nine doctors gave me up for dead. Freddie didn't. I was on a dialysis machine, semicomatose, in and out of consciousness, and there were fights going on outside my door. I heard them, but I didn't make sense of them. The nurses told me later that it had been terrible, Freddie screaming at all these medical men who were offering platitudes. "You must let your wife go, she'll be at peace. If it was my own mother, I'd let her go . . ."

How easy they let you go.

Mary Lasker, a close friend and a director of the National Cancer Institute, discussed my case with Freddie, recommended that he get Dr. Martin J. Cline to take over. Dr. Cline told the doctors, Freddie and me that chemotherapy might save me. "You're going to be awfully sick, but if you can get through the first two treatments, you'll become less sick each time," he said. "Are you willing to try it?"

"I don't think I have much choice," I said. "Either that, or fare-thee-well."

They call me the Miracle Woman, because I keep coming back.

In May of 1976, when Freddie had a musical called *So Long, 174th Street* opening in New York, I flew East to be with him, and because it was time for my chemotherapy, I went to Sloan-Kettering at Memorial Hospital. I sat in the waiting room with a hundred other people, some of them children, and I told a teenager I liked her shoes. It was a nice waiting room, painted in soft greens and full of apple blossoms, but everyone who was sitting there had cancer.

When your health breaks, your life becomes a compromise, and for me that's been difficult. It's not in my nature to like compromise, or to accept limitations. I'm volatile, and I had thought my God-given energy would never fail me. But I know that other people have had far more difficult times than I've had, and I never stop marveling at the human spirit.

There is a girl named Jacqueline du Pré, a prodigy of a cellist, whose career ended in 1973 when multiple sclerosis made it impossible for her to go on giving concerts. She was then twenty-eight years old.

In February of 1976, in the interests of helping to organize a new foundation for victims of her disease, she made a public appearance at London's Royal Festival Hall. She sat in a wheelchair and explained that she hoped to do some teaching. "I still play the cello because I think it's good exercise, but the sounds are atrocious," she said. "I can't feel the strings, so I don't know what notes I'm playing."

The bones, the muscles are not indestructible, but sometimes the heart seems to be.

"But When the Brightness Comes..."

PINDAR,

"Pythian Ode 8"

"TIME IS AN OUTRAGE, life is an outrage," Chanel once told an interviewer. "And the next few years will be worse." She was already in her seventies, the beautiful ankles beginning at last to swell, but she advised women not to fight the inevitable. "At forty you should forget how ravishing you were at twenty in your blue dress and your blond hair."

I don't believe for a minute that you can hang on to your youth. I think it's the worst, the saddest, the most futile struggle. I know a lot of women who've gone through cosmetic surgery, and it shows in photographs, something strange happens around the mouth.

Even the most temporary magic tricks aren't for me. When we made *Craig's Wife*, Billie Burke had these lifts which were hidden under her hair to pull up her forehead and pull back her neck. I was fascinated. "Pull my neck back," I said to the makeup man. He did. I couldn't talk; I couldn't move my head. "Take it off," I said, "it's awful." I never tried it again.

I've had enough trouble trying to stay myself, be myself. (All those brothers and sisters helped, of course. If you weren't yourself around them, you got knocked to the floor.) It's something you have to work at just as hard as you'd have to work at staying young, and it's the reason I tried to avoid being caught up in what I thought of as "the Hollywood scene."

One night at Jack Warner's house, many years ago, a bunch of ladies were in the powder room—which was a whole suite—and I heard Kay Francis say, "No, Roz is *in* Hollywood, but she's not *of* it."

"What the hell does that mean?" I said.

"It means you work here," she said, "but you're not part of Hollywood, and you never will be."

At first I was miffed. Didn't I function well with my colleagues? Wasn't I socially acceptable? Yet I came to realize she was right. I've said it before, in an earlier chapter: I never wanted the kind of life in which you dedicated your whole being to acting, and preparing for acting, and meeting only the people who could advance your acting career.

I wanted a home, a husband, children, a variety of experience. I wasn't willing to pay the price of superstardom, and my unwillingness made me very cautious. So my survival has been gratifying.

If you survive in this business at all—and I don't care if you're a superstar, a second-echelon star, a supporting player, that doesn't matter—it's a miracle of its own quality and size.

When I first came into film, I met a Russian director. "The day you begin to believe your publicity is the day you die," he said. "It's all over for you, whether the publicity is good or bad."

If you get knocked, you can't let it get you down, and certainly you can't wallow in the fact that you've been complimented, because your triumph has so much to do with other people. The good directors, the good authors are the ones who hand you most of your successes. Some writers provide you with parts that could be played blackface and upside down, and still come out all right. When you have a hit, you've usually had a damn good property. *His Girl Friday* had Hecht and MacArthur and Howard Hawks laboring to put Rosalind Russell over. Your failures have collaborators too. I've seen so many things spoiled by fools, but you just can't let the blood run until you're anemic, you have to pick yourself up and go on.

I think any career reads like a fever chart, or a chart of the stock market. It's up, down, in, out, over. An actor who endures for any number of years in this industry, which is so mercurial, has been fortunate.

And to endure more or less on your own terms, as I have, is to have been more fortunate than most. But then, I never kidded myself about what the movie business owed me. Some actors can't bear to live in California once they're no longer active in pictures. They condemn the new breed of studio heads for being money men who know profits, not pictures; they're resentful of scruffy-looking young directors (and refuse to admit their talent); they're humiliated that the parade has passed them by. I don't feel that way. I've had a wonderful time out here, but I don't expect anything of it—of the town, of the business, of the people with whom I once made deals because it was to our mutual advantage. I don't expect somebody to say now, "Look, we owe her something because she's been part of our lives, she's entertained us, she's made four pictures with us . . ."

Not at all. Why should I? Why should they? I think that's the kind of mistake people break their hearts over.

The irony is that if you *do* survive for long enough, some kind young folks are apt to turn you into a national monument when you aren't looking.

In 1974, for no particular reason that I could fathom, I became all the rage again. It had really started a couple of years before, with the board of Filmex, which runs film festivals. They honored me. They honor one performer every year. You come to a theatre, they run masses of your film, and after it's all over, you stand up and everybody applauds like mad and says wasn't it terrific.

John Springer, a publicist who'd been successful with a show of the same kind featuring Bette Davis, approached me about repeating my Filmex stint in the East. "When I'm in New York sometime," I said. "I'll come up from Washington after a meeting, and we'll do it."

In September of 1974 I appeared in what was billed as "A Tribute to Rosalind Russell," at New York's Town Hall. I thought nobody would come. "It's too early in the season," I said to John Springer. "The people aren't back from Long Island and Europe."

I was wrong. The house was sold out, the evening a success. After the film clips John Springer introduced me, and I fielded questions from the audience. Somebody out front wanted to know what I considered my top achievement. "Being alive," I said.

I heard my husband bragging about me later. "It wasn't just a standing ovation, it was a continuous standing," he was telling this person. "Then, afterward, they threw flowers at Roz like she was an opera star."

I don't know why he sounded so surprised. With a voice like mine, I should certainly get the same kind of floral offerings as any opera star.

A few months afterward I did a whole week of the same one-woman show at the historic Ford's Theatre in Washington. Again, the person who arranged it had more faith than I. "It's the kind of thing that's good for two or three performances," I told Frankie Hewett, "but you can't fill that theatre for a week."

"It'll be all right," she said, and it was. We filled that theatre for a week. The Washington run was fancy. Senators and Congressmen came, as well as Mamie Eisenhower, and the Henry Kissingers and Kay Graham, who owns the Washington *Post.* Mrs. Graham had invited the Kissingers, Freddie and me back to her house for supper after the show, and I was impressed. There aren't too many hostesses who have the staff to serve a full dinner at eleven-thirty or twelve o'clock at night.

The other amazing thing that happened to me in 1974 was that ANTA—the American National Theatre and Academy—tipped me a nod. I was given the National Artist Award, together with the information that the only other people who'd previously received this honor were Alfred Lunt and Lynn Fontanne. Not too bad, the company I keep.

There was a nice presentation bash, hosted by ANTA West, and I told the audience of actors and producers and writers and directors and comics and hoofers that I didn't think the theatre was dying. "It's alive because of you," I said. "I'm glad I was part of it." Then Donald Seawell, chairman of the board of ANTA, fastened the National Artist's medallion on my white Galanos gown, and suddenly the Duchess flashed into my head, the Duchess pinning a rhinestone elephant onto my burned white chiffon, and I felt a pang of loss for all that had been so merry and hopeful and dumb, for the innocence of the Russell girls all those years ago.

"We are things of a day," Pindar wrote five hundred years before Christ. "What are we? What are we not? The shadow of a dream is man, no more. But when the brightness comes, and God gives it, there is a shining of light on men, and their life is sweet."

My life has been sweet, and though this may sound funny, I feel it's been fairly normal, the kind of life Freddie and I would have had no matter what we'd worked at. We've lived in one house since we married, and there's a gardenia bush out front which was planted there for Freddie's father, whose theme song was "A Little White Gardenia." It was tiny when it went in; it's big now. Until recently I did a great deal of the gardening—I put in oleander bushes, pink ones alternating with white ones, but the pinks have taken over— because I enjoyed being out among the trees and the birds and the flowers.

I find my husband's glasses for him—"I'm losing my mind," he mutters—because, like all men, when he's looking for anything, he examines the ceiling first. And I worry about his weight. The other day he got out of the pool and tied some terrible-looking rag around his paunch and I told him he had to lose ten pounds.

"I don't," he said. "Do you know how old this thing is?"

"You mean the body or the wrapper?" I said.

"Well, if you'd buy me something that fits," he said, "I wouldn't look like this."

Sound familiar? Domestic? Ordinary? Thank God it is, and has been. I caught the right guy, he knows and understands me and cares about me, and that's been my chief blessing.

Since I lost my mother I don't go East so often, and when I do, we all meet at Mary Jane's house in Southport. My oldest brother, James, comes down there and so does my youngest sister, Josephine, and I see my nieces and my nephews and it's lovely. Phine stayed with my mother for a long while after the rest of us went off, but she finally went to work, became executive secretary to a Mr. Boak, who owned a factory, married him and moved to New Milford. Widowed now, she still lives there in a house full of antiques, goes to Antigua every winter and works for the Red Cross. I don't think Mother had thought Phine would ever marry. In a way, she wanted to see all of us married, but she'd grown to depend on Phine; they traveled to Cape Cod (to the same hotel, where they saw the same people) every summer, and to Florida in the winter, and Mother missed that companionship. But she forfeited gracefully. She knew Mr. Boak would take good care of her baby.

We were all her babies, and she would have liked to keep us

that way. She never discussed sex with any of us, I didn't know anything, and I tell Mary Jane that was probably wrong. Mary Jane disagrees. "Is it better now? They start learning about it in fourth grade, and by the time they're ten, there's no mystery left for them."

I have to say I'm not sure, I don't know what it would be like the other way.

If I could wave a magic wand and alter the past—or at least my character—I'd relax my tendency to push too hard, to be an extremist. It's always *mañana* time for me. Next month I'll take it easy; or in three months Freddie and I will go to Hawaii and we'll have a very fine rest together, and that'll be lovely. But it doesn't happen.

I think the older you get, the more you are struck with that "brightness" God gives, the more you find light alone to be a wonderful thing, the more you feel there's something else, another weight.

Mine has been a life with a lot of luck in it. I've had a good ride.

MOTION PICTURE CREDITS

TITLE	STUDIO
Evelyn Prentice (1934)	MGM
The President Vanishes (1934)	Paramount
Forsaking All Others (1935)	MGM
West Point of the Air (1935)	MGM
Reckless (1935)	MGM
Casino Murder Case (1935)	MGM
The Night Is Young (1935)	MGM
China Seas (1935)	MGM
Rendezvous (1935)	MGM
It Had to Happen (1936)	Twentieth Century-Fox
Under Two Flags (1936)	Twentieth Century-Fox
Trouble for Two (1936)	MGM
Craig's Wife (1936)	Columbia
Night Must Fall (1937)	MGM
Live, Love and Learn (1937)	MGM
Man-Proof (1938)	MGM
Four's a Crowd (1938)	Warner Brothers
The Citadel (1938)	MGM
Fast and Loose (1939)	MGM
The Women (1939)	MGM
His Girl Friday (1940)	Columbia
Hired Wife (1940)	Universal
No Time for Comedy (1940)	Warner Brothers
This Thing Called Love (1941)	Columbia
They Met in Bombay (1941)	MGM
The Feminine Touch (1941)	MGM

Design for Scandal (1941)	MGM
Take a Letter, Darling (1942)	Paramount
My Sister Eileen (1942)	Columbia
Flight for Freedom (1943)	RKO
What a Woman (1943)	Columbia
Roughly Speaking (1945)	Warner Brothers
She Wouldn't Say Yes (1945)	Columbia
Sister Kenny (1946)	RKO-Radio Pictures
The Guilt of Janet Ames (1947)	Columbia
Mourning Becomes Electra (1947)	RKO-Radio Pictures
The Velvet Touch (1948)	RKO-Radio Pictures
Tell It to the Judge (1949)	Columbia
A Woman of Distinction (1950)	Columbia
Never Wave at a WAC (1952)	RKO-Radio Pictures
The Girl Rush (1955)	Paramount
Picnic (1955)	Columbia
Auntie Mame (1958)	Warner Brothers
A Majority of One (1961)	Warner Brothers
Five-Finger Exercise (1962)	Columbia
Gypsy (1962)	Warner Brothers
The Trouble with Angels (1966)	Columbia
Oh Dad, Poor Dad, Mamma's Hung You in the Closet and I'm Feeling So Sad (1967)	Paramount-Seven Arts
Rosie (1967)	Universal
Where Angels Go . . . Trouble Follows (1968)	Columbia
Mrs. Pollifax—Spy (1971)	United Artists

INDEX